GIVE ME LIBERTY!

AN AMERICAN HISTORY

SECOND EDITION

STUDY GUIDE

VOLUME 2

ERIC FONER

GIVE ME LIBERTY!

AN AMERICAN HISTORY

SECOND EDITION

STUDY GUIDE

BY

Daniel Letwin
PENNSYLVANIA STATE UNIVERSITY

John Recchiuti
MOUNT UNION COLLEGE

Thomas Clarkin
SAN ANTONIO COLLEGE

VOLUME 2

W · W · NORTON & COMPANY · NEW YORK · LONDON

Copyright © 2008, 2006, 2005 by W. W. Norton & Company, Inc.

Printed in the United States of America

Layout/Composition by R. Flechner Graphics

Second Edition

ISBN 13: 978-0-393-93050-4 (pbk.)

W. W. Norton & Company, Inc., 500 Fifth Avenue, New York, NY 10110
www.wwnorton.com

W. W. Norton & Company Ltd., Castle House, 75/76 Wells Street, London W1T 3QT

1 2 3 4 5 6 7 8 9 0

CONTENTS

INTRODUCTION

Textbooks are vital to the study of history. While no two surveys present the American experience in quite the same way, they all share a common purpose—to weave together the essential events, developments, and issues of our national past into a coherent, comprehensible whole.

Seldom has any volume rendered the sweep of American history with the clarity, insight, and cohesiveness of Eric Foner's *Give Me Liberty! An American History*. Especially compelling is the centrality the author assigns "freedom"—a perpetually embattled and elusive ideal from the origins of colonial America to the present.

Give Me Liberty! offers an invaluable resource for your exploration of the American past. Yet no book can do the job on its own. The reading of history is, after all, a two-way street. What one gets out of a text turns largely on what one puts into it—and on what one does with the knowledge and insights thus acquired.

Helping the student get the most out of *Give Me Liberty!* is the purpose of this *Study Guide*. For each chapter of the text, a corresponding chapter in the *Study Guide* identifies central questions, highlights key themes and events, offers quiz and essay questions, and suggests resources for further study. Toward these ends, the *Study Guide* has a number of regular features, each discussed in turn below.

CHAPTER OBJECTIVES

Reading is essential to the study of history. Alas, not all reading is *effective* reading. We all know the experience of *ineffective* reading: scanning briskly through the pages of an assigned text . . . plowing through a thicket of facts and ideas . . . and promptly forgetting it all as soon as we're done! To maximize the effectiveness of our reading, it is important that we bring to the task some well-defined *questions*—questions that get at the underlying significance of the material in the text. The purpose of the Chapter Objectives that open each *Study Guide* chapter is to help the student focus his or her reading; and hence, to digest and retain its content more effectively.

Tips to consider:

- Consult these questions before reading the corresponding chapter of the text.
- As you read through the chapter, note where and how each of the questions are addressed.
- Once you have finished reading the chapter, review the questions again. While the material is fresh in your mind, you may want to jot down some thoughts regarding each question.
- Bear in mind: the questions listed in this section are not the *only* ones worth consideration. After completing the chapter, you might find it stimulating to come up with one or two questions of your own.

CHAPTER OUTLINE

The Chapter Outline distills, in schematic fashion, the progression of events, trends, and themes that make up the chapter.

Tips to consider:

- Scan the Outline quickly before reading the chapter. This will help bring the big picture into focus, and will reinforce your awareness of the Chapter Objectives.
- Review the Outline more closely after you've finished the chapter. This will help you retain its essential elements.
- Bear in mind: the Outline is intended to provide *signposts* to the chapter; it should not be taken as a *summary* of the chapter, or as a substitute for reading it!

CHRONOLOGY

The Chronology highlights key events from the period covered by the chapter. A glance at the Chronology can bring into sharp relief the progression of significant trends over time. It can also remind us of the variety of historical developments coinciding at any given time, and prompt us to consider how such contemporaneous trends might interrelate.

OBJECTIVE QUESTIONS

Each chapter contains a number of multiple-choice and true-or-false questions. (Answers to the Objective Questions are found at the end of each *Study Guide* chapter.) These questions will help you to test your command of the main themes and developments covered in the text chapter.

The true-or-false questions are self-explanatory. The multiple-choice questions come in two types. The first type—in most chapters, questions 1–3—asks you to identify the one choice that is historically *accurate*. The second type—in most chapters, questions 4–8—asks you to identify the one choice that is historically *inaccurate*. (This latter type of question always follows the form: *Which of the following is **not** . . . ?*)

Tips to consider:

- Do the Objective Questions while the chapter is fresh in your mind—but not before you've gone back and reviewed the Chapter Objectives, Outline, and Chronology.
- Bear in mind: by and large, the questions are geared toward the essential issues and patterns surveyed in the text rather than historical minutiae.
- If you find you're missing the answers to more than a few of the Objective Questions in a chapter, try to determine why that is. There may be various reasons and solutions for this. You may, for instance, be reading the chapter too quickly. Or, you may be reading it too *intensely*, focusing on each detail so closely that you lose the forest for the trees! Perhaps greater attention to the Chapter Objectives will sharpen our performance. If you continue to experience difficulties with the Objective Questions, you may find it useful to consult your instructor.
- With the second type of multiple-choice question, it is important to remember that three of the four choices are historically accurate—your mission here is to find the one that is *not*. This may take some getting used to at first, but there is a real payoff: since three of the four choices are historically accurate, these questions can be particularly useful as you review your written assignments, class sessions, and exams.
- Each week, make up a *Which of the following is **not** . . . ?* question of your own that addresses an important issue or event covered in the reading.

ESSAY QUESTIONS

Each chapter contains around ten Essay Questions. These vary in form: some ask for a formal paper on a particular problem, while others ask the student to imagine and "transcribe" a contemporary exchange among a set of characters from the specified period. Whichever form they take, the questions are all designed to help you pull together key themes and developments from the period in question, and subject them to substantial analysis.

Tip to consider:

- Your instructor may draw upon the Essay Questions for paper assignments. Even if they do not, thinking about these questions—imagining, or even outlining how you might tackle them—can be a useful way to review the text for class sessions and exams.

FURTHER READING

Give Me Liberty! is a highly distilled overview of American history. Each paragraph addresses topics that have been the focus of whole books. The bibliography is meant to point you toward some of the more useful or influential works in the field, for those who may wish to delve deeper into some particular aspect of the chapter.

Bear in mind: published works on American history run to the tens of thousands—inevitably, those listed in the Further Reading section represent no more than the tip of the iceberg!

VIDEOS

While reading lies at the heart of historical study, the sounds and sights offered by video can do much to enhance our feel for the past, and sharpen our empathy for those who came before us—in short, to make history come alive. Recent years have brought forth a rush of historical documentaries on the American past. Almost every chapter lists several of the more illuminating and evocative titles available on the period covered.

WEB RESOURCES

Each *Study Guide* chapter offers a sampling of some of the more substantial and well-regarded Web sites pertaining to American history. Students can use thee Web sites as points of entry into the vast ocean of materials on American history now available on the Internet—ranging from original documents, to scholarly writings, to bibliographies, to discussion groups, to multimedia items of every description.

Tips to consider:

- Bear in mind, while historical materials on the Web can wonderfully complement published works, they cannot replace them. Books and libraries still matter!
- Remember that the Internet is an unregulated arena, open to input from anyone with a computer. Just because it's on the Web does not mean it's accurate, or reliable!
- Remember that the Internet is a fluid, ever-changing place. When it comes to Web sites, what's here today—and perhaps included on the *Study Guide* list—may be gone tomorrow.

Likewise, valuable new sites on American history are constantly appearing. For possible inclusion in a future edition of the *Give Me Liberty! Study Guide,* readers are invited to send suggestions for relevant Web sites to: letwin@psu.edu.

Just as no two American history surveys are alike, no two people encounter our national past in quite the same manner. Every individual brings to the study of the past a unique perspective, reflecting a distinctive mix of background and personality, interests and knowledge, like experience and world view. Inevitably, then, each student will draw upon and respond to *Give Me Liberty!* in his or her own way. For every reader, it is the aim of the *Study Guide* to render this encounter as fruitful and engaging as possible.

CHAPTER 15

"What Is Freedom?": Reconstruction, 1865–1877

CHAPTER OBJECTIVES

- How did southerners—black and white, slave and free—experience the abolition of slavery?
- How did the freedpeople envision, and pursue, their freedom?
- How did the leading actors in the drama of Reconstruction—such as former slaves, southern planters, southern white yeoman, Radical Republicans, and President Johnson—contend over the shape of the postslavery South?
- How did the Reconstruction amendments to the Constitution transform the promise, and reality, of American freedom?
- What, at its peak, were the achievements of Reconstruction? How close did it come to bringing interracial democracy to the South?
- What ultimately accounts for the defeat of Reconstruction?

CHAPTER OUTLINE

I. Contested meanings of freedom at end of Civil War
   A. For southern blacks, an expansive quest
      1. Self-ownership
      2. Autonomous institutions
         a. Family
            i. Reuniting families separated under slavery
            ii. Adopting separate gender roles
         b. Church
            i. Worship
            ii. Social events
            iii. Political meetings

   c. Schools
     i. Motivations
     ii. Backgrounds of students and instructors
     iii. Establishment of black colleges
  3. Political participation
   a. Right to vote
   b. Engagement in political events
  4. Land ownership
 B. For southern whites, an imperiled birthright
  1. Postwar demoralization
   a. Loss of life
   b. Destruction of property
   c. Draining of planters' wealth and privilege
   d. Psychic blow of emancipation
     i. Inability to accept
     ii. Intolerance of black autonomy or equality
 C. For northern Republicans, "free labor"
  1. Middle approach between aspirations of freedpeople and planters
  2. Ambiguous role of federal government; Freedmen's Bureau
   a. Achievements in education and health care
   b. Betrayal of commitment to land reform
 D. Post-emancipation labor systems
  1. Task system (rice)
  2. Wage labor (sugar)
  3. Sharecropping (cotton, tobacco)
 E. Subversion of independent white yeomanry
  1. Spread of indebtedness, dependence on cotton production
  2. Sharecropping and crop lien systems
 F. Urban growth

II. Presidential Reconstruction
 A. Andrew Johnson
  1. Background and character
   a. Humble origins
   b. "Honest yeoman" identity
   c. Political career
   d. Hostility to southern secession and racial equality
  2. Approach to Reconstruction
   a. Pardons
   b. Reserving of political power to whites
 B. Southern white response
  1. Restoration of Confederate leaders and Old South elite
  2. Violence against freedpeople and northerners
  3. Black Codes

    C. Northern reaction
        1. Johnson satisfaction
        2. Republican outrage
    D. Republican goals and principles
        1. Moderate *and* Radical Republicans
            a. Equality of races before the law
            b. Federal enforcement
        2. Radical Republicans only
            a. Dissolution of Confederate-run state governments
            b. Enfranchisement of blacks
            c. Redistribution of land to former slaves
    E. Congressional Republicans vs. Johnson
        1. Passage of bill extending life of Freedmen's Bureau
        2. Passage of Civil Rights Bill
        3. Vetoes and override
        4. Fourteenth Amendment
            a. Terms and significance
            b. Approval by Congress, transmission to states
            c. Controversy in North
                i. Democrats vs. Republicans
                ii. Congress vs. Johnson
        5. 1866 midterm election
            a. Bitter campaign
            b. Republican sweep
            c. Growing breach between Johnson and Republicans

III. Radical Reconstruction
    A. Reconstruction Act
        1. Placement of South under federal military authority
        2. Call for new state governments, entailing black right to vote
    B. Tenure of Office Act
    C. Impeachment of Johnson
        1. Charges
        2. Acquittal
    D. 1868 presidential election
        1. Republican waving of "bloody shirt"
        2. Democratic race-baiting
        3. Ulysses S. Grant victory
    E. Fifteenth Amendment

IV. Significance of "Great Constitutional Revolution"
    A. Idea of national citizenry, equal before the law
    B. Expansion of citizenry to include blacks
    C. Empowerment of federal government to protect citizens' rights

    D. New boundaries of American citizenship
       1. Exclusion of Asian immigrants
       2. Exclusion of women
          a. Unfulfilled campaigns for women's rights
          b. Split within feminism over Reconstruction amendments

V. Radical Reconstruction in the South
    A. Black initiatives
       1. Mass public gatherings
       2. Grassroots protests against segregation
       3. Labor strikes
       4. Political mobilization
       5. Forming of local Republican organizations
          a. Union League
          b. Voter registration
    B. Reconstructed state governments
       1. Composition
          a. Predominance of Republicans
          b. Black Republicans
             i. Officeholding at federal, state, and local levels
             ii. Varied backgrounds
          c. White Republicans
             i. Carpetbaggers
             ii. Scalawags
             iii. Varied motivations of each
       2. Achievements
          a. Public education
          b. Affirmation of civil and political equality
          c. More equal allocation of public services and resources
          d. Measures to protect free labor
          e. Fairer system of justice
          f. Improvement in public facilities
       3. Shortcomings
          a. Uneven enforcement of laws
          b. Economic stagnation
          c. Persistence of black poverty

VI. Overthrow of Reconstruction
    A. Southern white opposition
       1. Grievances expressed
          a. Corruption
          b. Incompetence
          c. High taxes
          d. Black supremacy
       2. Underlying motivations

          a. Antipathy for racial equality
          b. Desire for controllable labor
      3. Use of terror
          a. Against any perceived threat to white supremacy
          b. Against Republicans, black and white
          c. Ku Klux Klan and other secret societies
  B. Northern response
      1. Measures to protect blacks' rights
          a. Enforcement Acts of 1870 and 1871
          b. Civil Rights Act of 1875
      2. Waning commitment to Reconstruction
          a. Liberal Republicans; Horace Greeley
          b. Resurgence of northern racism
          c. Economic depression
          d. Supreme Court decisions
             i. *Slaughterhouse Cases*
            ii. *U.S. v. Cruikshank*
  C. Death throes of Reconstruction
      1. 1874 Democratic gains in South; "Redeemers"
      2. Resurgence of terror
      3. Rise of electoral fraud
      4. Election of 1876 and Bargain of 1877

CHRONOLOGY

1865	Appomattox; end of Civil War
	Lincoln assassinated; Johnson becomes president
	Presidential Reconstruction begins
	Enactment of Black Codes begins in southern legislatures
	Congress refuses to admit southern representatives and senators
	Thirteenth Amendment ratified by the states
1866	Freedmen's Bureau extension and Civil Rights bills passed over Johnson's veto
	Congress passes Fourteenth Amendment (ratified in 1868)
	Republicans sweep congressional elections
1867	Reconstruction Act marks start of Congressional (Radical) Reconstruction
	Tenure of Office Act
1868	Readmission of most southern states
	Johnson impeached; narrowly acquitted
	Grant elected

1869	Congress passes Fifteenth Amendment (ratified in 1870)
1870	Remaining southern states readmitted under Congressional Reconstruction Force Act
1871	Ku Klux Klan Act
1872	Grant reelected
1873	Panic of 1873 triggers economic depression *Slaughterhouse Cases*
1874	Democrats claim electoral victories across South
1875	Civil Rights Act
1876	*U.S. v. Cruikshank* Disputed presidential election between Hayes and Tilden
1877	Bargain of 1877; end of Reconstruction

KEY TERMS

black families: White southerners had refused to recognize the legitimacy of slave marriages; slaves had relied upon ceremonies such as "jumping the broom" to publicly celebrate their unions. With the end of slavery, black southerners sought to legitimize their marriages, and throughout the region couples appeared before ministers to exchange their vows. Some former slaves also used their changed status to end relationships, seizing upon emancipation as a means to separate from an unloved partner.

presidential pardons: Republicans hoped that President Andrew Johnson would deal firmly with former Confederates. They had good reason to believe he would—his contempt for the elite planter class was no secret. However, the president surprised and dismayed observers, approving some 13,500 petitions for pardon; about half of those were granted to individuals owning more than $20,000. In addition, Johnson issued a series of amnesty acts, including one that pardoned all Confederate officials indicted for treason. This act, issued after the presidential election of 1868, applied to prominent individuals including Jefferson Davis and Robert E. Lee.

"swing around the circle": Andrew Johnson's effort to influence the outcome of the 1866 congressional elections proved disastrous. The president employed a rough-and-tumble style in which stump speakers challenged hecklers in the audience. While this approach may have been popular in the rural South, audiences in northern cities such as Cleveland and Cincinnati found the president's appearances repugnant. To make matters worse, Johnson's political foes may have planted hecklers in the crowds. Goaded by their hostile taunts, Johnson made wild statements. In one speech he declared that some members of Congress should be hanged. As a result, the "swing around the circle," as the speaking tour was called, further weakened Johnson even as he was rapidly losing support in Congress.

literacy tests: Southern states sought to evade the Fifteenth Amendment's protection of voting rights by implementing legal obstacles to voting. One such obstacle was the literacy test. Many states required prospective voters to read and interpret a written text, often a section of the state constitution. Because registrars had discretion as to when to require the literacy test, it quickly became a means to prevent African-Americans from voting. In 1904, the U.S. Supreme Court banned the use of literacy tests that were blatantly discriminatory, but allowed the states to continue to implement tests. It was not until the 1970s that Congress suspended the use of literacy tests throughout the United States.

Bradwell v. Illinois: The case of *Bradwell v. Illinois* involved Myra Bradwell, an Illinois woman who sought admission to the state bar so that she could practice law. Although she was clearly qualified, an Illinois court denied her application on the grounds that as a married woman Bradwell could not legally enter into contracts with clients. Her appeal to the state supreme court met with another objection. That court ruled that the state legislature never intended any woman, single or married, to become an attorney. The U.S. Supreme Court also rejected Bradwell's claim, ruling that the Fourteenth Amendment did not limit a state's ability to regulate professions. In a concurring opinion, Justice Joseph Bradley asserted that the "destiny and mission of woman are to fulfill the noble and benign offices of wife and mother." Almost a century would pass before the U.S. Supreme Court used the Fourteenth Amendment to overturn state laws that mandated sex discrimination. Meanwhile, however, the Illinois legislature passed a bill permitting women to practice law, with the first woman admitted to the bar in 1873.

Enforcement Acts: The third Enforcement Act, commonly called the Ku Klux Klan Act, had an immediate impact on Klan activities in South Carolina. President Ulysses Grant used the act to declare a state of rebellion in nine South Carolina counties. Grant suspended the writ of habeas corpus, allowing federal officials to detain suspected Klan members without having to explain or defend the detention in court. As federal troops combed the region, some 2,000 Klansmen fled. A federal grand jury indicted 3,000 people for violating the Enforcement Act; prosecutors allowed those who cooperated to receive suspended sentences. Ringleaders were tried, with some 250 receiving short jail terms, and another 65 receiving lengthy terms in federal prison. The success of the Ku Klux Klan Act in South Carolina revealed that such laws were effective when the federal government sought to enforce them.

Civil Rights Act of 1875: The lame-duck Congress that convened in December 1874 marked the end of Republican dominance. In the elections in the preceding month, Democrats had captured the House of Representatives. Hoping to safeguard black civil rights before losing the House, a group of Republicans introduced legislation that mandated equal access to public accommodations. Penalties included for violating the act included fines of up to $1000. After removing a controversial provision mandating the integration of schools and public cemeteries, Congress approved the legislation. The law led to some confusion, as it was not clear what the term "equal access" implied. For example, a Kentucky theater owner claimed that requiring black patrons to sit in the balcony constituted equal access. More important, many judges, even some outside the South, regarded the law as unconstitutional. This issue was resolved in 1883, when the U.S. Supreme Court heard five cases known collectively as the *Civil Rights Cases.* The court ruled that the 1875 law was unconstitutional because the Fourteenth Amendment banned discrimination by the states, not by individuals or private businesses. It was not until 1964 that Congress banned racial discrimination in public places, relying upon the Commerce Clause rather than the Fourteenth Amendment.

Slaughterhouse Cases: The *Slaughterhouse Cases,* which limited the application of the Fourteenth Amendment, arose from an effort to protect public health in Louisiana. The state hoped to limit threats to public health by requiring that livestock in New Orleans and its neighboring parishes be butchered at specific locations. To achieve this goal, the state provided a monopoly to one company. Butchers in the region complained that taking animals to the Crescent City Live-Stock Landing and Slaughtering Company was an unfair burden, increasing their expenses while lining the pockets of the company owners. Repeated efforts to end the monopoly in state courts failed. When the butchers hired John A. Campbell, a former justice on the U.S. Supreme Court, the butchers' cause earned national importance. Campbell argued that the monopoly violated the Fourteenth Amendment's guarantee of equal protection under the law. The U.S. Supreme Court ruled 5–4 against the butchers, declaring that the goal of the Fourteenth Amendment had been to protect black Americans, not to fundamentally alter the relationship between the federal government and the states. The dissenting justices offered a broader interpretation of the amendment, arguing that it guaranteed protections beyond those needed by African-Americans.

OBJECTIVE QUESTIONS

Multiple Choice

1. During Reconstruction, the black church functioned as a vital setting for
   A. political mobilization.
   B. worship.
   C. schooling.
   D. all of the above

2. One of the main purposes of the Freedmen's Bureau was to
   A. induce former slaves to work for free, at least until they had proved their usefulness to potential employers.
   B. ensure a fair and viable system of labor relations between former slaves and former slaveholders.
   C. encourage whites to work for blacks, as a way to deepen interracial understanding.
   D. encourage freedpeople to move out West, where they could make a new start.

3. Which of the following series of events is listed in proper sequence?
   A. assassination of Lincoln; passage by Congress of Fourteenth Amendment; passage of southern Black Codes; Johnson veto of Civil Rights Bill
   B. ratification of Thirteenth Amendment; Tenure of Office Act; impeachment of Johnson; election of Grant
   C. *Slaughterhouse Cases;* 1875 Civil Rights Act; passage by Congress of Fourteenth Amendment; Reconstruction Act
   D. Ku Klux Klan Act; election of Grant; ratification of Fifteenth Amendment; Bargain of 1877

4. Which of the following was *not* a widespread activity among newly emancipated blacks?
   A. seeking to obtain land of their own
   B. learning how to read and write
   C. moving about just to get the feel of freedom
   D. moving to the North in search of greater freedom and opportunity

5. Who among the following was *not* a leader of the Radical Republicans?
   A. Charles Sumner
   B. Thaddeus Stevens
   C. Andrew Johnson
   D. Benjamin Wade

6. Which of the following was *not* a central thrust of the Reconstruction amendments to the Constitution?
   A. redistribution of the former slaveowners' land among the freed slaves
   B. equal citizenship for blacks and whites
   C. the right to vote, regardless of race
   D. empowerment of the federal government to protect citizens' rights

7. Which of the following was *not* a major effect of Reconstruction (at its height) upon southern society?
   A. It saw the federal government take a direct role in the relations between black and white southerners.
   B. It saw the spread of schools and churches across the South, built by and for African-Americans.
   C. It inspired a mass exodus of southern blacks to lands that had never known slavery.
   D. It helped restrain southern whites from exploiting the labor of former slaves.

8. Which of the following was *not* a major cause of the decline of Reconstruction?
   A. the use of fraud and terror to prevent blacks from voting or running for office
   B. a deepening of mutual respect between black and white southerners, making Reconstruction seem no longer necessary
   C. a growing perception among northerners that southern blacks were unfit for equal citizenship
   D. a growing weariness in the North with the sectional issue and the burdens of enforcing Reconstruction

9. What was being reconstructed (constructed again) in Reconstruction?
   A. the West
   B. slavery
   C. the nation
   D. the Civil War

10. In the five years following the end of the Civil War, former slaves were guaranteed the following in three Amendments to the United States Constitution:
    A. forty acres and a mule; education; and equality
    B. the right to marry anyone of their choosing; freedom of assembly; land
    C. freedom from slavery; recognition as citizens; the vote for adult black men
    D. forty acres; education; and equal justice under law

11. The phrase, "forty acres and a mule," derived from:
    A. Lincoln's "10% Plan."
    B. The Wade-Davis Bill.

    C. Sherman's Field Order 15.

    D. The Emancipation Proclamation.

12. Which were central elements in the lives of post-emancipation blacks in the twenty years following the end of the Civil War?
    A. the family, the corporations, the university
    B. the family, the church, the school
    C. the boss, the cabin, the library
    D. the boss, the library, the farm

13. In the aftermath of the Civil War, the black church was a powerful influence in the South; what two denominations commanded the largest African-American following?
    A. Catholic and Protestant
    B. Episcopalian and Presbyterian
    C. Baptist and Methodist
    D. Lutheran and Church of Christ

14. As meant in the section on the free labor system, define "free labor":
    A. non-slave labor in a market economy
    B. voluntary labor done without pay
    C. labor you donate to a cause because you believe in it and so work for free
    D. labor that was without cost to the business owner

15. Which was *not* a principal task of the Freedmen's Bureau (1865–1870)?
    A. the establishment of schools
    B. to secure former slaves equal treatment before the courts
    C. to support black churches and businesses
    D. to provide aid to the poor and aged

16. In the summer of 1865, President Andrew Johnson ordered nearly all land in federal hands:
    A. given to freed blacks.
    B. given to poor blacks and whites.
    C. given to the railroads.
    D. returned to its former owners.

17. Sharecropping:
    A. allowed a black family to rent part of a plantation, with the crop divided between worker and owner at the end of the year.
    B. meant that black families shared their crops with each other, especially in times of hardship or drought.
    C. was a method of harvesting crops such that the soil was left intact for next year's planting.
    D. was a government-led economic initiative that sought to have people share the wealth in rural towns and in the countryside.

18. Following the Civil War, white and black farmers in the South:
    A. experienced extremely high prices for cotton.
    B. experienced rapidly rising prices.
    C. saw the price of cotton fall steadily.
    D. saw a leveling off of the price of cotton to pre-war levels.

19. Upon Lincoln's assassination, _____ became president.
    A. Ulysses S. Grant
    B. John Addams
    C. Andrew Jackson
    D. Andrew Johnson

20. In President Andrew Johnson's view, African-Americans ought to play what part in Reconstruction?
    A. none
    B. take up leadership positions in the Deep South
    C. take up leadership positions in the boarder states
    D. take up leadership positions in the federal government, but not in individual state governments

21. The Black Codes were:
    A. codes of honor by which newly freed black Americans lived.
    B. laws that sought to regulate the lives of former slaves.
    C. secret codes used by freed blacks in regions where the KKK was strongest.
    D. a secret code combining elements of Creole and Pidgin English.

22. Black Americans who refused to sign labor contracts to work for whites during Reconstruction:
    A. were often put on trains and sent out West.
    B. were often put on trains and sent to northern cities.
    C. were often convicted of vagrancy and fined; sometimes they were then auctioned off to work for the person who paid the fine.
    D. were convicted and sentenced to execution.

23. Radical Republicans in the Reconstruction Era shared the view that:
    A. the Union victory created a golden opportunity to institutionalize the principal of equal rights for all, regardless of race.
    B. the government should minimize its involvement in the economy and allow laissez faire to flourish.
    C. sought the repatriation of expatriate fugitives.
    D. allied themselves with the president in an effort to bring about "freedom and justice for all."

24. The Reconstruction Act of March 1867:
    A. allowed the Redeemers to reconstruct the South after their own lights.
    B. divided the South into five military districts and called for creation of new state governments, with black men given the right to vote.

    C. voided the Supreme Court's decision in *ex parte Milligan.*

    D. barred the president from removing certain officeholders, including cabinet members, without consent of the Senate.

25. The House of Representatives approved articles of impeachment against President Andrew Johnson for violation of what law?
    A. The Reconstruction Act
    B. The Fourteenth Amendment
    C. The Civil Rights Act
    D. The Tenure of Office Act

26. The Fifteenth Amendment to the United States Constitution:
    A. prohibited federal and state governments from denying any citizen the vote because of race.
    B. guaranteed freed slaves citizenship.
    C. ended slavery and indentured servitude.
    D. made the income tax constitutional.

27. "The destruction of slavery led feminists to search for ways to make the promise of free labor real for women." Define "feminists" in this context:
    A. persons who held a view advocating social, political, and other rights for women equal to those of men
    B. women who sought to destroy the nation's integrity by insisting that girls and young women receive separate educations
    C. women who wanted to volunteer their labor and time for causes they thought real
    D. men and women who wanted the promise of free labor extended to the destruction of slavery

28. The Enforcement Acts of 1870 and 1871:
    A. defined crimes that deprived citizens of their civil and political rights as federal offenses, and under these laws President Grant sent federal marshals to arrest hundreds of accused Klansmen.
    B. asserted South Carolina's right to nullify any federal law it deemed improper or unjust, and to enforce that decision.
    C. sought to sue for peace with Britain and Spain in the wake of the resurgence of international tensions surrounding imperialist filibustering.
    D. sought to enforce the Black Codes in places where they were not being properly adjudicated.

29. Which was *not* true of Liberal Republicans in the post-Civil War era?
    A. They nominated Horace Greeley for president.
    B. They formed their own political party.
    C. They believed the growth of federal power needed to be expanded.
    D. They were less committed to equal rights for blacks than the Radical Republicans had been.

30. In consequence of the "Bargain of 1877" President Rutherford B. Hayes:
    A. ordered all federal purchase orders for military uniforms to be purchased at bargain or discount prices.
    B. ordered federal troops withdrawn from the South.
    C. ordered federal troops to return to their barracks.
    D. ordered that future bargains, such as those promoted by the corrupt politicians involved in the Whiskey Ring, be made illegal.

True or False

1. After emancipation, many freedwomen elected to withdraw from work in the fields and focus their energies at home.
2. The Black Codes were laws passed by southern Republicans to promote black rights.
3. Charles Sumner and Thaddeus Stevens argued that planters' land should be confiscated and redistributed among former slaves.
4. "Scalawags" were southern white Republicans.
5. The Fifteenth Amendment granted the vote to white women but not black women.
6. Under Radical Reconstruction, blacks held most of the South's top elected positions.
7. During the 1872 elections, the Liberal Republicans argued that Reconstruction was a failure.
8. The Bargain of 1877 marked the formal end to Reconstruction.
9. Between 1880 and 1940 there were more white sharecroppers than black sharecroppers.
10. Presidential Reconstruction (1865–1867) was a success.
11. Black Codes denied black Americans the right to testify against whites, serve on juries or in state militias, or vote.
12. Black Codes sometimes assigned black children to work for their former masters without parental consent.
13. In 1866, the Civil Rights Bill became the first major law in American history to be passed over a presidential veto.
14. The period of Radical Reconstruction began in March 1867 with Congress's adoption of the Reconstruction Act over the president's veto and ended in 1877.

15. Prior to ratification of the Fourteenth Amendment the rights guaranteed in the Bill of Rights applied only to laws made by the federal government, not to laws made by individual states.

16. Susan B. Anthony and Elizabeth Cady Stanton, leading figures in the women's rights movement, were strong supporters of the Fifteenth Amendment.

17. During Radical Reconstruction, following ratification of the Fifteenth Amendment, the vast majority of eligible African-Americans registered to vote.

18. During Reconstruction some 2,000 African-Americans held public office, among them fourteen in the United States House of Representatives and two U.S. Senators.

19. Some 700 blacks sat in state legislatures during Reconstruction.

20. Robert Smalls, a black Representative in the United States House of Representatives, was elected to five terms in Congress.

21. Among the important accomplishments of Reconstruction state governments was the establishment of the South's first state-supported public schools.

22. During Reconstruction, a number of state governments initiated civil rights legislation that made it illegal for railroads, hotels, and other institutions to discriminate on the basis of race.

23. In consequence of the Reconstruction governments across the South, the region became a vibrant and successful hub of dynamic and expansive economic growth, allowing many African-Americans to escape from poverty.

24. While corruption was almost non-existent in the North, it was rampant in the South.

25. Opposition to Reconstruction resulted from the distaste many southerners had for tax increases that were needed to fund public schools and other improvements, and also because many white southerners could not accept black Americans voting, holding office, and enjoying equality before the law.

26. The KKK was founded in 1866 as a social club in Tennessee and served, in effect, as a military arm of the Democratic Party.

27. The Ku Klux Klan sought to uphold the American ideal of equality and justice for all.

28. In 1873, the country was plunged into an economic depression and support among Republicans for further reforms in the South weakened.

29. In the *Slaughterhouse Cases* (1873) the Supreme Court ruled that the Fourteenth Amendment had not altered traditional federalism.

30. "Redeemers" saved the South from the corrupt ways of Reconstruction politics and redeemed the South for fair and equal treatment for all Americans.

31. Black Americans continued to hold offices in the South into the 1890s.

32. The Civil Rights era of the 1950s and 1960s is sometimes called the Second Reconstruction.

ESSAY QUESTIONS

1. Describe the various ways in which southern blacks sought to experience their freedom following emancipation.

2. Compare the Reconstruction programs of Andrew Johnson and the Radical Republicans. How did they differ in their aims, their methods, their underlying beliefs, and their effects on the South?

3. Imagine a chance meeting, in 1865, among the following characters:

   - a former slave
   - a former slaveowner
   - a southern white yeoman farmer
   - a northern Republican
   - a follower of Andrew Johnson

   With remarkable candor, they launch into a freewheeling exchange on the question of what a "reconstructed" South should look like. (Each participant, it becomes clear, has his or her own conception of "freedom".) Transcribe this conversation.

4. Imagine another chance meeting, in 1877, among the same characters. Looking back on the rise and fall of Reconstruction over the past dozen years, they exchange views on Reconstruction's benefits and shortcomings, successes and failures. Transcribe this conversation.

5. Former slaves' definition of freedom resembled that of white Americans— self-ownership, family stability, religious liberty, political participation, and economic autonomy. But blacks formed a vision very much their own. Write an essay about the former slaves' vision of freedom.

6. Why was land ownership so important to ex-slaves?

7. Explain the profound changes in the nature of citizenship, the structure of constitutional authority, and the meaning of American freedom in the Reconstruction Era.

SOURCES FOR FURTHER RESEARCH

Books

GENERAL OVERVIEWS

Du Bois, W. E. B., *Black Reconstruction in America, 1860–1880* (1935)
Foner, Eric, *Reconstruction: America's Unfinished Revolution, 1863–1877* (1988)
Franklin, John Hope, *Reconstruction after the Civil War* (1960)

PARTICULAR ASPECTS

Carter, Dan T., *When the War Was Over: The Failure of Self-Reconstruction in the South, 1865–1867* (1985)
Cooper, Frederick, Thomas C. Holt, and Rebecca J. Scott, *Beyond Slavery: Explorations of Race, Labor, and Citizenship in Postemancipation Societies* (2000)
DuBois, Ellen C., *Feminism and Suffrage: The Emergence of an Independent Women's Movement in America, 1848–1869* (1978)
Edwards, Laura F., *Gendered Strife and Confusion: The Political Culture of Reconstruction* (1997)
Fields, Barbara, *Slavery and Freedom on the Middle Ground: Maryland During the Nineteenth Century* (1985)
Hahn, Steven, *A Nation under Our Feet: Black Political Struggles in the Rural South from Slavery to the Great Migration* (2003)
Holt, Thomas C., *Black over White: Negro Leadership in South Carolina during Reconstruction* (1978)
Hyman, Harold M., *A More Perfect Union: The Impact of the Civil War and Reconstruction on the Constitution* (1973)
Litwack, Leon F., *Been in the Storm So Long: The Aftermath of Slavery* (1979)
Rabinowitz, Howard N., ed., *Southern Black Leaders of the Reconstruction Era* (1982)
Rable, George C., *But There Was No Peace: The Role of Violence in the Politics of Reconstruction* (1984)
Ransom, Roger L., and Richard Sutch, *One Kind of Freedom: The Economic Consequences of Emancipation* (1977)

Richardson, Heather C., *The Death of Reconstruction: Race, Labor, and Politics in the Post–Civil War North* (2001)

Rodrigue, John C., *Reconstruction in the Cane Fields: From Slavery to Free Labor in Louisiana's Sugar Parishes, 1862–1880* (2001)

Schwalm, Leslie, *"A Hard Fight for We": Women's Transition from Slavery to Freedom in South Carolina* (1997)

Summers, Mark W., *Railroads, Reconstruction, and the Gospel of Prosperity: Aid Under the Radical Republicans, 1865–1877* (1984)

Trefousse, Hans L., *The Radical Republicans: Lincoln's Vanguard for Racial Justice* (1969)

Videos

Abolition: Broken Promises (50 minutes; Films for the Humanities and Sciences, 1998)

Dr. Toer's Amazing Magic Lantern Show (24 minutes, American Social History Project, 1987)

Reconstruction: The Second Civil War (180 minutes, PBS Video, 2004)

The Rise and Fall of Jim Crow: Episode 1: Promises Betrayed (1865–1896) (60 minutes, Quest Productions, Videoline Productions, and Thirteen/WNET, 2002)

Web Resources

The African American Odyssey, Volume V: Reconstruction and Its Aftermath, Library of Congress
http://memory.loc.gov/ammem/aaohtml/exhibit/aopart5.html

Freedmen and Southern Society Project, University of Maryland
http://www.history.umd.edu/Freedmen/

Freedmen's Bureau Online, Christine's Genealogy Web sites
http://www.freedmensbureau.com

ANSWERS TO OBJECTIVE QUESTIONS

Multiple Choice

1-D, 2-B, 3-B, 4-D, 5-C, 6-A, 7-C, 8-B, 9-C, 10-C, 11-C, 12-B, 13-C, 14-A, 15-C, 16-D, 17-A, 18-C, 19-D, 20-A, 21-B, 22-C, 23-A, 24-B, 25-D, 26-A, 27-A, 28-A, 29-C, 30-B

True or False

1-T, 2-F, 3-T, 4-T, 5-F, 6-F, 7-T, 8-T, 9-T, 10-F, 11-T, 12-T, 13-T, 14-T, 15-T, 16-F, 17-T, 18-T, 19-T, 20-T, 21-T, 22-T, 23-F, 24-F, 25-T, 26-T, 27-F, 28-T, 29-T, 30-F, 31-T, 32-T

| America's Gilded Age, 1870–1890

CHAPTER OBJECTIVES

- What were the key causes, features, and social impacts of the second industrial revolution?
- How did working people experience and respond to the industrial revolution?
- What gave rise to the urban boom of the late nineteenth century?
- How was the American West transformed during the closing decades of the nineteenth century?
- What were the respective programs and constituencies of the Democratic and Republican parties during these years?
- What were the leading points of social conflict in industrializing America?

CHAPTER OUTLINE

I. Second industrial revolution
   A. Astounding pace and magnitude
   B. Emergence of factory as foremost realm of industrial production
   C. Emergence of wage labor as prevalent source of livelihood
   D. Emergence of city as chief setting for manufacture
      1. Leading industrial cities
         a. New York
         b. Chicago
         c. Pittsburgh
      2. Single-industry cities
   E. Expansion of national market
      1. Eastern markets for western goods (agricultural, extractive)

    2. Western markets for eastern goods (manufactured)

    3. Central role of railroad

    4. National brands, chains, mail order firms

F. Technological innovations

    1. Leading breakthroughs

    2. Thomas A. Edison's research laboratories

G. Competition and consolidation

    1. Volatility of marketplace

    2. Downward pressure on prices; Great Depression of 1873–1897

    3. Ruthless competition among businesses

    4. Corporate initiatives to stabilize marketplace

       a. Pools

       b. Trusts

       c. Mergers

H. Industrial giants

    1. Vast accumulations of wealth and power

    2. Leading business figures

       a. Thomas A. Scott (railroad)

          i. Size and scope of Pennsylvania Railroad

          ii. Prototype of modern business organization

       b. Andrew Carnegie (steel)

          i. Personal rise

          ii. Vertical integration

          iii. Blend of philanthropy and dictatorial management

       c. John D. Rockefeller (oil)

          i. Cutthroat competition

          ii. Horizontal integration

          iii. Blend of philanthropy and dictatorial management

    3. Popular perceptions of

       a. Favorable; "captains of industry"

       b. Unfavorable; "robber barons"

I. Workers' conditions in industrial America

    1. Advantages for skilled labor elite

       a. High wages

       b. Areas of control

          i. Process of production

          ii. Pace of production

          iii. Training of apprentices

    2. Hardships for growing ranks of semi-skilled workers

       a. Economic insecurity

          i. Unreliability of employment and wage rates

          ii. Lack of pensions

          iii. Lack of compensation for injury or unemployment

    b. Working conditions
      i. Length of workday
      ii. Dangers of workplace
    c. Odds against collective action
   3. Breadth and depth of poverty
  J. Growing signs of class division
   1. New urban middle-class neighborhoods
   2. Exclusive world of the rich
    a. Home and neighborhood
    b. Resorts, social clubs, schools
    c. "Conspicuous consumption" (Thorstein Veblen)
    d. 1897 Waldorf-Astoria costume ball
   3. Contrasts of wealth and poverty
    a. Matthew Smith's *Sunshine and Shadow*
    b. Jacob Riis's *How the Other Half Lives*

II. Transformation of the West
  A. Overall themes
   1. Variety of regions within West
   2. Variant on global patterns of political and economic incorporation
    a. Displacement of indigenous peoples
    b. Promotion of business development
    c. Promotion of population settlement
    d. Vital role of government
  B. Farming empire
   1. Spread of land under cultivation
   2. Pace and diversity of settlement
   3. Wheat and corn production on Middle Border
   4. Hardships of Great Plains farming
    a. Hazards of nature
    b. Hard labor and solitude (especially for women)
   5. Call for large-scale irrigation
    a. John Wesley Powell
    b. Implications for small-scale farmers
   6. Increasing market orientation of small farmers
    a. Forms
      i. Sale of crops
      ii. Purchase of manufactured goods
    b. Impacts
      i. Dependence on loans
      ii. Vulnerability to shifts in world markets
   7. Budding trend toward large-scale farming
    a. Features
    b. California precedent

  C. Cowboys
     1. Diversity
     2. Myth vs. reality
     3. Rise and decline of cattle drives
  D. Corporate West
     1. Prominent manufacturing and trading centers
        a. San Francisco
        b. Los Angeles
     2. Large corporate enterprises
        a. Lumber
        b. Mining
        c. Railroad
     3. Displacement of independent prospectors, farmers
  E. Subjugation of Indians
     1. Earlier transformations of Plains Indians
        a. Eighteenth-century shift to hunting and farming
        b. Arrival and coalescence of rival tribes
     2. U.S.-Indian conflict on the Plains
        a. Emergence in 1850s
        b. During Civil War
        c. President Ulysses S. Grant's "peace policy"
        d. Systematic onslaught on Indian life
            i. By army, hunters
           ii. On villages, horses, buffalo
     3. U.S.-Indian conflict further west
        a. Defeat of the Navajo
            i. Destruction of orchards and sheep
           ii. Removal to reservation
        b. Defeat of the Nez Percé
            i. Pursuit of and capture by U.S. Army
           ii. Removal to reservation
          iii. Chief Joseph's Washington speech
     4. Continuation of Indian resistance
        a. Sioux-Cheyenne victory at Little Big Horn
        b. Apache escapes and raids
     5. Ongoing white encroachment
        a. New western states
        b. Railroads, soldiers, settlers
        c. Indian reservations
            i. Spread of
           ii. Impoverishment, exploitation
        d. Reduction of Sitting Bull to popular spectacle
     6. Federal assault on Indian culture
        a. Imposition of white American values

b. Elimination of treaty system
c. Dawes Act
 i. Provisions
 ii. Outcomes
7. Indian citizenship
 a. Conditional offers of American citizenship in nineteenth century
 b. Judicial obstructions to equal citizenship for Indians
  i. Western courts
  ii. Supreme Court
 c. Gradual expansion of Indian citizenship
8. Closing act
 a. Ghost Dance
 b. Wounded Knee massacre

III. Politics in a Gilded Age
 A. Origins and meanings of "Gilded Age"
 B. Political corruption
  1. Widespread unease over
  2. Manifestations of
   a. Corporate lobbyists
   b. Urban political machines; "Boss" Tweed
   c. Crédit Mobilier scandal
 C. The political parties
  1. Imprint of Civil War on each
  2. Social and regional bases of support
   a. Republican
   b. Democratic
  3. Close division of popular support
   a. Presidential elections
   b. Congressional elections
   c. Political stalemate
 D. The state of American political democracy
  1. Indications of vitality
   a. Closely contested elections
   b. Intense party loyalty
   c. High voter turnout
   d. Spectacular rallies and oratory
  2. Meager response to social problems of industrial era
   a. Minimal nature of federal government
    i. Size
    ii. Scale of activity
   b. Deference of both parties to business interests
   c. Divergence of parties over tariff policy
   d. Convergence of parties over fiscal policy

3. Achievements of national politics (and their limits)
    a. Civil Service Act
    b. Interstate Commerce Act
    c. Sherman Antitrust Act
E. Political ferment in the states
    1. Debate over role of government at state and local levels
        a. Potential points of intervention
        b. Actual points of intervention
    2. Popular campaigns for government action
        a. Greenback-Labor party
        b. Grange
        c. Labor movement
    3. Legacies of popular campaigns
        a. Mixed results in short-term
        b. Sowing of long-term debate on political and economic freedom

IV. Freedom in the Gilded Age
A. Debate over aspects of new social order
    1. Relations between classes
    2. Coexistence of poverty and wealth
    3. Advent of "permanent factory population"
B. Defenses of Gilded Age inequalities
    1. Justifications for concentration of wealth, low wages
    2. Uncoupling of principles of freedom and equality
C. New "liberal" reformers
    1. Fear of lower-class democracy
    2. Commitment to individual liberty and property rights
D. Social Darwinism
    1. Application of evolutionary science to social problems
    2. Implications for social policy
        a. Acceptance of poverty, material inequality
        b. Rejection of public relief, economic regulation
        c. Notion of "undeserving" poor
    3. William Graham Sumner; *What Social Classes Owe to Each Other*
E. Liberty of contract
    1. Link to Social Darwinism
    2. Themes
        a. Freedom as limited government and unrestrained market
        b. Sanctity of labor contract
            i.   As arbiter of free labor
            ii. As beyond reach of public intervention

     3. Promotion by the courts; overturning or distortion of regulatory legislation

       a. *Munn v. Illinois*

       b. *Wabash v. Illinois*

       c. Pro-business slant in ICC cases

       d. *U.S. v. E.C. Knight Co.*

       e. Use of Sherman Antitrust Act against labor

       f. *Lochner v. New York*

V. Labor and the republic

   A. 1877 railroad strike and emergence of "labor question"

   B. Resurgence of labor movement

     1. Knights of Labor

       a. Size and diversity

       b. Range of activities

     2. Variety of programs

     3. Common targets

       a. Ideologies of Social Darwinism and liberty of contract

       b. Growing loss of economic independence

       c. Inequalities of wealth and power

       d. Corruption of democracy by concentrated capital

   C. Middle-class reformers

     1. Unease over social conditions, concentrated capital, class conflict

     2. Range of social prescriptions

   D. Leading works of social criticism

     1. Henry George's *Progress and Poverty*

       a. Statement of problem

       b. "Single tax" solution

       c. Conceptions of freedom

       d. Mass popularity

     2. Laurence Gronlund's *The Cooperative Commonwealth*

       a. Popularization of socialist ideal in America

       b. Core socialist principles

       c. Socialism as outcome of peaceful evolution

     3. Edward Bellamy's *Looking Backward*

       a. Futuristic utopian novel

       b. Themes

         i. Embrace of cooperation, interdependence, equality, economic security, powerful state

         ii. Rejection of class strife, individualism, inequality, competition

       c. Impact

         i. Inspiration for Nationalist clubs

         ii. Influence on reform thought

E. Social Gospel movement
   1. Seedbed
      a. Emerging strain within Protestantism
      b. Variant within Catholicism
   2. Themes and initiatives
      a. Critique of Social Darwinism, laissez-faire doctrine, Gospel of Wealth
      b. Vision of equalization of wealth and power, checks on competition
      c. Efforts to ameliorate working-class conditions
      d. Promotion of cooperative organization of economy
F. 1886: Labor's great upheaval
   1. Explosive growth of Knights of Labor
   2. Nationwide May Day demonstration for eight-hour day
   3. Haymarket Affair (Chicago)
      a. Background
         i. Iron moulders' strikes of 1885 and 1886
         ii. Killing of strikers by police
      b. Bloodshed at Haymarket Square
      c. Scapegoating of labor movement
         i. As violent
         ii. As vehicle of immigrant radicals
      d. "Haymarket martyrs"
         i. Arrests, trial, and conviction of anarchists
         ii. Hangings, imprisonment, commutations
         iii. Albert and Lucy Parsons
G. Labor and politics
   1. Spread of independent labor political campaigns
      a. Connection to Knights of Labor
      b. Major goals
      c. Electoral successes
   2. New York mayoral campaign of Henry George
   3. Decline of Knights of Labor

CHRONOLOGY

1868   Matthew Smith publishes *Sunshine and Shadow*

1869   President Grant announces short-lived "peace policy" with Plains Indians
        Completion of transcontinental railroad
        Knights of Labor founded

1871   Congress eliminates treaty system of U.S.-Indian relations

1873	Panic of 1873; start of five-year depression *The Gilded Age* published by Mark Twain and Charles Dudley Warner
1876	Battle of Little Big Horn
1877	Bargain of 1877; end of Reconstruction Great Railroad Strike U.S. Army pursuit and capture of Nez Percé in Far West
1879	United States returns to gold standard Henry George publishes *Progress and Poverty*
1882	Thomas A. Edison opens first electric generating station, in Manhattan
1883	Railroads divide nation into four standard time zones Civil Service Act William Graham Sumner publishes *What Social Classes Owe to Each Other*
1884	*Elk v. Wilkins* Laurence Gronlund publishes *The Cooperative Commonwealth*
1886	Dedication of Statue of Liberty *Wabash v. Illinois* Nationwide May Day demonstration for eight-hour day Haymarket Affair Henry George's New York mayoral campaign
1886–87	Two harsh winters trigger collapse of western cattle boom
1887	Dawes Act Interstate Commerce Act
1888	Edward Bellamy publishes *Looking Backward*
1890	Jacob Riis publishes *How the Other Half Lives* Sherman Antitrust Act Wounded Knee massacre
1895	*U.S. v. E.C. Knight Co.*
1897	Waldorf-Astoria costume ball
1905	*Lochner v. New York*

KEY TERMS

standard gauge: The nation's railroad system grew erratically over the course of the nineteenth century. As a result, there were no uniform standards regarding the gauge, or distance between the rails, on railroad tracks. By the 1880s most railroads in the northern and western states had adopted a standard gauge of 4 feet 8.5 inches. In the southern states, however, some 13,000 miles of track had a gauge three inches wider. The difference in gauges necessitated moving goods and people onto different trains at points where the two gauges met, or using railroad cars with unusually wide wheels that worked on both gauges. To resolve this problem, railway workers gathered on Sunday May 30, 1886, to move 13,000 miles of southern rails three inches closer together, a monumental effort that brought uniformity to the nation's rail system.

Standard Oil: In 1870, the year it was founded, Standard Oil controlled some ten percent of the nation's oil refineries. Within a decade, it controlled ninety percent of the refining industry. The head of Standard Oil, John D. Rockefeller, propelled his company to dominance in part by shrewd manipulation of the railroads. Rockefeller would offer a particular railroad the opportunity to transport his oil; in return, the railroad would provide Standard Oil with rebates. If the railroad carried a competitor's product, it had to pay a fee, known as a drawback, to Standard Oil. The opportunity to transport vast quantities of oil was too good a deal for railroad owners to pass up, so they agreed to the rebates and drawbacks. Soon, many railroads became dependent upon Standard's business. For example, when the Pennsylvania Railroad continued to carry a rival's oil, Rockefeller stopped using that line. The loss of Standard's business ruined the Pennsylvania, and its owner decided to sell. The purchaser of the Pennsylvania Railroad was none other than Standard Oil.

bonanza farming: During the last three decades of the nineteenth century, large-scale agricultural enterprises called bonanza farms appeared in the West, especially in California and North Dakota. These operations, which often covered thousands of acres, relied upon investors for capital and professional managers to run day-to-day operations. Many bonanza farms used the latest technology, including steam-driven tractors, to increase yields. Initially successful, bonanza farms went into decline before the end of the century. Investors were unwilling to weather the poor economic performance that came with drought years. Small family farms, which were able to diversify or to endure market downturns, proved more successful in the West. Despite their failure, however, the bonanza farms pointed the way to the rise of agribusinesses in the twentieth century.

Cowboy Strike of 1883: Potential profits lured investors from as far away as Europe into the cattle ranching industry. Seeking to maximize their earnings, these investors limited cowboys' opportunities to make a living. In the past, cowboys often had been paid with calves, allowing them to build their own herds. In addition, they had been able to claim wild cattle, or mavericks, as their own. When ranch owners ended these practices, cowboys were forced to live on their low wages. In 1883 a group of Texas cowboys demanded higher wages and conducted a strike against five major ranches. Newspaper coverage of the event favored the owners, falsely claiming that the cowboys had planned violence. The Cowboy Strike of 1883 failed, as ranchers fired many strikers and had no trouble hiring replacements.

Ghost Dance: The religious revitalization movement that swept through Great Plains Indian communities in the early 1890s had its roots in the visions of Wovoka, a Paiute Indian prophet. Wovoka claimed that during a solar eclipse on New Years' Day in 1889, he entered a trance and met with the Creator. During his vision he learned that the Creator wanted the Indian people to lead peaceful and ethical lives. In addition, they were to perform a dance known as the Ghost Dance. Word spread throughout the Plains of the new prophet, and Indians from different nations met with Wovoka, often traveling by rail to meet him. Upon returning home, some groups modified his message. For example, the Lakota created the Ghost Dance Shirt, which supposedly provided protection from bullets. The Ghost Dance movement faded rapidly after the events at Wounded Knee in 1890. Some communities, however, continued to perform the Ghost Dance in the early twentieth century.

greenbacks: The cost of the Civil War led the United States government to print some $430 million in paper money, known as greenbacks because the bills were printed with green ink. At war's end, the federal government began withdrawing greenbacks from circulation. This policy led to deflation, in which the amount of money available in the economy declined. With the contraction of the money supply, each individual dollar became more valuable—it could buy more goods. Deflation benefits people who have money; their dollars can buy more. Debtors, however, face increased hardship, as they repay debts with bills more valuable than those they had borrowed. During the Gilded Age, indebted Americans often opposed the withdrawal of the greenbacks and advocated an increase in paper money.

civil service: Some civil servants earned impressive incomes. At a time when the average annual income was some $500 a year, the collector of the New York Customs House earned a salary of $12,000. In addition, the collector received a percentage of the value of seized goods. As a consequence, Chester A. Arthur, who held the position in the early 1870s, had an annual income of $50,000, equivalent to that of the president of the United States and five times that of a Supreme Court justice. Because the 1,300 Customs House employees had the opportunity to earn a great deal of money, politicians ensured that their political allies and cronies received positions there. An investigation in the 1870s revealed that some 200 employees did virtually no work whatsoever.

Sherman Antitrust Act: Congress struggled for two years before approving the Sherman Antitrust Act, which passed both houses with only a single dissenting vote. The legislation made it illegal to engage in "restraint of trade" or "monopolize or attempt to monopolize," and included a $5,000 fine for violations. In addition, any party injured by a trust could sue for triple damages. However, the law offered no clear definitions for restraint of trade or monopoly. As a consequence, the courts were reluctant to find alleged violators guilty. None of the eighteen lawsuits brought against trusts in the decade after the passage of the act resulted in a guilty verdict.

Lochner v. New York: In the late nineteenth century, many Americans labored long hours in unsafe working environments. Bakers in New York often worked 11 to 13 hours a day, seven days a week, in small basement shops that were frequently filthy. In 1895 the New York legislature passed the Bakeshop Act, which limited bakers to a ten-hour day and a sixty-hour week and created an inspections system. Five years later Joseph Lochner, a bakeshop owner in Utica, New York, received a fifty dollar fine for violating the law, as Lochner required his employees to work more than ten hours a day. He appealed his conviction, and in 1905 the U.S. Supreme Court issued its ruling in *Lochner v. New York.* The court invalidated the Bakeshop Act, arguing that the state could not regulate contracts between employers and employees. The court acknowledged that the state could provide for the safety of workers in hazardous workplaces such as mines but maintained that baking was not a dangerous profession. The ruling in *Lochner* made it difficult for states to establish a minimum wage or regulate the workplace until the *Lochner* precedent was modified in later rulings.

OBJECTIVE QUESTIONS

Multiple Choice

1. Two of the Gilded Age's leading business figures were:
   A. Henry George and Thomas A. Edison.
   B. Thomas A. Scott and Andrew Carnegie.
   C. Henry Demarest Lloyd and John D. Rockefeller.
   D. Terence V. Powderly and William Graham Sumner.

2. The phrase that best captures the vision of the Knights of Labor is:
   A. "Survival of the fittest."
   B. "Liberty of contract."
   C. "Cooperative commonwealth."
   D. "Laissez-faire."

3. Which of the following series of events is listed in proper sequence?
    A. Dawes Act; Wounded Knee massacre; Ghost Dance campaign; battle of Little Big Horn
    B. *Munn v. Illinois; Wabash v. Illinois; Interstate Commerce Act; Lochner v. New York*
    C. founding of Knights of Labor; Haymarket Affair; Great Railroad Strike of 1877; close of Reconstruction
    D. Sherman Antitrust Act; Interstate Commerce Act; Civil Service Act; Panic of 1873

4. Which of the following was *not* true of the second industrial revolution?
    A. A boom in automobile manufacture spurred the rise of oil, rubber, and steel production.
    B. More than any other sector, the railroad was the engine of the industrialization.
    C. Some companies rose to dominance by operating at a loss and underselling their rivals.
    D. Some companies beat out the competition by taking over more stages of production and distribution.

5. Which of the following was *not* a major reason for the decline and subjugation of the American Indian?
    A. Valuable natural resources out West gave U.S. settlers a powerful incentive to remove Indians.
    B. The widespread image of Indians as barbaric discouraged measures to protect their independence.
    C. Indifference to the advantages of guns and horses weakened Indian resistance to U.S. military power.
    D. The U.S. government regularly broke treaties designating which land would remain in the hands of the Indians.

6. Which of the following was *not* a theme of Social Darwinism?
    A. Charles Darwin's scientific theories help to explain—and justify—class inequalities in industrial society.
    B. The growing gulf between the haves and the have-nots poses a dire threat to American freedom.
    C. By and large, the poor have only themselves to blame for their misfortune.
    D. Government initiatives to ease the hardships of the poor are misguided.

7. Which of the following was *not* a focus of debate between Democrats and Republicans during the Gilded Age?
    A. laws governing cultural habits
    B. tariffs on imported goods
    C. memories of the Civil War and Reconstruction
    D. federal income tax levels

8. Which of the following was *not* a key episode of the "great upheaval" of 1886?
   A. America's first nationwide railroad strike
   B. the Haymarket Affair
   C. Henry George's New York mayoral campaign
   D. nationwide demonstrations for an eight-hour day

9. Which was *not* a central factor in the explosive economic growth in the second Industrial Revolution?
   A. the country's abundant natural resources
   B. growing supply of labor
   C. expanded markets for manufactured goods
   D. low tariffs

10. The federal government contributed to the dynamic and expansive growth of the American economy in the late 19th century by:
    A. granting land to railroads, removing Indians from desirable lands in the West, and enacting high tariffs.
    B. enacting federal child labor laws, minimum wage laws, and maximum power laws.
    C. banning segregation in federal buildings, and offering free education to freemen.
    D. ratifying the equal rights amendment act, and guaranteeing women the right to vote.

11. By 1913, the United States produced how much of the world's industrial output?
    A. five percent
    B. ten percent
    C. one-third
    D. half

12. Which census revealed for the first time that there were more non-farming jobs than farming jobs in the United States?
    A. 1860
    B. 1870
    C. 1880
    D. 1900

13. Between 1870 in 1920, how many immigrants arrived from overseas?
    A. 11 million
    B. one million
    C. 25 million
    D. 65 million

14. The Industrial Revolution in the United States took place principally in:
    A. the Southeast and Southwest.
    B. the mid-Atlantic states and the Southwest.
    C. the Northeast and the Midwest.
    D. the Southwest and Northwest.

15. The spirit of innovation contributed importantly to the dynamic and expansive growth of the American economy in the late nineteenth century. Which of the following was not an innovation of the 1870s and 1880s?
    A. the airplane
    B. typewriter
    C. telephone
    D. hand-held camera

16. In the late nineteenth and early twentieth centuries, the years from 1873 to 1897 were known as:
    A. the Great Depression.
    B. the Jazz Age.
    C. the Age of Jackson.
    D. Reconstruction.

17. All of the following were Captains of Industry except:
    A. John D. Rockefeller.
    B. Andrew Carnegie.
    C. J. P. Morgan.
    D. Samuel Gompers.

18. In 1890 the distribution of wealth in the United States was:
    A. about equally distributed.
    B. the top 1 percent of Americans owned more property than the remaining 99 percent
    C. unknown, as data on wealth was not then collected
    D. equal.

19. What Indian chief said, "If the white man wants to live in peace with the Indian he can live in peace. There need be no trouble. Treat all men alike. Give them the same law. Give them all and even chance to live and grow"?
    A. Chief Pontiac
    B. Sitting Bull
    C. Chief Joseph
    D. Chief Lakota

20. The 1887 Dawes Act:
    A. established federal railroad rates, making interlocking directorates illegal.
    B. established a federal minimum wage law for women and children.

C. led to the loss of tribal lands, and the erosion of Indian cultural traditions.

D. guaranteed federal employees an eight hour day.

21. The politics of Gilded Age America was said to be:
   A. A time of dishonesty and corruption in which corporations battled each other for special consideration by local state and federal governments.
   B. an era of golden opportunity for migrants, immigrants, and Native Americans.
   C. a glittering Jazz age and time for youthful rebellion.
   D. a golden age, like that of the period of the American founding, in the late 18th century.

22. The political "boss" of New York City in the early 1870s was:
   A. Charles Dudley Warner.
   B. Schuyler Colfax.
   C. William Marcy Tweed.
   D. James A. Garfield.

23. In the late nineteenth century, the Republican Party found particularly strong support among all of the following except:
   A. Protestant immigrants.
   B. African-Americans.
   C. Irish-Americans.
   D. Union veterans.

24. The first federal agency intended to regulate economic activity, and ensure that railroad rates were reasonable and favoritism avoided was:
   A. The Sherman Antitrust Act.
   B. The Dawes Act.
   C. The Interstate Commerce Commission
   D. The Civil Service Act.

25. What was the name of the organization that sought to organize both skilled and unskilled workers, women as well as men, blacks along with whites, and achieved a membership of nearly 800,000 in 1886?
   A. the Workingman's Union
   B. the Knights of Labor
   C. the American Federation of Labor
   D. the Congress of Industrial Organizations

26. The book in which Henry George proposed a "single tax" on real estate that would replace all other taxes:
   A. *Looking Backward*
   B. *Civic Engagement*
   C. *Progress and Poverty*
   D. *The Cooperative Commonwealth*

True or False

1. During the second industrial revolution, wage labor became America's leading employment arrangement.
2. With the mechanization of manufacture, skilled workers virtually disappeared from industrial America.
3. Wage reductions were commonplace during economic downturns.
4. The West was a remarkably homogeneous region—only in the twentieth century would it become ethnically diverse.
5. The extermination of the buffalo drastically undermined the livelihood of the Plains Indians.
6. The Democrats were the party of big government; the Republicans were the party of laissez-faire.
7. Neither of the two main political parties embraced any serious federal program to cushion citizens from poverty or unemployment.
8. The Knights of Labor regarded inequalities of wealth and power as a growing threat to American democracy.
9. During the two decades following the Civil War which were known as the golden age of the cattle kingdom, cowboys were highly paid.
10. The new Indian tribes that migrated to the Great Plains were greeted with open arms and friendly words by the Indians already living there.
11. The largest official execution in American history took place in December 1862 when 38 Sioux Indians were hanged.
12. Following the Civil War generals like Philip H. Sheridan set out to destroy the foundations of the Indian economy.
13. The most famous Indian victory in American history took place in June 1876 when When General George A. Custer and his 250 men perished.
14. On December 29, 1890, soldiers killed between 150 and 200 Indians, most women and children, near Wounded Knee Creek in South Dakota.
15. By the early 1890s, a pension system for Union soldiers, their widows and children, consumed more than 40 percent of the federal budget.
16. American presidents during the Gilded Age exerted strong, effective, executive leadership.
17. The Civil Service Act of 1883 marked the first step in establishing a professional civil service and removing officeholding from the hands of political machines.

18. The Sherman Antitrust Act of 1890, which banned combinations and practices that restrain free trade, proved an immediate success, both for its clarity of language and ease of enforcement.

19. According to Social Darwinism government should seek to help the poor, and build an activist state to regulate the nation's corporations.

20. Yale professor William Graham Sumner believed that America could achieve its ideals only with fair, progressive, taxation.

21. The term "Lochnerism" derived from the 1905 Supreme Court decision *Lochner v. New York,* in which the Court voided the state's law establishing a 10-hour day maximum for bakers.

22. The Social Gospel movement concentrated on attacking individual sins such as drinking and Sabbath-breaking and saw nothing immoral about the pursuit of riches.

23. The Haymarket Affair resulted in the hanging of four convicted anarchists.

ESSAY QUESTIONS

1. Compare the "second industrial revolution" described in this chapter to the "first industrial revolution" of the early–mid nineteenth century. In what ways did the second resemble the first? What about the second was new?

2. In what ways did the American West of the late nineteenth century represent a contrast to the East? In what ways did the two regions resemble each other?

3. "The Republicans and the Democrats of the late nineteenth century were different in name only; essentially, they represented the same outlooks and constituencies." In what ways do you agree with this statement? In what ways do you find it unpersuasive?

4. America during the Gilded Age was a land crackling with social protest and class tension. What were some of the different ways Americans explained such conflict and proposed to resolve it?

5. Consider the following statements:

   A. "The most conspicuous values of late nineteenth-century America were a commitment to justice for all and compassion for the problems of others."
   B. "The most conspicuous values of late nineteenth-century America were competition, personal gain, and indifference to the problems of others."

   In what ways does the reading support the first perspective? In what ways does it support the second?

6. Eric Foner writes, "for all its grandeur, the statue [of Liberty] could not conceal the deep social divisions and fears about the future of American freedom that accompanied the country's emergence as the world's leading industrial power." Write an essay on the deep social divisions and fears Americans experienced in the late nineteenth century.

7. Write an essay on "liberty of contract" in the market economy of the late nineteenth century.

8. Write an essay on how Native American Indians were treated in the late nineteenth century by the federal government.

9. Write an essay on the successes and setbacks working Americans confronted in the late nineteenth century.

10. Write an essay comparing Social Darwinism with the Social Gospel movement.

SOURCES FOR FURTHER RESEARCH

Books

GENERAL OVERVIEWS

Calhoun, Charles W., ed., *The Gilded Age: Essays on the Origins of Modern America* (1996)

Painter, Nell Irvin, *Standing at Armageddon: The United States, 1877–1919* (1987)

Trachtenberg, Alan, *The Incorporation of America: Culture and Society in the Gilded Age* (1982)

Wiebe, Robert H., *The Search for Order, 1877–1920* (1967)

PARTICULAR ASPECTS

Avrich, Paul, *The Haymarket Tragedy* (1983)

Bensel, Richard F., *The Political Economy of American Industrialization, 1877–1900* (2000)

Brown, Dee, *Bury My Heart at Wounded Knee: An Indian History of the American West* (1970)

Chandler, Alfred, *The Visible Hand: The Managerial Revolution in American Business* (1977)

Cronon, William, *Nature's Metropolis: Chicago and the Great West* (1991)

De Leon, Arnoldo, *Racial Frontiers: Africans, Chinese, and Mexicans in Western America, 1848–1940* (2002)

Deutsch, Sarah, *No Separate Refuge: Culture, Class, and Gender on the Anglo-Hispanic Frontier in the American Southwest, 1880–1940* (1987)

Emmons, David M., *The Butte Irish: Class and Ethnicity in an American Mining Town* (1989)

Fink, Leon, *Workingmen's Democracy: The Knights of Labor and American Politics* (1983)

Green, James, *Death in the Haymarket: A Story of Chicago, the First Labor Movement and the Bombing that Divided Gilded Age America* (2006)

Gutman, Herbert G., *Work, Culture, and Society in Industrializing America: Essays in American Working-Class and Social History* (1977)

Hofstadter, Richard, *Social Darwinism in American Thought* (1944)

Isenberg, Andrew C., *The Destruction of the Bison: An Environmental History, 1750–1920* (2000)

Jeffrey, Julie R., *Frontier Women: "Civilizing" the West? 1840–1880* (rev. ed., 1998)

Keller, Morton, *Affairs of State: Public Life in Late Nineteenth-Century America* (1977)

Kessler-Harris, Alice, *Out to Work: A History of Wage-Earning Women in the United States* (1982)

Limerick, Patricia Nelson, *Legacy of Conquest: The Unbroken Past of the American West* (1987)

Morgan, H. Wayne, *From Hayes to McKinley: National Party Politics, 1877–1896* (1969)

Paul, Rodman, *The Far West and the Great Plains in Transition, 1859–1900* (1988)

Shannon, Fred. A., *The Farmer's Last Frontier: Agriculture, 1860–1897* (1945)

Sproat, John G, *"The Best Men": Liberal Reformers in the Gilded Age* (1968)

Thomas, John L., *Alternative Americas: Henry George, Edward Bellamy, Henry Demarest Lloyd and the Adversary Tradition* (1983)

White, Richard, *"It's Your Misfortune and None of My Own": A New History of the American West* (1991)

Videos

Edison's Miracle of Light (60 minutes, Shanachie Home Video, 1995)

The Gilded Age (60 minutes, PBS Video, 1999)

The Iron Road (58 minutes, PBS Video, 1990)

Journey to America (59 minutes, PBS Video, 1990)

Mark Twain (220 minutes, PBS Video, 2002)

New York: A Documentary Film: Episode Three, Sunshine and Shadow, 1865–1898 (115 minutes, PBS Video, 1999)

The Richest Man in the World: Andrew Carnegie (120 minutes, PBS Video, 1997)

Transcontinental Railroad (120 minutes, PBS Video, 2003)

The West: The Grandest Enterprise Under God (84 minutes, West Film Project/WETA, 1994)

Web Resources

American Indians of the Pacific Northwest, Library of Congress
memory.loc.gov/ammem/award98/wauhtml/aipnhome.html

Chicago Anarchists on Trial: Evidence from the Haymarket Affair, 1886–1887,
Library of Congress
memory.loc.gov/ammem/award98/ichihtml/hayhome.html

H-SHGAPE Internet Resources, Society for Historians of the Gilded Age and
Progressive Era
www.h-net.org/~shgape/internet/index.html

The Haymarket Affair Digital Collection, Chicago Historical Society
www.chicagohistory.org/hadc/index.html

*The Northern Great Plains, 1880–1920: Photographs from the Fred Hultstrand
and F. A. Pazandak Photograph Collections,* Library of Congress
memory.loc.gov/ammem/award97/ndfahtml/ngphome.html

Prairie Settlement: Nebraska Photographs and Family Letters, 1862–1912,
Library of Congress
memory.loc.gov/ammem/award98/nbhihtml/pshome.html

ANSWERS TO OBJECTIVE QUESTIONS

Multiple Choice

1-B, 2-C, 3-B, 4-A, 5-C, 6-B, 7-D, 8-A, 9-D, 10-A, 11-C, 12-C, 13-C, 14-C,
15-A, 16-A, 17-D, 18-B, 19-C, 20-C, 21-A, 22-C, 23-C, 24-C, 25-B, 26-C

True or False

1-T, 2-F, 3-T, 4-F, 5-T, 6-F, 7-T, 8-T, 9-F, 10-F, 11-T, 12-T, 13-T, 14-T, 15-T,
16-F, 17-T, 18-F, 19-F, 20-F, 21-T, 22-F, 23-T

Freedom's Boundaries, at Home and Abroad, 1890–1900

CHAPTER OBJECTIVES

- What were the grievances, goals, and strategies of American Populism?
- How did the realities of life in the New South compare with its promise?
- What triggered the wave of segregation and disfranchisement measures in the South at the turn of the century?
- What were the signs and causes of the narrowing conception of nationhood in late-nineteenth-century America?
- What motivated the imperial expansion of America at the close of the nineteenth century?

CHAPTER OUTLINE

I. Agrarian revolt
   A. The farmers' plight
      1. Generally
         a. Falling agricultural prices
         b. Growing economic dependency
      2. Regional variants
         a. In trans-Mississippi West
         b. In South
   B. Farmers Alliance
      1. Origins and spread
      2. Strategies
         a. Initial cooperative approach; "exchanges"
         b. Turn to "subtreasury plan," political engagement
   C. Advent of People's (Populist) party
      1. Scope of following

2. Grassroots mobilization
3. Guiding vision
   a. Commonwealth of small producers as fundamental to freedom
   b. Restoration of democracy and economic opportunity
   c. Expansion of federal power
4. Omaha platform
D. Populist coalition
   1. Interracial alliance
      a. Extent
      b. Limits
   2. Involvement of women
      a. Mary Elizabeth Lease
      b. Support for women's suffrage
   3. Electoral showing for 1892
E. Prospects for Populist-labor alliance
   1. Context
      a. Economic collapse of 1893
      b. Resurgence of conflict between labor and capital
      c. Sharpening of government repression of labor
   2. Key episodes
      a. Miners strike at Coeur d'Alene, Idaho
      b. Coxey's Army
      c. Pullman strike
   3. Populist appeals to industrial workers in 1894
      a. Some success among miners
      b. Minimal success among urban workers; preference for Republicans
F. Election of 1896
   1. Campaign of William Jennings Bryan
      a. Joint support by Democrats and Populists
      b. Electrifying rhetoric
      c. Themes
         i. "Free silver"
         ii. Social Gospel overtones
         iii. Vision of activist government
      d. National tour to rally farmers and workers
   2. Campaign of William McKinley
      a. Insistence on gold standard
      b. Massive financial support from big business
      c. National political machine; Mark Hanna
   3. Outcome
      a. Sharp regional divide
      b. McKinley victory

4. Significance and legacy
   a. Emergence of modern campaign tactics
   b. Launching of Republican political dominance
   c. Fading of Populism

II. The segregated South
   A. Redeemers in power
      1. Dismantling of Reconstruction programs
      2. Convict lease system
   B. Failures of the New South
      1. Limits of economic development
      2. Persistence of regional poverty
   C. Black life
      1. Rural
         a. Varied prospects around region
         b. Elusive quest for land
      2. Urban
         a. Network of community institutions
         b. The black middle class
         c. Racially exclusive labor markets
            i. For black men
            ii. For black women
      3. Pockets of interracial unionism
      4. Kansas Exodus
   D. Decline of black politics
      1. Narrowing of political opportunity for black men
      2. Shifting of political initiative to black women
         a. National Association of Colored Women
         b. Middle-class orientation
         c. Pursuit of equal rights and racial uplift
         d. Range of activities
   E. Disfranchisement
      1. Persistence of black voting following Reconstruction
      2. Mounting alarm over specter of biracial insurgency
      3. Elimination of black vote, state by state
      4. Justifications and motivations
      5. Effects
         a. Massive purging of blacks from voting rolls
         b. Widespread disfranchisement of poor whites as well
         c. Emergence of southern white demagogues
      6. The North's blessing
         a. Senate
         b. Supreme Court

    F. Segregation
1. Fluidity of race relations following Reconstruction
2. Green light from Supreme Court for legal segregation
    a. *Civil Rights Cases*
    b. *Plessy v. Ferguson*
        i. "Separate but equal" doctrine
        ii. Justice Harlan dissent
3. Spread of segregation laws across South
4. Unreality of "separate but equal"
5. Segregation as component of overall white domination
6. Social etiquette of segregation
7. Effects on other "non-white" groups

    G. Rise of lynching
1. Motivations
2. Shocking brutality
3. The "rape" myth
4. Ida B. Wells's antilynching crusade
5. A distinctively American phenomenon

    H. Uses of historical memory
1. Civil War as "family quarrel" among white Americans
2. Reconstruction as horrible time of "Negro rule"
3. Erasure of blacks as historical actors

III. Contrasting notions of nationhood
    A. New nativism
1. Against "new immigrants" from southern and eastern Europe
    a. Depictions of "new immigrants"
        i. As lower "races"
        ii. As threat to American democracy
    b. Campaigns to curtail
        i. Immigration Restriction League
        ii. Efforts to bar entry into United States
        iii. State disfranchisement measures
2. Against immigrants from China
    a. Congressional exclusion of Chinese women
    b. Congressional exclusion of all Chinese
        i. Passage in 1882
        ii. Renewal in 1892, 1902
    c. Discrimination and violence against Chinese-Americans
    d. Uneven positions of Supreme Court on rights of Chinese
        i. *Yick Wo v. Hopkins*
        ii. *United States v. Wong Kim Ark*
        iii. *Fong Yue Ting*
    e. Precedent for legal exclusion of other groups

B. Booker T. Washington and the scaling back of black demands
   1. Background on Washington
   2. 1895 Atlanta address
   3. Washington approach
      a. Repudiation of claim to full equality
      b. Acceptance of segregation
      c. Emphasis on material self-help, individual advancement, alliance with white employers
C. American Federation of Labor and the scaling back of labor's outlook
   1. Rise of the AFL, Samuel Gompers
   2. AFL-Gompers approach
      a. Repudiation of broad reform vision, political engagement, direct confrontation with capital
      b. Emphasis on bargaining with employers over wages and conditions; "business unionism"
      c. Narrower ideal of labor solidarity
         i. Concentration on skilled labor sectors
         ii. Exclusion of blacks, women, new immigrants
D. Ambiguities of the "women's era"
   1. Widening prospects for economic independence
   2. Expanding role in public life
      a. Growing network of women's organizations, campaigns
      b. Women's Christian Temperance Union
   3. Growing elitism of women's suffrage movement
      a. Ethnic
      b. Racial

IV. Becoming a world power
   A. The new imperialism
      1. Traditional empires
      2. Consolidation and expansion of imperial powers
      3. Cultural justifications for imperial domination
   B. Abstention of United States from scramble for empire before 1890s
      1. Continuing status as second-rate power
      2. Confinement of national expansion to North American continent
      3. Minimal record of overseas territorial acquisition
      4. Preference for expanded trade over colonial holdings
   C. Emerging calls for American expansion
      1. Leading advocates
         a. Josiah Strong (*Our Country*)
         b. Alfred T. Mahan (*The Influence of Sea Power Upon History*)

     2. Themes
       a. Moral
         i. Global application of manifest destiny
         ii. Uplift of "inferior races"
       b. Economic
         i. Expanded markets for American goods
         ii. Protection of international trade
       c. Strategic
     3. Influence
  D. Intervention in Hawaii
     1. American trade and military agreements
     2. Economic dominance of American sugar planters
     3. Overthrow of Queen Liliuokalani
  E. Rise of assertive nationalism
     1. Contributing factors
       a. Depression-era quest for foreign markets
       b. Concern over economic and ethnic disunity
     2. Manifestations
       a. Rituals
         i. Pledge of Allegiance
         ii. "Star-Spangled Banner"
         iii. Flag Day
       b. Yellow journalism
  F. Spanish-American War
     1. Background
       a. Long Cuban struggle for independence from Spain
       b. Renewal of struggle in 1895
         i. Harsh Spanish response
         ii. Growing American sympathy for Cuban cause
     2. Toward intervention
       a. Destruction of battleship *Maine*
       b. War fever, fanned by yellow press
       c. U.S. declaration of war; Teller Amendment
     3. The war
       a. In Philippines
         i. Admiral George Dewey's victory at Manila Bay
         ii. Landing of American troops
       b. In Cuba and Puerto Rico
         i. Landing of American troops
         ii. Naval victory off Santiago
         iii. Theodore Roosevelt's Rough Riders; legendary charge up San Juan Hill
       c. Swift defeat of Spain

G. From liberator to imperial power
 1. Postwar attainment of overseas empire
  a. Varied arrangements
   i. Annexation of Hawaii
   ii. Acquisition of Philippines, Puerto Rico, Guam
   iii. Qualified sovereignty for Cuba; Platt Amendment
  b. Value as outposts for U.S. naval and commercial power
 2. Open Door policy
 3. Initial welcome in former Spanish colonies for U.S. forces
  a. As agent of expanded trade and social order
  b. As agent of social reform and national self-rule
 4. Growing disenchantment in Philippines
  a. Founding of provisional government by Emilio Aguinaldo
  b. U.S. failure to recognize; insistence on retaining possession
 5. Philippine war
  a. Bloodiness and brutality
  b. Controversy in United States
  c. Outcome
 6. Legacy of poverty and inequality in American possessions
H. Status of territorial peoples
 1. Limits on claims to American freedom
  a. Foraker Act
  b. *Insular Cases*
 2. Divergent futures for American territories
  a. Hawaii (statehood)
  b. Philippines (independence)
  c. Guam ("unincorporated" territory)
  d. Puerto Rico (commonwealth)
I. American debate over imperial expansion
 1. Opponents (Anti-Imperialist League): "republic or empire?"
 2. Proponents: "benevolent" imperialism

V. America at dawn of twentieth century

CHRONOLOGY

1875	Congress bars Chinese women from entry into United States
1879–80	Black "exodus" to Kansas
1882	Congress bars all Chinese from entry into United States
1883	*Civil Rights Cases*
1885	Josiah Strong publishes *Our Country*

1886	*Yick Wo v. Hopkins* Founding of American Federation of Labor
1890	Founding of National American Woman Suffrage Association Alfred T. Mahan publishes *The Influence of Sea Power Upon History*
1892	Homestead steel strike Coeur d'Alene miners strike Tennessee miners rebellion against convict lease Omaha platform of People's party adopted Congress renews restriction on Chinese immigration Populist presidential candidate James Weaver gains over one million votes
1893	Economic collapse launches four-year depression *Fong Yue Ting* American-backed overthrow of Queen Liliuokalani in Hawaii
1894	Coxey's Army Pullman strike Founding of Immigration Restriction League
1895	Booker T. Washington's Atlanta address *In Re Debs* Resumption of Cuban movement for independence from Spain
1896	*Plessy v. Ferguson* William McKinley defeats William Jennings Bryan in presidential election
1897	Passage of Dingley tariff Bill barring illiterate foreigners from entry into United States vetoed by President Cleveland
1898	*United States v. Wong Kim Ark* Spanish-American War Annexation of Hawaii
1899	Announcement of Open Door policy
1899–1903	Philippine War
1900	Gold Standard Act Foraker Act McKinley defeats Bryan, is reelected
1901–04	*Insular Cases*
1902	Congress makes permanent restriction on Chinese immigration

KEY TERMS

agricultural expansion and decline: The nation's agricultural sector grew dramatically during the late nineteenth century, as American farmers brought an additional 430 million acres under cultivation between 1860 and 1900. The subjugation of the American Indians opened lands for farming on the Great Plains, and the expansion of the nation's railroad system enabled farmers in the West to send the crops to markets. In addition, new technologies improved efficiency and productivity. For example, a single person in 1900 could harvest as much wheat as twenty men had four decades earlier. As a result, yields increased. U.S. farmers produced 254 million bushels of wheat in 1870; in 1900, they harvested 599 million bushels. Production of other crops grew at a similar pace. However, these remarkable increases in production were matched by falling prices for farm goods. A bushel of wheat that sold for $1.20 in 1870 was worth only 71 cents some twenty years later.

Coxey's Army: A longtime reformer and member of the Populist Party, Jacob Coxey knew that the U.S. Congress had little interest in providing assistance to working Americans during the Panic of 1893. Seeking to prod legislators into passing a road improvements bill that would create jobs, the Ohio businessman announced that he would "send a petition to Washington with boots on." He hoped for 100,000 marchers; only 500 men arrived in the nation's capital in March 1894, although they drew a crowd of more than 15,000 onlookers. Events of the day proved anticlimactic. The police prevented Coxey from speaking, and he was arrested for walking on the grass. In 1944, fifty years after his army had marched in Washington, D.C., the ninety-year-old Coxey mounted the Capitol steps and delivered the speech he had intended to present a half-century earlier.

black voting: During the late nineteenth century the continuing disfranchisement of African Americans in the South weakened the Republican Party in that region. President Benjamin Harrison, a Republican, supported legislation to allow federal officials to oversee elections in the southern states. This measure would protect black voters, thus ensuring Republican influence in the region. Henry Cabot Lodge of Massachusetts sponsored the legislation in the House, which passed the bill by a narrow vote of 155 to 149. Many Senate Republicans, however, believed that the measure would only inflame tensions between the North and the South. They conspired with their Democratic counterparts to kill the measure, which was never taken up for consideration. It was not until 1957 that Congress would pass civil rights legislation.

Yick Wo v. Hopkins: In the 1880s, Chinese immigrants owned and operated three-quarters of the laundries in San Francisco. Among them was Yick Wo, a laundry owner for over two decades, whose business had received a stamp of approval from city inspectors in 1884. The following year, the city of San Francisco adopted an ordinance requiring laundries in wooden buildings to obtain a special permit. Some eighty non-Chinese applicants received their permits, but of the nearly two hundred Chinese laundry owners who applied, all were rejected but one (and that one was apparently issued in error). Yick Wo and some 150 fellow Chinese laundry owners were arrested for violating the ordinance. Yick Wo refused to pay the $10 fine and appealed his case. In its unanimous ruling, the U.S. Supreme Court declared that the enforcement of the city ordinance in a discriminatory manner violated the Fourteenth Amendment.

The U.S. Navy: After the Civil War, the United States Navy went into decline. Most of its ships were dedicated to coastal or river patrols. An 1881 naval committee reported that the sea-going navy consisted of only thirty-five ships, many of them made of wood in an era of iron. Its report ranked the U.S. Navy twelfth in the world, behind nations such as Chile and China. Growing imperialist fervor and a realization that naval construction could spark economic growth at home prompted Congress to order the expansion of the navy. In the fifteen years between 1883 and 1898, the navy ordered construction of some 110 ships.

sinking of the U.S.S. *Maine:* The cause of the explosion that ripped apart the U.S.S. *Maine* as it sat in Havana Harbor in 1898 has intrigued historians and the general public. In March 1898, just four weeks after the incident, a U.S. Navy commission concluded that an external explosion had destroyed the ship. Thirteen years later navy experts examined portions of the sunken vessel. They claimed that a portion of the hull was bent inward, confirming the findings of the 1898 commission. However, these findings remained a matter of dispute. In 1976 retired Admiral Hyman G. Rickover headed an inquiry that concluded spontaneous combustion in the *Maine*'s coal bunker caused munitions on board to explode. The matter remains an historical mystery, unlikely to be resolved.

the press and war: In an effort to control public opinion, the McKinley administration censored news reports regarding the war in the Philippines. General Elwell Otis, commander of U.S. combat forces in the Philippines, prevented the distribution of unfavorable reports, a fact that became public in July 1899. The administration also attempted to control the flow of information into the Philippines. Edward Atkinson, a Boston businessman and officer in the Anti-Imperialist League, mailed some 500 pamphlets with titles such as "The Hell of War and Its Penalties" to U.S. military personnel in the Philippines. The postmaster general seized the pamphlets before they left the United States, raising concerns about freedom of speech in the United States.

OBJECTIVE QUESTIONS

Multiple Choice

1. The immigrants facing the harshest reception in late-nineteenth-century America were those arriving from
   A. eastern Europe.
   B. the Caribbean.
   C. China.
   D. Scandinavia.

2. A leading opponent of American imperialism was
   A. Rudyard Kipling.
   B. Albert Beveridge.
   C. Theodore Roosevelt.
   D. William Jennings Bryan.

3. Which of the following series of events is listed in proper sequence?
   A. founding of People's (Populist) party; William Jennings Bryan's "cross of gold" speech; birth of Farmers Alliance; Coxey's Army
   B. Kansas Exodus; *Civil Rights Cases;* Booker T. Washington's Atlanta address; *Plessy v. Ferguson*
   C. Sinking of battleship *Maine;* publication of Josiah Strong's *Our Country;* Platt Amendment; overthrow of Hawaii's Queen Liliuokalani
   D. Battle of Manila Bay; founding of Immigration Restriction League; Homestead steel strike; founding of National American Woman Suffrage Association

4. Which of the following was *not* a grievance of the Farmers Alliance and the Populists?
   A. excessive interest rates
   B. excessive power of the labor unions
   C. excessive power of the banks and railroads
   D. inadequate government response to the plight of ordinary farmers

5. Which of the following was *not* a leading strategy of the Populists?
   A. using vigilante tactics to intimidate farmers who failed to join the cause
   B. creating cooperative enterprises through which to distribute their crops on more reasonable terms
   C. holding public events to give their followers a sense of power and community
   D. declaring political independence from the two major political parties

6. Which of the following was *not* a factor behind the spread of segregation and disfranchisement laws in the South?
    A. growing tolerance, and even encouragement, by the federal government for white supremacy
    B. a desire to discourage further biracial insurgencies
    C. a growing insistence by blacks that whites simply leave them alone
    D. an overall narrowing of the American conception of nationhood

7. Which of the following was *not* a central principle of the American Federation of Labor?
    A. Labor should avoid entanglement in politics.
    B. Bargaining with employers over day-to-day issues is the most promising avenue for labor.
    C. Organized labor should pursue concrete gains rather than dreamy reforms.
    D. It is vital that unions include workers of all backgrounds, regardless of race, ethnicity, sex, or skill.

8. Which of the following was *not* a major reason for America's imperial expansion?
    A. a desire to broaden the exposure of Americans to different cultures
    B. a sense of strategic rivalry with other imperial powers
    C. a conviction that it was America's mission to uplift "less civilized" peoples
    D. a quest on the part of business for new markets for goods

9. The largest citizens' movement of the nineteenth century was:
    A. the abolitionist movement.
    B. the Farmers Alliance.
    C. the prohibitionist movement.
    D. The American Federation of Labor.

10. The "subtreasury plan" was:
    A. a policy of opening banks in each state.
    B. a plan developed by the undersecretary of commerce that would ensure equitable international exchange.
    C. another name for the black market.
    D. a plan to establish federal warehouses where farmers could store crops until they were sold.

11. The 1892 People's Party platform, written by Ignatius Donnelly and adopted at the party's Omaha convention, proposed all of the following except:
    A. direct election of United States senators.
    B. a graduated income tax.
    C. recognition of the rights of workers to form labor unions.
    D. a decentralization over the control of currency.

12. The 1892 presidential election was won by:
    A. Grover Cleveland, the Democrat.
    B. William Henry Harrison, the Republican.
    C. James Weaver, the Populist.
    D. William Jennings Bryan, the Independent.

13. The leader of the band of several hundred unemployed men who marched on Washington in May 1894 to demand economic relief was:
    A. George Pullman.
    B. Richard Olney.
    C. Jacob Coxey.
    D. Eugene V. Debs.

14. What was the name of the railroad car company against which workers struck in 1894?
    A. Pullman
    B. American Railway Company
    C. The Chicago and Sacramento
    D. the Maine and California

15. The nation's urban working class voters shifted their support en masse to the Republican Party in 1894 in significant degree because:
    A. Republicans claimed that raising tariff rates would restore prosperity by protecting manufacturers and industrial workers from the competition of cheap imported goods.
    B. They did not shift their support to the Republican Party, since the Republican Party is the party of big business, and big business is opposed to the interests of the working class.
    C. in solidarity with farmers across the nation, working people believed it was time for a change.
    D. a sharp upturn in the economy and the return to "good Times" meant increasingly that the American people shared a common cause and interests.

16. The congressman from Nebraska who was the Democratic Party nominee for president in 1896, and who called for the "free coinage" of silver was:
    A. James G. Blaine.
    B. William Jennings Bryan.
    C. William McKinley.
    D. Grover Cleveland.

17. The 1897 Dingley Tariff:
    A. lowered tariff rates.
    B. fulfilled one of the Populist Party's political party platform promises.
    C. raised tariff rates to their highest level in American history to that time.
    D. lowered tariff rates east of the Mississippi, while raising them in the Far West.

18. The coalition of merchants, planters, and business entrepreneurs who dominated politics in the American South after 1877 called themselves:
    A. Carpetbaggers.
    B. Redeemers.
    C. Reconstructionists.
    D. the Ku Klux Klan.

19. The Redeemers in the South:
    A. increased state budgets and improved schooling across the region.
    B. increased spending on public schools without measurably increasing taxes.
    C. slashed state budgets, cut taxes, and reduced spending on hospitals and public schools.
    D. vigorously enforced the fifteenth amendment.

20. During the 1880s, the South as a whole:
    A. sank deeper and deeper into poverty.
    B. flourished, as industrial expansion and agricultural diversification made the "New South" the richest region in the country.
    C. became increasingly culturally diverse as new immigrants and freedmen worked together in the region's mines, mills, and factories.
    D. built thousands of new public schools, hundreds of hospitals, and scores of new factories

21. Between 1879 and 1880, an estimated 40,000–60,000 African-Americans migrated to:
    A. South Carolina.
    B. California.
    C. Massachusetts.
    D. Kansas.

22. The name for the coalition of black Republicans and anti-Redeemer Democrats that governed the state of Virginia from 1879 to 1883 was:
    A. the Readjuster movement.
    B. the Farmers' Alliance.
    C. the Populist-Republican coalition.
    D. the Arkansans.

23. Which was *not* one of the devices used by Southern whites to keep blacks from exercising suffrage?
    A. the poll tax
    B. literacy tests
    C. the grandfather clause
    D. a religious test

24. What landmark United States Supreme Court decision gave approval to state laws requiring separate facilities for whites and blacks?
    A. the Slaughterhouse Cases
    B. the Civil Rights Cases
    C. *Plessy v. Ferguson*
    D. *Brown v. The Board of Education of Topeka, Kansas*

25. In 1900, in the entire South, how many public high schools for blacks existed?
    A. only a few but their numbers were growing
    B. As a result of Reconstruction politics, there were hundreds of high schools across the South for black Americans.
    C. more than 500
    D. none

26. From 1880 to the mid-twentieth century, the number of people lynched reached nearly:
    A. 200.
    B. 250.
    C. 1000.
    D. 5000.

27. What 1893 United States Supreme Court decision authorized the federal government to expel Chinese aliens without due process of law?
    A. *The United States v. Wong Kim Ark*
    B. *Yick Wo v. Hopkins*
    C. *Fong Yue Ting*
    D. Saum Song Bo

28. Who was the African-American leader who delivered a speech in 1895 at the Atlanta Cotton Exposition urging black Americans to adjust to segregation and stop agitating for civil and political rights?
    A. W.E.B. DuBois
    B. Frederick Douglass
    C. Samuel Armstrong
    D. Booker T. Washington

29. What was the name of the labor organization of principally white, male, skilled workers that arose in the 1880s and was headed by Samuel Gompers?
    A. the American Federation of Labor
    B. the Knights of Labor
    C. the Congress of Industrial Organizations
    D. the Federated Amalgamated Union

30. Which was *not* principally one of the networks by which women exerted a growing influence on public affairs in the late nineteenth century?
    A. temperance associations
    B. social reform organizations
    C. political party organizations
    D. women's clubs

31. The Women's Christian Temperance Union began by demanding the prohibition of alcoholic drinks, but developed into an organization:
    A. calling for a comprehensive program of economic and political reforms, including the right to vote.
    B. opposed to women's suffrage.
    C. that held meetings specifically to help men and women control their tempers.
    D. that promoted workers' unions in the temperance industry.

32. What was the name of the naval officer and his 1890 book that argued that no nation could prosper without a large fleet of ships engaged in international trade, protected by a powerful navy operating overseas bases?
    A. J. M. Price, *Seapower Comes of Age*
    B. Theodore Roosevelt, *The History of the United States Navy*
    C. Alfred T. Mahan, *The Influence of Sea Power upon History*
    D. Josiah Strong, *Our Country*

33. "The splendid little war" of 1898 was:
    A. the Spanish-American War.
    B. the Mexican-American War.
    C. the Great War.
    D. the Philippine War.

34. In February 1898, what ship exploded in Havana Harbor with a loss of nearly 270 lives:
    A. the battleship *Arizona*
    B. the battleship *McKinley*
    C. the battleship *Maine*

35. Who was the future American president who made a national name for himself by charging up San Juan Hill with the Rough Riders?
    A. William McKinley
    B. William Howard Taft
    C. Woodrow Wilson
    D. Theodore Roosevelt

36. What was the name of the 1899 policy established by Secretary of State John Hay with regard to China?
    A. the Open Door policy
    B. the Chinese Exclusion Act

    C. the Monroe Doctrine
    D. the Hay Corollary

37. What war lasted from 1899 to 1903, in which 4,200 Americans and over 100,000 Filipinos perished?
    A. There was no such war.
    B. the Spanish-American War
    C. the Cuban-Filipino Conflict
    D. the Philippine War.

True or False

1. Ironically, the Farmers Alliance found greater support among industrial workers than among small farmers.

2. Southern Populists forged notable alliances between black and white farmers.

3. Government intervention was vital to the defeats of the 1892 Homestead strike and the 1894 Pullman strike.

4. Turn-of-the-century segregation laws were passed in clear defiance of Supreme Court rulings.

5. As the subordination of blacks grew more rigid, American attitudes toward immigrants grew more tolerant.

6. Like the American Federation of Labor, the National American Woman Suffrage Association was infused with the social elitism of the times.

7. Only after Spain threatened to invade America did the United States elect to go to war.

8. The American war to suppress Filipino independence proved to be much longer and bloodier than the Spanish-American War had been.

9. An oversupply of cotton on the world market, which led to a sharp decline in prices, contributed to a farmers' revolt and gave rise to the Populist Movement.

10. In a show of democratic solidarity on the part of the American people, the Farmers Alliance, especially in the southern states, welcomed black farmers into the Alliance.

11. In 1894 a coalition of white Populists and black Republicans won control of North Carolina, bringing the state into a sort of "second Reconstruction."

12. Populists in Western states endorsed women's suffrage.

13. The economic upturn in 1893 led to increased harmony between capital and labor across the country.

14. In the late nineteenth century urban workers rallied in support of Populist farmers.

15. In 1894, in one of the most decisive shifts in congressional power in American history, the nation's urban working class shifted en masse to the Republican Party, and Republicans gained 117 seats in the House of Representatives.

16. By the 1890s, although financiers and industrial managers voted for the Republican Party, workers in industry voted solidly Democratic.

17. The election of 1896 is sometimes called the first modern presidential campaign, in part, because of the amount of money spent—William McKinley raised some $10 million, while William Jennings Bryant raised only around $300,000.

18. By 1900, southern per capita income was only sixty percent of that of the national average.

19. With the exception of some dockworkers' and mine laborers' unions, blacks were excluded from membership in the few unions that existed in the South in the late nineteenth century.

20. In the late nineteenth century, black women were largely excluded from jobs as secretaries, typists, and department store clerks.

21. In the late nineteenth century, black women frequently found work as domestic servants.

22. In the 1880s and 1890s, blacks no longer served in the United States Congress.

23. Until the Great Migration of black Americans from the rural South to the urban North during World War I, the vast majority of African-Americans lived in the South.

24. In 1915, the United States Supreme Court invalidated the "grandfather clause" for violating the Fifteenth Amendment.

25. Southern Democrats persistently raised to the threat of "Negro domination" to justify denying blacks the right to vote.

26. Tom Watson, who had earlier been a leading figure in forging an interracial Populist coalition had, by the early twentieth century, emerged as a power in Georgia, whipping up prejudice against African-Americans, Catholics, and Jews.

27. One consequence of the bitter attacks on African-Americans' political rights across the South was that, by 1940, 97 percent of adult black Southerners were not registered to vote.

28. The 1890s saw not only widespread disfranchisement, but also segregation in the South.

29. In *Plessy v. Ferguson,* John Marshall Harlan, in dissent, insisted, "Our Constitution is color-blind."

30. Segregation was more than a form of racial separation. It was one part of an all-encompassing system of white domination.

31. Beginning about 1880, "new immigrants" were welcomed with open arms by the American people.

32. In 1882 and again in 1902, the United States Congress passed laws excluding immigrants from China.

33. "The Age of Imperialism" is the name given to the last quarter of the nineteenth century by historians.

34. Most Americans who looked to expand America's influence overseas were interested not in territorial possessions, but in expanded trade.

ESSAY QUESTIONS

1. Compare the experiences of struggling farmers in the South and West with those of industrial workers, and the movements they mobilized to address their respective conditions.

2. The late-nineteenth and early-twentieth centuries saw a sharp decline in the status of African-Americans, particularly in the South. What were the indications of this decline? Why did it happen?

3. During the 1890s, the author observes, "social movements that had helped to expand the nineteenth-century boundaries of freedom now redefined their objectives so that they might be realized within the new economic and intellectual framework." Discuss how this narrowing of freedom's boundaries is reflected in the positions taken by black leader Booker T. Washington, labor leader Samuel Gompers, and feminist leader Carrie Chapman Catt.

4. "The reasons for America's imperial expansion overseas during the late-nineteenth and early-twentieth centuries were essentially no different than the reasons for its earlier expansion across the North American continent." In what ways do you agree with this statement? In what ways do you find it unpersuasive?

5. Imagine a public exchange between an advocate and an opponent of American imperial expansion in the aftermath of the Spanish-American War. Transcribe this debate.

6. Write an essay on the challenges African-Americans faced during the Gilded Age.

7. Write an essay on how workers responded to the challenges they faced in Gilded-Age America.

8. Write an essay on how women responded to the challenges they faced in the late nineteenth century.

9. Write an essay on American foreign policy in "the Age of Imperialism."

10. Write an essay on the experiences of new immigrants from Europe and Asia in Gilded-Age America.

SOURCES FOR FURTHER RESEARCH

Books

GENERAL OVERVIEWS

Painter, Nell Irvin, *Standing at Armageddon: The United States, 1877–1919* (1987)

PARTICULAR ASPECTS

Aleinikoff, Alexander, *Semblances of Sovereignty: The Constitution, the State, and American Citizenship* (2002)
Ayers, Edward L., *The Promise of the New South: Life After Reconstruction* (1992)
Blair, William A., *Cities of the Dead: Contesting the Memory of the Civil War in the South, 1865–1914* (2004)
Blight, David, *Race and Reunion: The Civil War in American Memory* (2001)
Brands, H.W., *The Reckless Decade: America in the 1890s* (2002)
Factor, Robert I., *The Black Response to America: Men, Ideals, and Organization from Frederick Douglass to the NAACP* (1970)
Goodwyn, Lawrence, *The Populist Moment: A Short History of the Agrarian Revolt in America* (1978)
Greene, Julie, *Pure and Simple Politics: The American Federation of Labor, 1881–1915* (1997)
Hahn, Steven, *The Roots of Southern Populism: Yeoman Farmers and the Transformation of the Georgia Upcountry, 1850–1890* (1983)
Hahn, Steven, *A Nation under Our Feet: Black Political Struggles in the Rural South from Slavery to the Great Migration* (2003)
Harlan, Louis B., *Booker T. Washington: The Making of a Black Leader* (1973)

Higginbotham, Evelyn, *Righteous Discontent: The Women's Movement in the Black Baptist Church, 1880–1920* (1993)
Kraditor, Aileen S., *The Ideas of the Woman Suffrage Movement, 1890–1920* (1962)
Krause, Paul, *The Battle for Homestead, 1880–1892: Politics, Culture, and Steel* (1992)
LaFeber, Walter, *The New Empire: An Interpretation of American Expansion, 1860–1898* (1963)
Lebsock, Suzanne, *A Murder in Virginia: Southern Justice on Trial* (2003)
Linn, Brian M., *The Philippine War, 1899–1902* (2000)
Litwack, Leon F., *Trouble in Mind: Black Southerners in the Age of Jim Crow* (1998)
McClain, Charles J., *In Search of Equality: The Chinese Struggle Against Discrimination in Nineteenth-Century America* (1994)
McMillen, Neil R., *Dark Journey: Black Mississippians in the Age of Jim Crow* (1989)
Perez, Louis A., *The War of 1898: The United States and Cuba in History and Historiography* (1998)
Sanders, Elizabeth, *Roots of Reform: Farmers, Workers, and the American State, 1877–1917 (1999)*
Schneirov, Richard, Shelton Stromquist, and Nick Salvatore, eds., *The Pullman Strike and the Crisis of the 1890s: Essays on Labor and Politics* (1999)
Shapiro, Karin A., *A New South Rebellion: The Battle Against Convict Labor in the Tennessee Coalfields, 1871–1896* (1998)
Woodward, C. Vann, *Origins of the New South, 1877–1913* (1951)

Videos

Crucible of Empire: The Spanish-American War (120 minutes, PBS Video, 1999)
America, 1900 (170 minutes, PBS Video, 1998)
Ethnic Notions (58 minutes, California Newsreel, 1986)
The Homestead Strike (60 minutes, History Channel, A&E Home Video, 2006)
Ida B. Wells: A Passion For Justice (58 minutes, PBS Video, 1989)
The River Ran Red (58 minutes, WQED Productions, 1993)

Web Resources

The African American Odyssey, Volume VI: The Booker T. Washington Era, Library of Congress
http://memory.loc.gov/ammem/aaohtml/exhibit/aopart6.html
Anti-Imperialism in the United States, 1898–1935, Jim Zwick
http://www.boondocksnet.com/ai/index.html

The Chinese in California, 1850–1925, Library of Congress
  http://memory.loc.gov/ammem/award99/cubhtml/cichome.html

H-SHGAPE Internet Resources, Society for Historians of the Gilded Age and Progressive Era
  http://www.h-net.org/~shgape/internet/index.html

The History of Jim Crow, produced as part of the PBS documentary The Rise and Fall of Jim Crow
  http://www.jimcrowhistory.org/home.htm

The Spanish-American War in Motion Pictures, Library of Congress
  http://lcweb2.loc.gov/ammem/sawhtml/

The World of 1898: The Spanish-American War, Library of Congress
  http://lcweb.loc.gov/rr/hispanic/1898/

The World's Columbian Exposition, Julie K. Rose
  http://xroads.virginia.edu/~MA96/WCE/title.html

1896—The Presidential Campaign: Cartoons and Commentary, Rebecca Edwards and Sarah DeFeo, Vassar College
  http://projects.vassar.edu/1896/1896home.html

ANSWERS TO OBJECTIVE QUESTIONS

Multiple Choice

1-C, 2-D, 3-B, 4-B, 5-A, 6-C, 7-D, 8-A, 9-B, 10-D, 11-D, 12-A, 13-C, 14-A, 15-A, 16-B, 17-C, 18-B, 19-C, 20-A, 21-D, 22-A, 23-D, 24-C, 25-D, 26-D, 27-C, 28-D, 29-A, 30-C, 31-A, 32-C, 33-A, 34-C, 35-D, 36-A, 37-D

True or False

1-F, 2-T, 3-T, 4-F, 5-F, 6-T, 7-F, 8-T, 9-T, 10-F, 11-T, 12-T, 13-F, 14-F, 15-T, 16-F, 17-T, 18-T, 19-T, 20-T, 21-T, 22-F, 23-T, 24-T, 25-T, 26-T, 27-T, 28-T, 29-T, 30-T, 31-F, 32-T, 33-T, 34-T

CHAPTER 18 | The Progressive Era, 1900–1916

CHAPTER OBJECTIVES

- What were some of the leading trends—cultural and material—in early-twentieth-century American life?
- What did Americans see as the chief strengths and problems of their country at the outset of the twentieth century?
- What were the meanings and underlying spirit of "Progressivism"?
- What were the various motivations, goals, and philosophies of Progressivism? Who were the Progressives, and what were they trying to reform?
- How did the character and impact of Progressive efforts vary across such arenas as voluntary organizations, social movements, the arts, the professions, party politics, and government?
- How did Progressivism transform conceptions of freedom and the mission of government in American society?
- What were the chief goals of early-twentieth-century women's activism? How did feminism relate to Progressivism?

CHAPTER OUTLINE

I. Introduction
    A. Progressive era
        1. Surge in production, consumption, urban growth
        2. Persistence of social problems
    B. Progressivism
        1. Broad-based elements
        2. Loosely-defined meanings

          3. Varied and contradictory character

     C. New notions of American freedom

II. An urban age

     A. Early-twentieth-century economic explosion

          1. "Golden age" for agriculture

          2. Growth in number and size of cities

          3. Stark contrasts of opulence and poverty

     B. Popular attention to dynamism and ills of the city

          1. Painters and photographers

          2. Muckrakers

             a. Lewis Hine's photography

             b. Lincoln Steffens's *The Shame of the Cities*

             c. Ida Tarbell's *History of the Standard Oil Company*

          3. Novelists

             a. Theodore Dreiser's *Sister Carrie*

             b. Upton Sinclair's *The Jungle*

     C. Immigrants and immigration

          1. Height of "new immigration" from southern and eastern Europe

          2. Immigration from agrarian to industrial centers as a global process

             a. Volume and flows

             b. Causes

             c. Circumstances of immigrants

          3. Ellis Island

          4. Influx of Asian and Mexican immigrants in West

          5. Immigrant presence in industrial cities

          6. Aspirations of new immigrants

             a. Social and legal equality, freedom of conscience, economic opportunity, escape from poverty

             b. Means to acquire land back home

             c. Material prosperity as central to "freedom"

          7. Circumstances of new immigrants

             a. Close-knit "ethnic" neighborhoods

                i. Social institutions

               ii. Preservation of native languages

              iii. Churches

             b. Low pay, harsh working conditions

     D. The new mass-consumption society

          1. Outlets for consumer goods

             a. Department stores

             b. Neighborhood chain stores

             c. Retail mail order houses

          2. Expanding range and availability of consumer goods

      3. Leisure activities
         a. Amusement parks
         b. Dance halls
         c. Theaters; vaudeville
         d. Movies; "nickelodeons"
  E. Women in urban public life
      1. Employment
         a. Racial and ethnic stratification
         b. Working woman as symbol of female emancipation; Charlotte Perkins Gilman's *Women and Economics*
      2. Leisure, entertainment
  F. "Fordism"
      1. Background on Henry Ford, Ford Motor Company
      2. Production innovations
         a. Standardized output
         b. Lower prices
         c. Assembly line
      3. Strategies to attract and discipline labor
         a. Five-dollar day
         b. Anti-union espionage
      4. Linking of mass production and mass consumption
  G. Impact of mass-consumption ideal
      1. Recasting of "American way of life," "freedom"
      2. Challenges to material inequalities
         a. Labor unionism
         b. Critique of corporate monopoly
         c. Doctrine of "a living wage"; Father John A. Ryan

III. Changing ideas of freedom
  A. Varieties of Progressivism
  B. Industrial labor and the meanings of freedom
      1. Frederick W. Taylor's "scientific management"
         a. Principles of
         b. Mixed response to
            i. Favorable: as way to enhance efficiency
            ii. Unfavorable: as threat to worker independence
      2. New talk of "industrial freedom," "industrial democracy"
  C. Socialist party
      1. High watermark of American socialism
         a. Membership
         b. Elected officials
         c. Newspapers
         d. Eugene V. Debs

2. Program
   a. Immediate reforms
   b. Public ownership of railroads and factories
   c. Democratic control of economy
3. Breadth of following
   a. Urban immigrant communities
   b. Western farming and mining regions
   c. Native-born intelligentsia
4. Rising presence of socialism throughout Atlantic world
D. Labor movement
1. American Federation of Labor
   a. Surge of growth
   b. Boundaries of membership
      i. Skilled industrial and craft laborers
      ii. White, male, and native-born
   c. Moderate ideology; ties with business Progressives
      i. National Civic Federation
      ii. Collective bargaining for "responsible" unions
      iii. Alternative strain of rigid employer anti-unionism
2. Industrial Workers of the World
   a. Inclusion of workers from all stations and backgrounds
   b. Trade union militancy
   c. Advocate of workers' revolution
   d. William "Big Bill" Haywood
   e. Support and guidance for mass, multiethnic strikes
3. High points of broad-based labor struggle
   a. Lawrence "Bread and Roses" textile strike; march of strikers' children
   b. New Orleans dock workers strike
   c. Paterson silk workers strike; Paterson pageant
   d. Colorado Fuel and Iron miners strike; Ludlow Massacre
4. Suppression of labor radicalism and emergence of "civil liberties" issue
E. Shadings of feminism
1. Appearance of term "feminism"
2. "Lyrical Left"
   a. New cultural "bohemia"
   b. Radical reassessments of politics, the arts, sexuality
3. Rise of personal freedom
   a. Freudian psychology
   b. Free sexual expression and choice
   c. Pockets of open gay culture
4. Birth control movement
   a. Emma Goldman
   b. Margaret Sanger

IV. The Politics of Progressivism
    A. Global scope of Progressive impulse
        1. Common strains arising from industrial and urban growth
        2. International networks of social reformers
        3. Influence of European "social legislation" on American reformers
    B. Shared premises
        1. Commitment to activist government
        2. View of freedom as a positive concept
            a. "Effective freedom"; "power to do things"
            b. John Dewey, Randolph Bourne
        3. Trans-Atlantic scope of Progressive impulse
    C. Progressivism in municipal and state politics
        1. Agendas
            a. Curbing of political machines
            b. Regulation of public utilities, railroads, and other business interests
            c. Taxation of property and corporate wealth
            d. Improvement and enhancement of public space
            e. Humanizing of working and living conditions
        2. Significant municipal and state Progressives
            a. Mayors Hazen Pingree (Detroit) and Samuel "Golden Rule" Jones (Toledo)
            b. Governors Hiram Johnson (California) and Robert M. La Follette (Wisconsin)
    D. Progressive democracy
        1. Expansion and empowerment of electorate
            a. Popular election of U.S. senators, judges
            b. Primary elections
            c. Initiatives, referendums, recalls
            d. Women's suffrage
        2. Contraction and curtailment of electorate
            a. Disfranchisement of southern blacks
            b. Spread of appointed city commissions or managers
            c. Narrowing of voting rights for the poor
            d. Preference for government by experts; Walter Lippmann's *Drift and Mastery*
    E. Women reformers
        1. Challenge to political exclusion
        2. Crusades to uplift condition of immigrant poor, women, and child laborers
            a. Settlement house movement
            b. Government measures to alleviate problems of housing, labor, health
            c. Racist aspect

        3. Leading figures
- a. Jane Addams (Hull House)
- b. Julie Lathrop (Children's Bureau)
- c. Florence Kelley (National Consumers' League)

F. Revival of suffrage movement
1. National American Woman Suffrage Association
2. Scattered progress at state and local levels
3. Gathering focus on constitutional amendment

G. Ambiguities of "maternalist" reform
1. Drive to improve conditions of working women while reconfirming their dependent status
   - a. Mothers' pensions
   - b. Maximum working hours for women (*Muller v. Oregon;* Brandeis brief)
2. Stamping of gender inequality into foundation for welfare state

H. Native American Progressivism
1. Profile of Indian reformers
   - a. Intellectuals
   - b. Pan-Indian
   - c. Society of American Indians
2. Shared aims
   - a. Highlight plight of Native Americans
   - b. Promote justice for Native Americans
3. Differing aims
   - a. Endorsement of federal Indian policy
   - b. Full citizenship rights
   - c. Self-determination
4. Carlos Montezuma

V. Progressive presidents
A. Progressivism and the rise of the national state
B. Theodore Roosevelt
1. Succession to presidency; reelection in 1904
2. Limits on corporate power
   - a. "Good trusts" and "bad trusts"
   - b. Northern Securities case
3. Mediation between labor and capital; 1902 coal strike arbitration
4. Regulation of business
   - a. Hepburn Act
   - b. Pure Food and Drug Act
   - c. Meat Inspection Act
5. Mixed reaction from business

6. Conservation movement
   a. Late-nineteenth-century antecedents
      i. Early national parks
      ii. Sierra Club; John Muir
   b. Wildlife preserves and national parks
   c. Balance between development and conservation; Gifford Pinchot
   d. Water as a key point of contention
C. William Howard Taft
   1. Anointment as successor by Roosevelt; electoral victory over Bryan
   2. Partial continuation of Progressive agenda
      a. Antitrust initiatives
         i. Standard Oil case
         ii. American Tobacco case
         iii. Upholding of "good trust"/"bad trust" distinction by Supreme Court
      b. Support for graduated income tax (Sixteenth Amendment)
   3. Conservative drift; Pinchot-Ballinger affair
D. Election of 1912
   1. Distinctive outlooks on political and economic freedom
      a. Woodrow Wilson (Democrat; "New Freedom")
      b. Theodore Roosevelt (Progressive; "New Nationalism")
      c. William Howard Taft (Republican; conservative wing)
      d. Eugene V. Debs (Socialist)
   2. Wilson victory
E. Wilson's first-term program
   1. Underwood tariff
   2. Labor
      a. Clayton Act
      b. Keating-Owen Act
      c. Adamson Act
   3. Farmers: Warehouse Act
   4. Supervision of economy
      a. Federal Reserve System
      b. Federal Trade Commission

CHRONOLOGY

1900   Galveston creates first city commission government

1901   Socialist party formed
        William McKinley assassinated; Theodore Roosevelt becomes president

1902	Federal government files Northern Securities antitrust suit
	Roosevelt mediates anthracite coal strike
1904	Lincoln Steffens publishes *The Shame of the Cities*
	Roosevelt reelected
1905	Industrial Workers of the World formed
	Roosevelt creates U.S. Forest Service
1906	Upton Sinclair publishes *The Jungle*
	Pure Food and Drug Act and Meat Inspection Act
	Hepburn Act
1908	*Muller v. Oregon*
	Ford Motor Company introduces Model T
	William Howard Taft elected president
1909	Ballinger-Pinchot controversy
	Wave of garment worker strikes; "Uprising of the Twenty Thousand"
1910	Roosevelt delivers New Nationalism speech
1911	Triangle Shirtwaist Fire
	Society of American Indians founded
	Frederick W. Taylor publishes *The Principles of Scientific Management*
1912	IWW leads Lawrence, Massachusetts ("Bread and Roses") textile strike
	Four-way election between Woodrow Wilson (Democrat), Theodore Roosevelt (Progressive), William Howard Taft (Republican), and Eugene V. Debs (Socialist); Wilson elected
1913	Avant-garde Armory art exhibit opens in New York City
	Sixteenth Amendment ratified
	Seventeenth Amendment ratified
	Ford company adopts moving assembly line
	Federal Reserve Act
1914	Ludlow Massacre
	Federal Trade Commission established Clayton Act
	Ford company introduces five-dollar day
1916	Adamson Act
	Margaret Sanger organizes New York Birth Control League
	Keating-Owen Child Labor Act
	Wilson reelected

KEY TERMS

population growth: Both urban and rural populations grew in the late nineteenth century, but the rate of urban growth far exceeded that of the rural regions. In 1870, some 6.2 million Americans lived in cities; three decades later, their number had risen to 30.2 million. During that same time period, the rural population grew from 25.2 million to 45.8 million. In the three decades between 1870 and 1900, the decade with the slowest rate of growth in the cities was the 1890s, during which the urban population increased by 36.4 percent. In the same time period, the highest rate of growth in rural areas was 25.7 percent.

child labor: Founded in 1904, the National Child Labor Committee sought enforcement of state laws prohibiting child labor. In 1909 the group called for federal legislation banning the practice. Years later, Congress passed the Keating-Owen Child Labor Act. The legislation relied upon the Congress's power to regulate interstate commerce to end child labor, banning the shipment of goods across state lines of any products made by children. The U.S. Supreme Court, however, struck down the law in *Hammer v. Dagenhart*. Roland Dagenhart, who worked with his two children in North Carolina, had sued in order to keep his children working. The court determined that the Congress's use of the commerce clause to regulate manufacturing within a state was unconstitutional. It was not until 1938 that the Congress passed child labor legislation that the Supreme Court approved.

Mexican immigration: During the first decade of the twentieth century, some 50,000 Mexicans migrated to the United States. Their numbers grew during the decade that followed, with some 219,000 arriving. The growth of Mexican immigration continued into the 1920s, when an additional 459,000 migrated to the United States. Two factors promoted this trend. First, Mexico underwent a catastrophic civil war in the 1910s, leading hundreds of thousands to flee their homeland. Second, the expansion of agriculture in the United States offered economic opportunities, however limited, to Mexican immigrants. The exclusion of Japanese immigrants in the early twentieth century contributed to the increased demand for farm laborers that drew Mexicans north.

commission form of city government: On September 8, 1900, an enormous hurricane struck Galveston, Texas, destroying much of the city and taking as many as 12,000 lives. In an effort to hasten the rebuilding process, city leaders replaced the existing government with a commission of experts, each heading a city department. The commission form of government in Galveston proved successful, and by 1918 some 500 cities throughout the nation had adopted it. However, critics noted that because commission members were elected at-large, minority neighborhoods saw their political power decline. As a result, many southern cities abandoned the commission system during the civil rights era of the 1960s. Even Galveston abandoned it, turning to a city manager system in 1960.

censoring the movies: Even as reformers such as Margaret Sanger called for open discussion of controversial topics such as human sexuality, some Americans called for censorship of motion pictures containing material deemed unfit or obscene. In 1907 the city of Chicago granted its police force the authority to close "immoral scenes"; other cities enacted similar measures. In an effort to avoid government regulation of the industry, in 1909 movie producers in New York agreed to voluntarily submit films to a review board. Six years later the U.S. Supreme Court validated state regulation of the movies, ruling that motion pictures did not have free speech protections guaranteed under the First Amendment because they were a form of entertainment.

Seventeenth Amendment: Article I of the U.S Constitution required state legislatures to select their state's senators to the U.S. Congress. However, the Constitution did not require any specific procedure for legislatures to follow. As a result, each state's method of selecting senators varied, and deadlocks within legislatures led to occasional unfilled seats. In 1866, Congress mandated a selection process in which the two houses of each state voted separately. If they did not agree on a senator, the two bodies met in joint session and voted until a senator was elected. By the time the Seventeenth Amendment passed, however, many states had allowed voters to choose a candidate in primary elections and required their legislatures to honor the voters' choice. Thus, the Seventeenth Amendment acknowledged a trend already taking place at the state level.

Muller v. Oregon: On September 4, 1905, a foreman at the Grand Laundry in Portland, Oregon, required an employee named Mrs. Elmer Gotcher to work more than ten hours. The foreman violated Oregon law, which limited women's work in business and factories to a ten-hour maximum. Mrs. Gotcher complained, and a court fined laundry owner Curt Muller ten dollars for violating the Oregon statute. When Muller's appeal reached the U.S. Supreme Court, women were divided in their positions on the case. Some women favored legislation that provided protections for women in the workplace and society. Feminists, however, argued that the laws in Oregon and nineteen other states placed women on an unequal footing with men, diminishing efforts to secure the vote. The court's ruling in *Muller v. Oregon* granted women protection in the workplace, but also limited their access to higher paying jobs in industry.

coal miners' strike of 1902: On May 12, 1902, some 140,000 men who worked in the nation's anthracite coal mines went on strike. They made three demands. First, they called for an eight-hour workday. Second, the miners called for a twenty percent increase in pay. Finally, they wanted the mine operators to recognize their union, the United Mine Worker (UMW). Mine owners refused to negotiate, assuming the strike would collapse. However, they misjudged the resolve of the miners, who vowed to continue. The owners also misjudged public sentiment. Because the miners were open to negotiation and avoided open violence, the American people sided with the workers. As winter approached and the price of coal rose from $5 a ton to as high as $20, the public demanded action. It was in this environment that President Theodore Roosevelt arranged negotiations between the two groups. Roosevelt's commission awarded the miners a ten percent wage increase, and hours were reduced. The owners received something, too. They did not have to recognize the union, and the commission recommended an increase in the price of coal, a suggestion that was quickly implemented.

Roosevelt and conservation: Roosevelt made extensive use of executive orders to expand the nation's land reserves by some 150 million acres during his presidency. His ambitious conservation program met opposition from some westerners, who argued that Roosevelt's agenda stifled economic development in the region. One such opponent was Senator Charles Fulton of Oregon, a member of the president's own Republican Party. In 1907, Fulton attached an amendment to an agricultural appropriations bill prohibiting the further creation of reserves in Oregon and five other western states unless Congress approved. Before he signed the agricultural bill that would limit his ability to promote conservation, Roosevelt created twenty-one new national forests and increased the size of several more, adding some seventeen million acres to national reserves. He then signed the agriculture legislation. Opponents decried the president's actions, but could do nothing to stop him.

OBJECTIVE QUESTIONS

Multiple Choice

1. Progressive-era writers and photographers seeking to expose the underside of urban-industrial society were known as:
   A. Muckrakers.
   B. Bushwhackers.
   C. Ditch-diggers.
   D. Stand-patters.

2. Progressive-era feminists were:
   A. fewer in number than during the Gilded Age.
   B. engaged in a wide range of social causes.
   C. more interested in Freudian psychology than in the right to vote.
   D. all of the above

3. Which of the following series of events is listed in proper sequence?
   A. Pure Food and Drug Act; publication of *The Jungle;* assassination of President McKinley; election of Woodrow Wilson
   B. Northern Securities case; Pinchot-Ballinger controversy; reelection of Roosevelt; Hepburn Act
   C. creation of Federal Reserve System; election of William Howard Taft; Triangle Shirtwaist Fire; Lawrence textile strike
   D. assassination of President McKinley; Meat Inspection Act; unveiling of Woodrow Wilson's "New Freedom" program; Federal Reserve Act

4. Which of the following was *not* a theme of Upton Sinclair's *The Jungle?*
   A. the hardship and uncertainty of immigrant life
   B. the disruptive effects of unions on industrial efficiency
   C. the harsh labor conditions at meatpacking plants
   D. the unsanitary preparation of meats at the packing houses

5. Which of the following was *not* a significant part of Theodore Roosevelt's Progressive agenda?
   A. curbing the power of the railroads
   B. protecting consumers
   C. expanding the rights of all Americans regardless of race
   D. conserving natural resources

6. Which of the following was *not* a key element of the Progressive ideology?
   A. Human beings and their society can be improved, perhaps even perfected, through collective effort.
   B. Government has proven so corrupt and ineffective that it can never be a vehicle for improving society; Progressives must rely on their own voluntary initiatives.
   C. For all of its achievements, unregulated capitalism has generated dehumanizing conditions for millions of Americans.
   D. Government runs best when left to the professionals.

7. Which of the following was *not* a significant motivation behind Progressivism?
   A. a desire to free American culture from its obsession with morality and values
   B. a desire to bring greater efficiency to government and the economy
   C. a desire to make society more fair and just
   D. a desire to lessen conflict among different groups of Americans

8. Which of the following was *not* true of the 1912 election?
   A. Of the four candidates (Wilson, Taft, Roosevelt, and Debs), only Taft leaned at all toward the laissez-faire philosophy so familiar in the late nineteenth century.
   B. Of the four candidates, only Debs challenged the legitimacy of capitalism.

C. Wilson's victory ushered in a new wave of Progressive reform, affecting such areas as the tariff, the banking system, and the livelihoods of farmers and workers.

D. Once elected, Wilson surprised many by shifting toward a conservative, anti-Progressive position.

9. The 1909 "uprising of the 20,000" was:
   A. an organized effort on the part of manufacturers to secure property rights in the face of Populist opposition.
   B. an interracial rebellion of sharecroppers in Alabama, Louisiana, and Arkansas.
   C. a walkout of garment workers, which led to a victory for the International Ladies' Garment Workers Union.
   D. a mass meeting of farmworkers in Wichita, Kansas, at which they sought to advance the subtreasury plan.

10. The organization of middle-class and upper-class women and impoverished immigrants founded in 1903 to bring women workers into unions was called the:
    A. Women's Christian Temperance Union.
    B. International Ladies' Garment Workers Union.
    C. National Consumers' League.
    D. Women's Trade Union League.

11. The term "Progressive" that came into common use around 1910 describes:
    A. a loosely defined political movement of individuals and groups who hoped to bring about social and political change in American life.
    B. a type of life insurance, and auto insurance then available.
    C. a self-help movement in which one was to take pro-active measures in seeking to overcome one's aggressive tendencies.
    D. a movement that sought to recapture America's lost glory through an active policy of global imperialism.

12. Which was *not* a group associated with the Progressive movement?
    A. forward-looking businessmen
    B. labor activists, who desired to empower industrial workers
    C. sharecroppers in the Northwest
    D. social scientists who believed that their research would help to solve social problems

13. The Progressive Era was a time of:
    A. desultory economic performance in the economy, and decreasing wages.
    B. economic recession.
    C. explosive economic growth, rapid population rise, and increased industrial production, and "a Golden Age" for American agriculture.
    D. economic downturn for agriculture in America, and uneven growth in the industrial economy.

14. All of the following were muckrakers, except:
    A. Lincoln Steffens.
    B. Ida Tarbell.
    C. Upton Sinclair.
    D. Theodore Roosevelt.

15. Between 1901 and 1914,
    A. 13 million immigrants came to the United States.
    B. there was a net outflow of population from the United States to other countries.
    C. 17 million Asian immigrants arrived on America's shores.
    D. 3 million immigrants came to the United States.

16. In Charlotte Perkins Gilman's view, as she wrote in her influential book *Women and Economics* (1898):
    A. American women were freer, wealthier, and healthier than ever before in human history, and should celebrate these newfound achievements.
    B. the new industrial economy afforded women more opportunities and freedoms than ever before, even if economic growth was uneven across the country.
    C. prevailing gender norms condemned women to a life of domestic drudgery; women were oppressed, and a housewife was an unproductive parasite.
    D. Socialism, not capitalism, was the way forward.

17. The Progressive Era economic system based on mass production and mass consumption came to be called:
    A. Progressive-era plenty.
    B. Fordism.
    C. the Affluent Society.
    D. the American Way.

18. Pope Leo XIII's 1894 *Rerum Novarum,* and the Catholic priest Father John A. Ryan's *A Living Wage* (1906), called for all of the following except:
    A. a decent standard of living for working people.
    B. an endorsement of the rights of working people to organize unions.
    C. repudiating competitive individualism in favor of a more cooperative vision of the good society.
    D. the view that the Catholic Church should in no way become involved in discussions of wages, working conditions, and the ethical basis of the free market economy.

19. The view that the foremost social problem in America lay in the
    contradiction between "political liberty" and "industrial slavery" was
    held by:
    A. Woodrow Wilson.
    B. Louis D. Brandeis.
    C. Henry Ford.
    D. John A. Ryan.

20. Which of the following was *not* one of the principal "varieties of
    Progressivism"?
    A. the proposal to return to a competitive marketplace of small producers
    B. acceptance of large corporations, with the view that the government
       ought to regulate them
    C. the proposal to relocate freedom from the economic and political
       worlds to the private realm of personal fulfillment
    D. the proposal to embrace Social Darwinism, and laissez-faire economics

21. Which was *not* a goal of the Socialist Party in the United States at its 1901
    founding?
    A. free college education
    B. legislation to improve the conditions of laborers
    C. democratic control over the economy through public ownership of
       factories
    D. support for the Soviet Union and nonaligned nations around the world

22. Who was the leading Socialist Party figure who ran for the presidency of the
    United States on several occasions?
    A. Ben Handford
    B. Hiram Revels
    C. Eugene V. Debs
    D. Bill Haywood

23. What was the name of the organization that advocated a workers' revolution
    to seize control of the means of production and abolish the state, and which
    organized women, blacks, Asian-Americans, as well as white men?
    A. Industrial Workers of the World
    B. the National Civic Federation
    C. the American Chambers of Commerce
    D. the Federated Employers International

24. The 1912 mill-workers strike that had the greatest impact on public
    consciousness in Progressive-Era America took place in:
    A. Chicago, Illinois.
    B. New York City.
    C. Lawrence, Massachusetts.
    D. New Orleans, Louisiana.

25. The 1914 Ludlow Massacre was:
    A. a precursor to the Sioux Indian attack against General George Armstrong Custer.
    B. an attack by militia against a tent city of striking workers in Colorado.
    C. a premeditated attack against Native Americans in South Dakota by the federal militia.
    D. a massacre of frontier settlers by Sioux, Cheyenne, Algonquin, and Narragansett Indians.

26. In 1907, at a time when segregation had become much the norm throughout the South, in which city did a strike of 10,000 black and white dockworkers take place, as a remarkable expression of interracial solidarity?
    A. Charleston, South Carolina
    B. Wilmington, North Carolina
    C. New Orleans, Louisiana
    D. Newport News, Virginia

27. A principal organization in the early twentieth century that battled for civil liberties and the right of individual freedom of speech was:
    A. the American Chambers of Commerce.
    B. the Industrial Workers of the World.
    C. the National Civic Federation.
    D. the Ladies' Christian Temperance Union.

28. What was the name of the organization that sponsored the 1914 debate at New York City's Cooper Union on the question "What is feminism?", and whose definition of feminism emphasized greater economic opportunities, the vote, and open discussions of sexuality?
    A. the Feminist Alliance
    B. the Lyrical Left
    C. the Women's Christian Temperance Organization
    D. Heterodoxy

29. In Progressive-Era America, what particular locale became known as a center of sexual experimentation, attracting women interested in free sexual expression and, with its aura of tolerance, attracted many homosexuals?
    A. Greenwich Village in New York City
    B. Hoboken, New Jersey
    C. The Bronx, New York
    D. Westerville, Ohio

30. Who was the woman best known during the second decade of the twentieth century for promoting birth control?
    A. Margaret Sanger
    B. Florence Kelley
    C. Mary Kingsbury Simkhovitch
    D. Frances Perkins

31. Who was the Progressive-era mayor of Toledo who founded night schools, built new parks, established kindergartens, and supported the right of workers to unionize?
    A. Hazen Pingree
    B. Samuel "Golden Rule" Jones
    C. Mary "raise less corn and more hell" Lease
    D. "Big" Bill Haywood

32. Who was the early-twentieth-century governor of Wisconsin, who made that state a "laboratory for democracy," developed what came to be known as the Wisconsin Idea, taxed corporate wealth, and initiated state regulation of public utilities?
    A. Robert M. LaFollette
    B. Hazen Pingree
    C. Randolph Bourne
    D. Samuel Jones

33. The amendment to the United States Constitution that provides that United States senators will be chosen by popular vote rather than by state legislatures is:
    A. The Fifteenth Amendment
    B. The Sixteenth Amendment
    C. The Seventeenth Amendment
    D. The Eighteenth Amendment

True or False

1. In the Progressive era, industry was on the rise and agriculture was in decline.

2. Immigrants from southern and eastern Europe showed little interest in emerging forms of popular entertainment such as amusement parks, dance halls, and nickelodeons.

3. One of the main principles of Frederick W. Taylor's "scientific management" was the submission of workers to the dictates of their supervisors.

4. As president, Theodore Roosevelt was determined to break up every business trust he could find.

5. At times Progressives sought to expand popular democracy, and at times they sought to restrict it.

6. Theodore Roosevelt's "New Nationalism" called for vigorous federal intervention in the economy, while Woodrow Wilson's "New Freedom" called on government to stay out of business affairs.

7. Women reformers devoted little attention to labor conditions, regarding that as a "man's issue."

8. The new radical "bohemia" that thrived in places like Greenwich Village explored fresh ways of thinking about politics, culture, and sexuality.

9. In the early twentieth century, New York City was a center of finance, publishing, and entertainment, but there was almost no manufacturing going on in the city.

10. The 1911, Triangle Fire was a fire in a triangular region of Massachusetts between the towns of Worcester, Boston, and Salem.

11. Historians call the period of American history from the closing years of the nineteenth century into the second decade of the twentieth century the Progressive era.

12. The Progressive era was a time of economic expansion that produced millions of new jobs and brought unprecedented material wealth to millions of Americans.

13. During the Progressive era more than a million claims for free government land were filed under the Homestead Act of 1863, while the populations of Texas, Oklahoma, Kansas, Nebraska, and the Dakotas grew rapidly.

14. During the Progressive era, the Imperial Valley of California was transformed by irrigation and became a major area of commercial farming.

15. Cities formed a principal focus of Progressive-era politics and a new mass-consumer society.

16. Directly or indirectly, J. P. Morgan controlled 40 percent of the financial and industrial capital in the United States in the opening years of the twentieth century.

17. By 1910, almost 60 percent of workers in leading manufacturing and mining industries were foreign-born.

18. Millions of Europeans immigrated to the United States to flee oppressive governments and poverty, and with a desire to share the "freedom and prosperity" the United States afforded.

19. A cornucopia of goods was available to Progressive-era Americans in downtown department stores, chain stores, and retail mail order houses.

20. Not all Americans shared in the mass-consumption society in Progressive-era America; persistent poverty in the South, low wages, and an unequal distribution of income kept many Americans from participating in the nation's growing wealth.

21. Among the many leisure activities in Progressive-era America were amusement parks, dance halls, vaudeville theaters, and silent motion pictures, called "nickelodeons."

22. There was little change in traditional gender roles in Progressive-era America.

23. By the 1910s, women worked not only as domestic servants, but also as office workers, telephone operators, and store clerks.

24. Free speech and American civil liberties became significant public issues in the early twentieth century, in workers' struggles for the right to strike, and in labor radicals' work against restraints on open-air speaking.

25. Mabel Dodge's New York living room was the location of a famed "salon" in which bohemian intellectuals and intelligentsia gathered to discuss issues of sexual liberation, modern trends in art, and labor unrest.

26. "Social legislation" includes governmental action taken to address urban problems and the insecurities of working-class life.

27. The politics of Progressivism was almost solely a North American phenomenon.

28. The initiative, referendum, and recall were all early-twentieth-century means by which democracy was expanded.

29. During the Progressive era, city managers and nonpartisan commissions ran many municipalities.

30. One current of Progressive-era political thought promoted the view that experts—college professors and others able to apply scientific methods to modern social problems—ought to direct government policy.

31. By 1900, more than 80,000 women in the United States had earned college degrees.

32. At a time when college-educated women were excluded from politics (in almost every state women could not vote), they became spearheads for reform by opening settlement houses—houses in impoverished areas of cities—from which they administered kindergartens, employment bureaus, health clinics, and other endeavors, which both empowered themselves and their immigrant neighbors.

33. The most prominent female reformer in Progressive-era America was Florence Kelley.

34. In 1903, Alabama passed a law restricting child labor, and by 1915 all Southern states had followed suit.

35. Julia Lathrop was the first woman to head a federal agency; in 1912 she took up leadership of the Children's Bureau.

36. The National Consumers' League was a leading advocate for legislation for women and children in Progressive-era America.

37. After 1900, the campaign for women's suffrage became a mass movement; membership in the American Woman Suffrage Association was more than 2 million by 1917.

38. By 1900, more than half of the states allowed women to vote on school issues, and four Western states allowed women full suffrage.

39. Massachusetts became the first state east of the Mississippi to allow women the right to vote in presidential elections.

40. After 1910, mothers' pensions—aid given to mothers of young children who lacked male support—were established by many states; though, to be sure, the amounts of the monthly checks given to such mothers was small and often inadequate.

41. Feminists who supported mothers' pensions believed these pensions would empower single women.

42. The Supreme Court's decision in *Mueller v. Oregon* (1908) unambiguously empowered women.

43. Louis D. Brandeis held that economic entitlements must be based on special service to the nation.

44. By 1913, twenty-two states had enacted workmen's compensation laws.

45. The most striking political development of the early twentieth century was the rise of the national state.

46. The first World Series was played in 1903.

47. Herbert Croly proposed a new synthesis of American political traditions in which "Jeffersonian ends" would be achieved by employing "Hamiltonian means."

48. Theodore Roosevelt was the youngest president in American history.

49. President William McKinley was assassinated by an anarchist in September 1901.

50. President Theodore Roosevelt's political program was called the New Deal.

51. President Theodore Roosevelt distinguished between "good" and "bad" corporations, and in the Northern Securities Company case made his mark as a trust buster.

52. An example of President Roosevelt's activism was his handling of the anthracite coal strike of 1902, in which he threatened a federal takeover of the mines.

53. A significant step in the expansion of federal power over the economy was taken in 1906 with passage of the Hepburn Act, which allowed the ICC to set railroad rates.

54. Another important example of federal intervention and a new activism on the part of the national government into the economy was passage of the Pure Food and Drug Act (1906) by which the federal government became the agent policing the labeling and quality of food and drugs.

55. Yet another example of Theodore Roosevelt's expansion of the powers of the federal government was the actions he took vis-à-vis the conservation movement; under his leadership, and relying on the advice of Gifford Pinchot, conservation became a concerted federal policy.

56. Gifford Pinchot held that logging, mining, and grazing on public lands should be eliminated.

57. President William Howard Taft pursued antitrust policy far less aggressively than Roosevelt had.

58. William Howard Taft opposed the graduated income tax.

59. The Sixteenth Amendment made the income tax constitutional.

60. By 1912, in spite of its long tradition of backing states' rights and a laissez-faire approach to the economy the Democratic Party nominated Woodrow Wilson as its presidential candidate; Wilson had been a Progressive governor of New Jersey.

61. "The New Nationalism" was the name of the program on which Woodrow Wilson ran for the presidency in 1912.

62. The 1912 Progressive Party platform set out a blueprint for a modern welfare state.

63. President Woodrow Wilson proved to be a weak executive leader, taciturn and secretive.

64. Wilson met fierce resistance by the Republican-controlled Congress during his first term.

65. The Underwood Tariff sharply raised duties on imports.

66. The Underwood Tariff imposed a graduated income tax on the richest five percent of Americans.

67. The Keating-Owen Act of 1916 legalized child labor.

68. The Federal Reserve System (1913), and the Federal Trade Commission (1914) were major examples of the remarkable expansion of the role of the federal government in the economy during the Progressive era.

ESSAY QUESTIONS

1. How did the new ideal of material consumption affect the way Americans thought about "freedom"?

2. Describe the chief motivations and philosophies behind Progressivism, along with some of the important variations and tensions within it.

3. In what ways did women's activism shape the Progressive movement? How, in turn, did Progressivism affect the situation of American women?

4. What were the main conservative critiques of Progressivism? What were the main radical critiques?

5. How were American conceptions of "freedom" altered by Progressivism?

6. Imagine a chance meeting, in 1912, among the following characters:

   • a working-class immigrant from southern or eastern Europe
   • a native-born, middle-class professional
   • a black advocate of racial equality
   • a women's suffragist
   • a factory owner
   • a small farmer

   With remarkable candor, they fall into a spirited debate over the meanings and effects of Progressivism. Among the questions they debate: "What have been the impacts of Progressivism on life in America? Has Progressive reform gone too far, not far enough, or is it just right?" Transcribe this unusual conversation.

7. Eric Foner writes, "Only energetic national government, Progressives believed, could create the social conditions of freedom." Write an essay describing how, in the Progressive view, energetic government and freedom were linked.

8. By 1916, Eric Foner writes, "the Progressive era had given birth to a new American state." Write an essay on the social ferment and political mobilizations that had given rise to the new laws, administrative agencies, and independent commissions of this "new American state."

9. Compare and contrast the goals of the New Freedom, New Nationalism, Progressive Party, and Socialist Party in the 1912 election.

10. Compare and contrast the presidencies of Theodore Roosevelt, William Howard Taft, and Woodrow Wilson.

11. Write an essay on the place of women in Progressive-era America detailing their status, successes, and the major issues they faced.

SOURCES FOR FURTHER RESEARCH

Books

GENERAL OVERVIEWS

Dawley, Alan, *Struggles for Justice: Social Responsibility and the Liberal State* (1991)
Diner, Steven J., *A Very Different Age: Americans of the Progressive Era* (1998)
McCormick, Richard L., *Progressivism* (1983)
McGerr, Michael, *A Fierce Discontent: The Rise and Fall of the Progressive Movement in America, 1890–1921* (2003)
Wiebe, Robert H., *The Search for Order, 1877–1920* (1967)

PARTICULAR ASPECTS

Bodnar, John, *The Transplanted: A History of Immigrants in Urban America* (1985)
Cameron, Ardis, *Radicals of the Worst Sort: Laboring Women in Lawrence, Massachusetts, 1860–1912* (1993)
Cott, Nancy, *The Grounding of Modern Feminism* (1987)
Glenn, Susan A., *Daughters of the Shtetl: Life and Labor in the Immigrant Generation* (1990)
Glickman, Lawrence B., *A Living Wage: Workers and the Making of American Consumer Society* (1997)
Grantham, Dewey W., *Southern Progressivism: The Reconciliation of Progress and Tradition* (1983)
Greene, Julie, *Pure and Simple Politics: The American Federation of Labor and Political Activism, 1881–1917* (1998)
Hofstadter, Richard, *The Age of Reform: From Bryan to F.D.R.* (1955)
Johnston, Robert D., *The Radical Middle Class: Populist Democracy and the Question of Capitalism in Progressive Era Portland* (2003)
Keller, Morton, *Regulating a New Society: Public Policy and Social Change in America, 1900–1933* (1994)
Kloppenberg, James T., *Uncertain Victory: Social Democracy and Progressivism in European and American Thought, 1870–1920* (1986)
Lukas, J. Anthony, *Big Trouble* (1997)

Maddox, Lucy, *Citizen Indian: Native American Intellectuals, Race, and Reform* (2005)

Meyer, Stephen, *The Five Dollar Day: Labor Management and Social Control in the Ford Motor Company, 1908–1921* (1981)

Montgomery, David, *The Fall of the House of Labor: The Workplace, the State, and American Labor Activism, 1865–1925* (1987)

Muncy, Robyn, *Creating a Female Dominion in American Reform, 1890–1935* (1991)

Orsi, Robert A., *The Madonna of 115th Street: Faith and Community in Italian Harlem, 1880–1915* (1985)

Peiss, Kathy, *Cheap Amusements: Working Women and Leisure in Turn-of-the-Century New York* (1986)

Rauchway, Eric, *Murdering McKinley: The Making of Theodore Roosevelt's America* (2003)

Rodgers, Daniel T., *Atlantic Crossings: Social Politics in a Progressive Age* (1998)

Stansell, Christine, *American Moderns: Bohemian New York and the Creation of a New Century* (2000)

Stromquist, Shelton, *Re-Inventing "The People": The Progressive Movement, the Class Problem, and the Origins of Modern Liberalism* (2006)

Westbrook, Robert, *John Dewey and American Democracy* (1991)

Videos

Heaven Will Protect the Working Girl (28 minutes, American Social History Productions, 1993)

The Jungle (51 minutes, Discovery Channel/Films for the Humanities and Sciences, 2000)

Margaret Sanger (87 minutes, Films for the Humanities & Sciences, 1998)

New York: A Documentary Film: Episode 4, The Power and the People, 1898–1918 (120 minutes, PBS Home Video, 1999)

One Woman, One Vote (114 minutes, PBS Video, 1995)

Mr. Sears' Catalogue (59 minutes, PBS Video, 1990)

TR: The Story of Theodore Roosevelt (240 minutes, PBS Video, 1996)

Unforgivable Blackness: The Rise and Fall of Jack Johnson (220 minutes, PBS Video, 2005)

Web Resources

America at Work, America at Leisure: Motion Pictures from 1894–1915, Library of Congress
    http://memory.loc.gov/ammem/awlhtml/awlhome.html

American Variety Stage: Vaudeville and Popular Entertainment, 1870–1920,
Library of Congress
  http://memory.loc.gov/ammem/vshtml/vshome.html

*Before and After the Great Earthquake and Fire: Early Films of San Francisco,
1897–1916*, Library of Congress
  http://memory.loc.gov/ammem/papr/sfhome.html

Child Labor in America, 1908–1912: Investigative Photos of Lewis W. Hine,
The History Place
  http://www.historyplace.com/unitedstates/childlabor/index.html

Ellis Island History, Ellis Island Immigration Museum
  http://www.ellisisland.com/indexHistory.html

Emergence of Advertising in America: 1850–1920, Digital Scriptorium and the
John W. Hartman Center for Sales, Advertising & Marketing History Rare
Book, Manuscript, and Special Collections Library, Duke University
  http://scriptorium.lib.duke.edu/eaa/browse.html

The Evolution of the Conservation Movement, 1850–1920, Library of Congress
  http://memory.loc.gov/ammem/amrvhtml/conshome.html

H-SHGAPE Internet Resources, Society for Historians of the Gilded Age and
Progressive Era
  http://www.h-net.org/~shgape/internet/index.html

Progressive Era to New Era, 1900–1929, Library of Congress
  http://memory.loc.gov/ammem/ndlpedu/features/timeline/progress/
  progress.html

The Triangle Factory Fire, Kheel Center for Labor-Management Documentation
and Archives, Cornell University
  http://www.ilr.cornell.edu/trianglefire/

*Votes for Women: Selections from the National American Woman Suffrage
Association Collection, 1848–1921*, Library of Congress
  http://memory.loc.gov/ammem/naw/nawshome.html

The Wilbur and Orville Wright Papers, Library of Congress
  http://memory.loc.gov/ammem/wrighthtml/

1912: Competing Visions for America, Ohio State University
  http://ehistory.osu.edu/osu/mmh/1912/default.cfm

ANSWERS TO OBJECTIVE QUESTIONS

Multiple Choice

1-A, 2-B, 3-D, 4-B, 5-C, 6-B, 7-A, 8-D, 9-C, 10-D, 11-A, 12-C, 13-C, 14-D,
15-A, 16-C, 17-B, 18-D, 19-B, 20-D, 21-D, 22-C, 23-A, 24-C, 25-B, 26-C,
27-B, 28-D, 29-A, 30-A, 31-B, 32-A, 33-C

True or False

1-F, 2-F, 3-T, 4-F, 5-T, 6-F, 7-F, 8-T, 9-F, 10-F, 11-T, 12-T, 13-T, 14-T, 15-T, 16-T, 17-T, 18-T, 19-T, 20-T, 21-T, 22-F, 23-T, 24-T, 25-T, 26-T, 27-F, 28-T, 29-T, 30-T, 31-T, 32-T, 33-F, 34-T, 35-T, 36-T, 37-T, 38-T, 39-F, 40-T, 41-T, 42-F, 43-F, 44-T, 45-T, 46-T, 47-T, 48-T, 49-T, 50-F, 51-T, 52-T, 53-T, 54-T, 55-T, 56-F, 57-F, 58-F, 59-T, 60-T, 61-F, 62-T, 63-F, 64-F, 65-F, 66-T, 67-F, 68-T

CHAPTER 19

Safe for Democracy: The United States and World War I, 1916–1920

CHAPTER OBJECTIVES

- How and for what purposes did the United States intervene in the affairs of neighboring nations during the Progressive era?
- What gave rise to World War I?
- What considerations led America eventually to enter the war? How did Americans debate the question?
- Through what means, and with what effects, did American leaders seek to rally the country around the war? What kinds of divisions persisted despite these efforts?
- How did World War I transform the lives of Americans and the direction of their society?
- How did the war alter American visions of freedom and democracy?
- What made the postwar period such a tempestuous time in American history?

CHAPTER OUTLINE

I. An era of intervention
   A. Theodore Roosevelt and Roosevelt Corollary
      1. Panama
         a. U.S.-backed separation of Panama from Colombia
         b. U.S. acquisition of Panama Canal Zone
         c. Construction of Panama Canal
      2. Dominican Republic
      3. Cuba
   B. William Howard Taft and Dollar Diplomacy
      1. Nicaragua

    2. Honduras
    3. Dominican Republic
  C. Woodrow Wilson and "moral imperialism"
    1. Haiti
    2. Dominican Republic
    3. Mexico
      a. Mexican Revolution under leadership of Francisco Madero
      b. Assassination of Madero and outbreak of Civil War
      c. Wilson dispatch of troops, skirmishes with Pancho Villa

II. America and the Great War
  A. Outbreak of European war
    1. Assassination of Archduke Franz Ferdinand
    2. Allied Powers (Britain, France, Russia, Japan) versus Central Powers (Germany, Austria-Hungary, Ottoman Empire)
    3. Protracted, bloody stalemate
  B. Implications of European war
    1. Undermining of faith in human progress and reason
    2. Indication of power of nationalism in modern world
  C. American response
    1. Mixed sentiments
      a. Sympathy for Allied Powers
        i. British roots
        ii. Association of Britain with democracy, Germany with tyranny
      b. Opposition to Allied Powers, and/or U.S. involvement
        i. German, Irish, Russian (anti-czarist) roots
        ii. Antiwar feminists, pacifists, social reformers
    2. The road to American involvement
      a. Initial declaration of neutrality
      b. British and German blockades
      c. American business ties to Britain
      d. Sinking of *Lusitania*
      e. "Preparedness" policy
      f. German suspension of submarine warfare against neutrals
      g. Reelection of Wilson; "He Kept Us Out of War"
      h. German resumption of open submarine warfare
      i. Zimmerman Note
      j. First Russian Revolution (Menshevik); overthrow of czar
      k. American declaration of war against Germany
  D. From American entry to Armistice
    1. Second Russian Revolution (Bolshevik)
      a. Vladimir Lenin's break with Allies
      b. Withdrawal of Russia from war

      2. Wilson's Fourteen Points
      3. Defeat of German advance; Allied counteroffensive
      4. German surrender

III. The war at home
   A. Perceived prospects for fulfillment of Progressive vision
      1. Economic rationalization
      2. Spirit of national unity and purpose
      3. Social justice
   B. Expansion of federal powers
      1. Military conscription
      2. Economic intervention
         a. Areas
            i. War production (War Industries Board)
           ii. National transportation (Railroad Administration)
          iii. Coal and oil (Fuel Administration)
          iv. Farming and food preparation (Food Administration)
            v. Labor relations (National War Labor Board)
         b. Varied degrees of intervention
            i. Coordination of overall war production (WIB)
          ii. Control of some sectors (railroads)
          iii. Regulation of some sectors (coal, oil, labor relations)
         c. Partnership between business and government
            i. Guaranteed profit
          ii. Suspension of antitrust
         d. Labor-management-government cooperation
            i. Uninterrupted production
          ii. Federal mediation
          iii. Labor's right to organize
          iv. Improved wages and working conditions
      3. Raising of revenue
         a. Corporate and income tax increases
         b. Liberty bonds
   C. Propaganda war
      1. Widespread opposition to American entry
         a. Industrial Workers of the World
         b. Socialist party
      2. Committee on Public Information; George Creel
         a. Modes of propaganda
            i. Pamphlets
          ii. Posters
          iii. Advertisements
          iv. Motion pictures
            v. Four-Minute speeches

        b. Themes
- i. Social cooperation
- ii. Expanded democracy and freedom
- iii. Demonization of Germans

D. Revitalization of Progressive causes
1. Women's suffrage
   a. Optimism that wartime patriotism will gain women the vote
   b. Insistence that women should enjoy "democracy" at home
      - i. National Women's party
      - ii. Alice Paul
   c. Support from Wilson
   d. Postwar ratification of Nineteenth Amendment
2. Prohibition
   a. Sources of support
      - i. Employers
      - ii. Urban reformers
      - iii. Women
      - iv. Anti-immigrant Protestants
      - v. Anti-Germans
   b. Progress
      - i. Passage of state laws
      - ii. Postwar ratification of Eighteenth Amendment

E. Repression of dissent
1. Instruments
   a. Federal government
      - i. Espionage Act
      - ii. Sedition Act
   b. State governments
   c. Vigilante organizations
2. Themes
   a. Definition of "patriotism" as support for government, war, economic status quo
   b. Definition of "un-Americanism" as labor radicalism, opposition to war
3. Means
   a. Criminalization of dissent; conviction of Eugene V. Debs
   b. Investigations of suspected dissidents
   c. Mass arrests
   d. Public harassment and intimidation
   e. Suppression of labor protest
   f. Terror
4. Minimal reaction from Progressives

F. The "race problem"
 1. Progressive-era conceptualization
  a. Ethnic groups as "races"
  b. Inbred "racial" characteristics
  c. Racial diversity as threat to American civilization
 2. Progressive solutions
  a. Mainstream
   i. "Americanization"
   ii. Eugenics
  b. Insistence by some on respect for other cultures
 3. Wartime Americanization
  a. Government-sponsored
  b. Pressure on immigrants to demonstrate patriotism
  c. Suppression of German-American culture
 4. Heightened interest in immigration restriction, eugenics
G. Ambiguous status of groups neither black nor white
 1. Mexicans in Southwest
 2. Puerto Ricans
 3. Asian-Americans
H. Status and response of African-Americans
 1. Progressive era
  a. Barriers to political rights, employment opportunity, consumer economy
  b. Progressives' indifference or aversion to black freedom
   i. Activists
   ii. Intellectuals
   iii. Presidents
  c. W. E. B. Du Bois and revival of black protest
   i. Du Bois's background
   ii. *The Souls of Black Folk*
   iii. Challenge to Booker T. Washington's accommodationism
   iv. "Talented tenth"
   v. Niagara movement
   vi. National Association for the Advancement of Colored People
 2. World War I era
  a. Optimism that wartime patriotism would gain blacks equal rights
   i. "Close ranks"
   ii. Minimal gains
  b. Great migration
   i. Scale and direction
   ii. Motivations and aspirations
   iii. Disappointing realities

       c. Anti-black violence, North and South

       d. New spirit of militancy

          i. Silent Protest Parade

          ii. Garveyism

IV. 1919

    A. Upheaval around world

       1. Inspirations and manifestations

          a. Russian Revolution

          b. Spread of communist-led governments

          c. General strikes

          d. Peasant movements

          e. Anti-colonial campaigns

       2. Underlying aspirations

          a. Socialism

          b. "Industrial democracy"

          c. National self-determination

       3. Counter-mobilization

          a. Allied intervention in Soviet Union

          b. Limits of Wilson's internationalism

       4. Receding of postwar radicalism around world

    B. Labor upheaval in America

       1. Breadth and magnitude

       2. Spirit and themes

          a. Appropriation of wartime rhetoric of freedom and democracy

          b. Social and ideological diversity

       3. Leading instances

          a. Seattle general strike

          b. Boston police strike

          c. Coal strike

          d. Steel strike

       4. Anti-union mobilization

          a. Employers

          b. Government

          c. Private organizations

       5. Defeats of postwar strikes

       6. Red Scare

          a. Methods

            i. Federal raids on offices of labor and radical organizations; Palmer Raids

            ii. Arrests

            iii. Deportations

            iv. Secret files

        b. Outcomes
           i. Devastation of labor and radical organizations
          ii. Broad outrage over abuse of civil liberties

V. Forging of postwar international order
   A. Wilson's performance abroad
      1. Rapturous reception in Paris
      2. Hardheaded diplomacy at Versailles
   B. Treaty of Versailles
      1. Wilsonian elements
        a. League of Nations
        b. New sovereign nations in Europe
      2. Harsher elements
        a. French occupation of Saar basin and Rhineland
        b. Restrictions on German military
        c. Crippling reparations for Germany
      3. Limits of national sovereignty
        a. Denial of independence for French and British colonies
        b. League of Nations "mandates" for former Ottoman lands
        c. Reallotment of former German colonies
   C. Seeds of instability for twentieth-century world
   D. Wilsonian internationalism in postwar America
      1. Short-term setbacks
        a. League of Nations debate
        b. Wilson's stroke, incapacity
        c. Senate rejection of Versailles treaty
        d. Eclipse of Progressivism; "return to normalcy"
      2. Long-term legacy for American foreign policy
        a. Blend of idealism and power politics
        b. Appeals to democracy, open markets, global mission
        c. Impulse for military intervention abroad

CHRONOLOGY

1903	W. E. B. Du Bois publishes *The Souls of Black Folk*
	Roosevelt engineers Panamanian "independence" from Columbia; treaty with new Panama government grants U.S. sovereignty over Canal Zone
1904	Roosevelt Corollary issued
	U.S. forces seize customs houses of Dominican Republic
1905	Du Bois mobilizes Niagara movement
1906	U.S. troops sent to Cuba

1909	Founding of National Association for the Advancement of Colored People
1911	United States intervenes in Nicaragua Mexican Revolution
1914	Assassination of Archduke Ferdinand sparks outbreak of World War I Wilson declares neutrality Completion of Panama Canal U.S. occupation of Vera Cruz, Mexico
1915	Sinking of *Lusitania* Wilson launches policy of military "preparedness" U.S. Marines occupy Haiti Wilson hosts premier of *Birth of a Nation* at White House
1916	Pershing pursues Pancho Villa into Mexico U.S. Marines occupy Dominican Republic Wilson reelected
1917	Germans resume open submarine warfare United States breaks off relations with Germany Zimmerman Note United States declares war on Germany U.S. troops mobilized, sent overseas Federal war mobilization agencies established Espionage Act Anti-black riot in East St. Louis Silent Protest Parade in New York City Rounding up and abandonment of Bisbee, Arizona copper miners Russian Revolution
1918	Sedition Act Influenza epidemic devastates Europe, Asia, Americas Wilson unveils Fourteen Points Armistice in Europe American military intervention in Soviet Union
1919	Chicago race riot Nationwide strike wave, involving four million workers Ratification of Eighteenth Amendment Treaty of Versailles signed in Paris; later rejected by U.S. Senate
1919–20	Palmer Raids
1920	Ratification of Nineteenth Amendment Election of Harding; "return to normalcy"

KEY TERMS

yellow fever: Yellow fever, or "yellow jack" as it was often known, is a viral disease transmitted by the *Aedes aegypti* mosquito. Historians believe that this mosquito and the disease arrived in the Americas on the slave ships making the Middle Passage. Scholars have tallied some 230 major yellow fever epidemics in North America between its arrival in the 1600s and 1905, the date of the last major outbreak. Americans lived in fear of the disease; a 1793 epidemic in Philadelphia took some 5,000 lives. The occupation of Cuba at the Spanish-American War prompted fears that soldiers returning from duty on that island would bring the fever into the United States. In response, the U.S. Army initiated efforts to combat the disease. Mosquito eradication efforts led to declines in yellow fever cases, proving the connection between the insects and the illness. Army officers used their experiences in Cuba to successfully battle yellow fever in Panama, thereby allowing for the construction of the canal.

Vera Cruz Incident: President Woodrow Wilson went to extremes in his effort to oust the Huerta government in Mexico. In April 1914, Mexican officials in the port city of Tampico arrested crew members of the U.S.S. *Dolphin.* In search of gasoline, the Americans had mistakenly entered a restricted area. Mexican commanders quickly released the Americans with an apology, but the U.S. commander demanded a twenty-one gun salute to the American flag. President Wilson supported this demand, seeing it as a humiliation for Huerta if he agreed to the salute, and as a pretext for military action if the Mexican president refused. Huerta agreed on the condition that U.S. forces return the salute, which Wilson refused. The U.S. president then asked Congress for a resolution allowing him to protect the nation's honor, a measure that threatened military action. Events overtook the congressional debate after Wilson learned that a German ship was headed to the port of Vera Cruz with a weapons shipment. Wilson ordered the navy to seize the port, which led to a battle and numerous casualties. The Tampico and Vera Cruz incidents did not reflect well upon the Wilson administration at home or abroad, as the president who declared his commitment to peace seemed to be spoiling for a fight with the nation's southern neighbor.

Sinking of the *Lusitania*: On May 1, 1915, newspapers in New York City ran two advertisements side by side. One announced the sailing of the luxury liner *Lusitania;* the second was a warning from the German government declaring that "travelers sailing in the war zone on ships of Great Britain or her allies do so at their own risk." The warning was largely ignored as the British liner sailed with 702 crew members and 1,257 passengers. Despite news regarding submarine sightings, the ship's captain was unworried, declining to hold lifeboat drills. Such exercises probably would not have mattered—the *Lusitania* sank a mere eighteen minutes after the German torpedo struck its side, trapping hundreds of passengers and crew members below decks. The tragedy outraged the American public and contributed to the decline of neutrality in the United States.

Selective Service Act: Conscription, or the drafting of individuals to serve in the U.S. military, had proven problematic during the Civil War. In 1863, the federal government required all men between the ages of twenty and thirty-five, and all single men up to age forty-five, to register. However, draftees could hire substitutes to serve in their stead or pay a fee exempting them from service. Such exemptions led to widespread resentment and contributed to the deadly New York City riot of July 1863. Determined not to repeat the mistakes of the past, the Wilson administration carefully drafted the Selective Service Act of 1917. Few exemptions were permitted, and these were based on religious or economic concerns. Ministers and conscientious objectors were not drafted, nor were men who were in professions deemed essential to the national economy. The legislation allowed local draft boards to make the final selections, permitting board members to take into consideration personal concerns, such as family obligations, as they determined who would serve. Widely perceived as fair, the Selective Service Act of 1917 elicited few protests.

state sedition acts: Several states passed laws similar to the Sedition Act. Montana convicted seventy-four people of sedition under its law. Forty men and one woman served prison time as a result of their convictions—some were found guilty for statements such as "This is a rich man's war." In April 2006, nearly nine decades after the convictions, Montana Governor Brian Schweitzer issued a blanket pardon to those found guilty. Schweitzer acted after a University of Montana journalism professor and his students researched the implementation of the law and began public discussions of its effects on the people of the state.

Brownsville Affair: The incident in Brownsville, Texas, that prompted President Theodore Roosevelt to dishonorably discharge 156 African-Americans began in late July 1906, when the Twenty-Fifth United States Infantry arrived at Fort Brown. Unhappy with the arrival of black soldiers, the people of Brownsville engaged in discrimination and instances of physical abuse. Two weeks after the soldiers arrived, a shootout killed a local bartender and wounded a police officer. Witnesses claimed that a dozen or so black soldiers were responsible. The soldiers, who maintained all along that they had no knowledge of the shooting, gave investigators little to go on. President Roosevelt authorized the dishonorable discharges, although no soldier was ever convicted in the shootings. In doing so, he ignored the testimony of white commanders who said the men were in the barracks and clear indicators that evidence linking them to the violence had been planted. In an effort to correct this injustice, President Richard Nixon awarded the soldiers honorable discharges in 1972. The sole surviving member of the group received a pension for his military service.

Bailey v. Alabama: In the years after the Civil War, white southern landowners sought means to control agricultural workers, ensuring that they had access to cheap labor. Alabama's peonage law made breaking a labor contract a crime punishable by hard labor. The very act of quitting was considered evidence of intent to defraud the employer. Laws such as this made sharecroppers and other laborers reluctant to break contracts, no matter how unfair, because they faced such severe penalties. The case of *Bailey v. Alabama* arose when Alonzo Bailey quit his job with the Riverside Company in Alabama after working there for only one month. Bailey had signed a year-long contract and accepted a cash advance that he did not return. After an Alabama jury convicted him of violating the peonage law, Bailey appealed. The U.S. Supreme Court ruled that Bailey's decision to quit did not indicate intent to defraud his employer. In their ruling, the justices noted that peonage servitude (forced labor to repay a debt) violated the Thirteenth Amendment's prohibition on involuntary servitude.

Garvey and African nationalism: Marcus Garvey sought to instill a sense of pride in African-Americans in part by revising popular images of Africa. By the 1920s, most of Africa had been colonized by European powers, and popular depictions of the continent were entirely negative, offering images of poverty and primitivism. Garvey maintained that far from being a backward land, Africa was a center of civilization before the rise of Europe. He claimed that support for Africa would allow that region to return to its position of power in world affairs, a process that would benefit peoples of African heritage across the globe. Garvey's promotion of African nationalism and celebration of its culture foreshadowed the black nationalist movements of the 1960s.

The United States in Russia: U.S. troops first arrived in Russia as part of an Allied expeditionary force in 1918. Concerned about the rise of Bolshevism and fearing that the Germans might seize some 750,000 tons of supplies stored in Murmansk, the Allies, including approximately 5,000 Americans, landed in that port city in late June. The Russians responded aggressively, hemming in the Allied troops for about a year, at which point the American troops departed. A second group of Americans, around 10,000 soldiers, arrived in the eastern port of Vladivostok in August 1918. This force was sent to limit Japanese influence in the region and to aid the Czech League, a group of eastern Europeans trying to flee Russia. The Americans fought with Russian troops, leaving only after the Czech League was safely out of the country.

Red Scare bombings: During the first Red Scare, the use of bombs to terrorize public officials helped foster public anxiety. On April 28, 1919, a leaky package arrived in the mail for the mayor of Seattle. An examination revealed it to be a bomb. The following day the maid of a retired Georgia senator had both hands blown off when she opened a package. On the lookout for similar parcels, post office officials located a total of thirty-four additional packages mailed to prominent Americans, including cabinet members, Supreme Court justices, and members of Congress. A little over a month later, bombs exploded in eight American cities on the same night. One bomb destroyed the front of the house of Attorney General Mitchell A. Palmer (the bomber was killed in the explosion). The bombings gave credence to fears that radicals intended to use violence to overthrow the government and contributed to the hysteria that marked the Red Scare.

OBJECTIVE QUESTIONS

Multiple Choice

1. A leading characterization of U.S. foreign policy in the early twentieth century was:
   A. "Benign Neglect."
   B. "Dollar Diplomacy."
   C. "Golden-Rule Diplomacy."
   D. "Preemptive Engagement."

2. The outbreak of World War I in 1914 was triggered by:
   A. the Zimmerman note.
   B. the Russian Revolution.
   C. the assassination of Archduke Ferdinand.
   D. the sinking of the *Lusitania*.

3. Which of the following series of events is listed in proper sequence?
   A. completion of Panama Canal; overthrow of Mexican dictator Porfirio Diaz; American occupation of Haiti; founding of independent Panama
   B. announcement of "preparedness" policy; assassination of Archduke Ferdinand; reelection of Wilson; sinking of *Lusitania*
   C. establishment of Committee on Public Information; Seattle general strike; U.S. declaration of war on Germany; ratification of Nineteenth Amendment
   D. publication of Du Bois's *The Souls of Black Folk;* founding of NAACP; Silent Protest Parade in New York City; Chicago race riot

4. Which of the following was *not* a significant development in American race relations during the first two decades of the twentieth century?
   A. a growing impatience among black leaders with the accommodationist approach of Booker T. Washington
   B. the ascent of racial equality to the top of the Progressive agenda
   C. a mass migration of southern blacks to the industrial centers of the North
   D. a series of anti-black riots around the country during and following World War I

5. Which of the following was *not* a feature of public debate over whether the United States should enter the war in Europe?
   A. Advocates held that American entry was essential to the causes of democracy and free trade.
   B. Opponents held that American entry would imperil the causes of social justice at home.
   C. Labor generally opposed American entry; business generally endorsed it.

    D. Ethnic background had a lot to do with where Americans stood on the question.

6. Which of the following was *not* a significant effect of World War I on American society?
    A. the withdrawal of the federal government from domestic affairs, so that it could concentrate on the war overseas
    B. an influx of women into many occupations previously reserved for men
    C. the vigorous suppression of antiwar dissent
    D. a growing demand on the part of labor for greater democracy at the workplace

7. Which of the following was *not* a significant development in postwar America?
    A. a surge of labor militancy and radicalism across the country
    B. a fierce federal assault on the rights of labor and radical activists
    C. the constitutional enfranchisement of women
    D. the constitutional enfranchisement of African-Americans

8. Which of the following was *not* a principle espoused in Wilson's Fourteen Points?
    A. national self-determination
    B. free trade among nations
    C. the abolition of colonial rule around the globe
    D. the founding of an international structure to ensure the peaceful resolution of conflict among nations

9. The "open door" policy refers to:
    A. a key principle of American foreign relations that emphasizes the free flow of trade, investment, and information.
    B. the policy of many employers by which trade unions were deemed illegal.
    B. a liberal policy on the part of industrial capitalists by which they hired many women, African-Americans, and Asian-Americans.
    D. the economic opportunities afforded by the market economy in early-twentieth-century America.

10. President Woodrow Wilson's foreign policy that called for active intervention to remake the world in America's image, and which asserted the view that greater freedom worldwide would follow from increased American investment and trade abroad was called:
    A. The Good Neighbor Policy.
    B. international realism.
    C. liberal internationalism.
    D. isolationism.

11. The right to dissent from government policy during World War I:
    A. was encouraged by President Woodrow Wilson and others.
    B. met sweeping repression.
    C. was discouraged by Congress, but actively encouraged by President Wilson.
    D. was not much of an issue, as the nation united in common wartime cause.

12. Between 1901 and 1920, the U.S. Marines landed in Caribbean countries:
    A. never, since the Marines had not yet been founded as a military force.
    B. half a dozen times.
    C. with the help of the British, French, and Spanish.
    D. more than twenty times.

13. President Theodore Roosevelt won the Nobel Peace Prize for helping to negotiate a settlement of:
    A. the tensions between Colombia and Panama over the Panama Canal.
    B. the Russo-Japanese War of 1905.
    C. tensions between Colombia, Venezuela, and British Guiana.
    D. border disputes between the United States and Mexico.

14. What was the West African proverb which President Theodore Roosevelt was fond of?
    A. It takes a village to raise a child.
    B. The word of a friend makes you cry; the word of an enemy makes you laugh.
    C. Speak softly and carry a big stick.
    D. Until the lion has his or her own storyteller, the hunter will always have the best part of the story.

15. The American foreign policy principle that held that the United States had a right to exercise "an international police power" in the Western Hemisphere was called:
    A. the Monroe Doctrine.
    B. Dollar Diplomacy.
    C. the Roosevelt Corollary.
    D. the International Police Addendum.

16. Dollar Diplomacy, the U.S. foreign policy that emphasized economic investment and loans from American banks, rather than direct military intervention, was the policy of:
    A. William McKinley.
    B. Theodore Roosevelt.
    C. William Howard Taft.
    D. Woodrow Wilson.

17. In 1916, President Woodrow Wilson sent more than 10,000 troops into Mexico in an effort (that proved unsuccessful) to arrest:
    A. "Pancho" Villa, who had killed seventeen Americans in an attack on Columbus, New Mexico.
    B. Che Guevara, the leader of an indigenous uprising that sought to curtail American influence in the region.
    C. Vera Cruz, a leading figure in the Mexican government under Porfirio Diaz.
    D. Santa Anna, who had led the murderous raid against the Alamo.

18. During World War I, Germany, Austria-Hungary, and the Ottoman Empire were called:
    A. the Allies.
    B. the Triple Entente.
    C. the Junta.
    D. the Central Powers.

19. Which of the following was *not* a military technology used during World War I:
    A. machine guns
    B. tanks
    C. airplanes
    D. atomic bombs

20. How many soldiers perished during World War I worldwide?
    A. 620,000
    B. 950,000
    C. 1.2 million
    D. 10 million

21. Of the great ideologies that had arisen in the nineteenth century, which, by 1920, had proven most powerful?
    A. socialism
    B. nationalism
    C. idealism
    D. internationalism

22. What was the name of the British liner sunk by a German submarine in May 1915, which resulted in the deaths of more than a thousand passengers, including 124 Americans?
    A. the Lusitania
    B. the Ireland
    C. the Essex
    D. the Arabia

23. The United States entered World War I in April of 1917 only after Germany resumed submarine warfare against its ships in the Atlantic, and:
    A. after the discovery of a plot to assassinate President Woodrow Wilson.
    B. after discovery of the Zimmermann telegram.
    C. major riots broke out in all of America's principal cities.
    D. after bombardment of New York by German submarines.

24. In November 1917, in the midst of World War I, a communist revolution broke out in what country?
    A. Germany
    B. Japan
    C. China
    D. Russia

25. President Woodrow Wilson articulated the clearest statement of American war aims and his vision of a new postwar international order in:
    A. his Second Inaugural.
    B. the Fourteen Points.
    C. the Treaty of Versailles.
    D. the Treaty of Bretton Woods.

26. The federal organization established to explain the war to the American people, and which trained some 75,000 Four-Minute Men to deliver short talks in support of America's war effort was called:
    A. the War Industries Board.
    B. the American Minutemen Association.
    B. the War Labor Board.
    D. Committee on Public Information.

27. Who was the leader of the National Women's Party, an organization that employed militant tactics in favor of women's suffrage?
    A. Susan B. Anthony
    B. Jeannette Rankin
    C. Alice Paul
    D. Elizabeth Cady Stanton

28. What did prohibition (the Eighteenth Amendment, ratified in 1919) prohibit?
    A. a federal income tax
    B. employer liability laws
    C. white slavery (i.e. prostitution)
    D. manufacturer, sale, or distribution of alcoholic beverages

29. Randolph Bourne's vision of America was one in which:
    A. with suppression of dissent within the United States, the American melting pot would create liberty and justice for all.
    B. a cosmopolitan, democratic society in which immigrants and natives would together create a new "trans-national" culture.

C. assimilation was deemed compulsory.

D. a strong military would make America preeminent in the world.

30. During World War I, popular words of German origin were changed; "hamburger" became:
    A. "liberty sandwich"
    B. "liberty cabbage"
    C. "ground chuck"
    D. "American sandwich"

31. The worst race riot in American history occurred in 1921 when more than 300 blacks were killed and over 10,000 were left homeless after white mobs burned an all-black section of this city to the ground:
    A. East St. Louis, Illinois
    B. Phillips County, Arkansas
    C. Tulsa, Oklahoma
    D. Akron, Ohio

32. Who was the leader of the Universal Negro Improvement Association, a movement for African independence and black self-reliance?
    A. W. E. B. Du Bois
    B. William Monroe Trotter
    C. Fanny Lou Hammer
    D. Marcus Garvey

True or False

1. President Roosevelt declined to assert U.S. authority over the Canal Zone until the citizens of Panama had had a chance to vote on the matter.

2. Presidents Roosevelt, Taft, and Wilson shared a common belief that the United States had a right, even a duty, to intervene from time to time in the affairs of other countries.

3. Following the outbreak of World War I, the Allied and Central Powers each acted to block American trade with their adversaries.

4. President Wilson won reelection in 1916 on the slogan, "We Must Fight to Make the World Safe for Democracy."

5. After America entered the conflict, antiwar opposition disappeared.

6. While many were troubled by the ongoing slaughter overseas, most Progressives regarded wartime mobilization as an extraordinary chance to remake American society.

7. During American involvement in the war, all expressions of German-American culture came under sharp assault.

8. The coming of peace abroad quickly ushered in a restoration of social tranquility at home.

9. The United States produced a third of the world's manufactured goods by 1914.

10. By 1900, measured by its acquisition of new territories, the United States was an imperialist power, the equal of Great Britain and France.

11. Most Progressives opposed America's entry into World War I as jingoistic, imperialist venturing.

12. In intervening in Caribbean countries in the early twentieth century the United States generally sought to promote peace, democracy, and freedom.

13. In 1903, when Panama declared its independence from Colombia, the United States stationed a gunboat off the Panamanian coast, preventing the Colombian army from taking back the area.

14. In 1904, President Theodore Roosevelt arranged an "executive agreement" that gave a group of American bankers control over the finances of the Dominican Republic.

15. American troops occupied Cuba from 1906 to 1909.

16. President Woodrow Wilson repudiated Dollar Diplomacy.

17. President Woodrow Wilson authorized more military interventions into Latin America than any other president in American history.

18. When U.S. troops landed at Vera Cruz, Mexico in an effort to stop weapons from being delivered to Victoriano Huerta's forces, the Marines were greeted as liberators by the Mexican people.

19. More people were killed by the flu (epidemic of influenza) at the end of World War I, than died during all the years of fighting in that war.

20. At the outbreak of war in Europe in the summer of 1914, the U.S. population quickly unified in its support for Great Britain and France.

21. Ten of the twelve states that by 1916 had adopted women's suffrage were carried by Wilson in the election that year; without women's votes Wilson would not have been reelected.

22. No one was ever convicted under the 1917 Espionage Act or the 1918 Sedition Act.

23. Eugene Victor Debs, a Socialist Party leader, was imprisoned for delivering an antiwar speech.

24. The American Protective League was an organization dedicated to the protection of American civil liberties and free speech.

25. In 1911, the United States immigration commission listed forty-five immigrant "races" in a dictionary published that year.

26. Eugenics studied the mental characteristics of different ethnicities and races, only to discover that, for the most part and overwhelmingly, all human beings possess "good genes."

27. Settlement house workers, social scientists, and progressives in general, placed demands for black suffrage at the forefront of their efforts.

28. Having grown up in the South, President Woodrow Wilson was particularly sensitive to the needs of African-Americans and he worked actively to promote civil rights.

29. W. E. B. Du Bois asserted the need for the "talented tenth" of the African-American community to step forward and take the lead in education and training to challenge inequality faced by black Americans.

30. The 1905 Niagara movement derived its name from the fact that a group of black leaders met at Niagara Falls, Canada (since no hotel on the American side would accommodate them).

31. The National Association for the Advancement of Colored People (NAACP) launched a long battle for the enforcement of the Fourteenth and Fifteenth Amendments.

32. Major strides toward the advancement of equality for American blacks was one significant consequence of the war's aftermath due to the heroism, courage, determination, and patriotism demonstrated by black soldiers during World War I.

33. Between 1910 and 1920, half a million blacks moved away from the South; many migrated into northern cities like Chicago, New York, Akron, Buffalo, and Trenton.

34. When black workers took up jobs in East St. Louis, Illinois in 1917, traditional race prejudices were dropped as white American workers recognized the need for all Americans to pull together to win the war.

35. During 1919, more than 250 people died in riots in northern cities.

36. The year 1919 was a time of comparative political tranquility and harmony in the United States.

37. In the 1919 Seattle shipyard workers strike, American Federation of Labor unions and workers in the IWW battled each other in sometimes fierce hand combat.

38. In the 1919 steel strike, workers demanded union recognition, higher wages, and an eight-hour day.

39. Attorney General A. Mitchell Palmer sent federal agents to raid the offices of radical and labor organizations in November 1919 and January 1920 as part of the Red Scare.

40. When President Woodrow Wilson traveled to Paris at the end of World War I, he was met by tens of thousands of cheering citizens.

41. The Treaty of Versailles that ended World War I was a savvy and fair, if short, document that equitably distributed culpability for the war among all warring factions.

42. Reparations payments at the end of World War I demanded Germany pay, in effect, to repair the damages it had inflicted on the Allies (reparations payments were estimated variously to be between $33 billion and $56 billion).

43. President Woodrow Wilson's Fourteen Points had asserted the principle of "self-determination;" in this spirit, W. E. B. Du Bois organized a Pan-African Congress in Paris that put forward the idea of a self-governing nation to be carved out of Germany's African colonies. Koreans, Indians, Irish, and others also pressed claims for self-determination.

ESSAY QUESTIONS

1. What explains America's decision to enter the European war and to side with the Allied Powers?

2. World War I was greeted by Progressives with a remarkable blend of optimism and dismay. How might this ambivalent reaction be explained?

3. "It took a world war to bring America's fractious population into a state of harmony and unity." How well does this statement capture the effects of wartime mobilization?

4. Any campaign to rally a diverse and divided people around a common cause must draw upon three key elements: 1) material incentives; 2) ideological persuasion; and 3) coercion. Identify and assess how each of these elements figured in America's wartime mobilization. Illustrate your discussion with examples from the text.

5. The year following the end of World War I was one of the rockiest moments in American history—a time of labor, racial, ethnic, and political strife. What explains this turbulence?

6. Imagine a chance meeting, in 1920, among the following characters:
   - a labor organizer
   - a women's suffragist

- a black advocate of racial equality
- a German-American community leader
- an industrialist
- a Progressive-style social reformer
- a socialist
- a laissez-faire conservative

With passion and directness, they launch into a discussion of the recent war and its consequences for American society. Among the questions they debate: "In what ways were the freedoms, rights, and opportunities of Americans advanced over the course of the wartime era? In what ways were they diminished? Is America ultimately better off for its entry into World War I?" Incorporating at least *four* of the above characters, transcribe this conversation.

7. Write an essay on the balance between security and freedom. What debates and laws shaped this issue, during World War I?

8. Write an essay on the struggle for civil rights in the second decade of the twentieth century.

9. Write an essay on the issues, conflicts, and contrasting world views taken up by American workers in the second decade of the twentieth century.

10. Write an essay about the United States' involvement in World War I.

11. Write an essay about the United States in the aftermath of World War I, including in your essay a discussion of the Red Scare, segregation and racism, labor turmoil, presidential initiatives and actions, prohibition, and women's suffrage.

SOURCES FOR FURTHER RESEARCH

Books

GENERAL OVERVIEWS

Dawley, Alan, *Changing the World: American Progressives in War and Revolution* (2003)

Hawley, Ellis W., *The Great War and the Search for a Modern Order: A History of the American People and Their Institutions, 1917–1933* (1992)

Kennedy, David M., *Over Here: The First World War and American Society* (1980)

Knock, Thomas J., *To End All Wars: Woodrow Wilson and the Quest for a New World Order* (1992)

PARTICULAR ASPECTS

Bederman, Gail, *Manliness and Civilization: A Cultural History of Race and Gender in the United States, 1880–1917* (1995)

Brophy, Alfred L., *Reconstructing the Dreamland: The Tulsa Riot of 1921: Race, Reparations, and Reconciliation* (2002)

Gardner, Lloyd C., *Safe for Democracy: The Anglo-American Response to Revolution, 1913–1923* (1984)

Gilmore, Glenda E., *Gender and Jim Crow: Women and the Politics of White Supremacy in North Carolina, 1896–1920* (1996)

Green, Elna C., *Southern Strategies: Southern Women and the Woman Suffrage Question* (1997)

Grossman, James R., *Land of Hope: Chicago, Black Southerners, and the Great Migration* (1989)

Hahn, Steven, *A Nation under Our Feet: Black Political Struggles in the Rural South from Slavery to the Great Migration* (2003)

Healy, David, *Drive to Hegemony: The United States in the Caribbean, 1898–1917* (1988)

Knock, Thomas J., *To End All Wars: Woodrow Wilson and the Quest for a New World Order* (1992)

LaFeber, Walter, *The American Search for Opportunity, 1865–1913* (1993)

Lewis, David Levering, *W. E. B. Du Bois: Biography of a Race, 1868–1919* (1993)

McCartin, Joseph, *Labor's Great War: The Struggle for Industrial Democracy and the Origins of Modern American Labor Relations* (1997)

Meier, August, *Negro Thought in America, 1880–1915* (1966)

Mitchell, David J., *1919: Red Mirage* (1970)

Preston, William, Jr., *Aliens and Dissenters: Federal Suppression of Radicals, 1903–1933* (1963)

Renda, Mary A., *Taking Haiti: Military Occupation and the Culture of U.S. Imperialism, 1915–1940* (2001)

Stein, Judith, *The World of Marcus Garvey: Race and Class in Modern Society* (1986)

Tuttle, William M., Jr., *Race Riot: Chicago in the Red Summer of 1919* (1970)

Weinstein, James, *The Decline of Socialism in America, 1912–1925* (1967)

Woodruff, Nan E., *American Congo: The African American Freedom Struggle in the Arkansas and Mississippi Delta, 1900–1950* (2003)

Videos

The Great War: 1918 (58 minutes, PBS Video, 1990)

The Great War and the Shaping of the 20th Century (8 hours, PBS Home Video, 1996)

Iron Jawed Angels (125 minutes, HBO and Spring Creek Productions, 2004)
The Killing Floor (118 minutes, Made in USA Productions and American
   Playhouse, 1985)
The Rise and Fall of Jim Crow: Episode 2: Fighting Back (1896–1917), and
   Episode 3: Don't Shout Too Soon (60 minutes each, Quest Productions,
   Videoline Productions, and Thirteen/ WNET, 2002)
Up South: African-American Migration in the Era of the Great War (30 minutes,
   American Social History Project, 1996)

Web Resources

The African American Odyssey, Volume VII: World War I and Postwar Society,
Library of Congress
   http://memory.loc.gov/ammem/aaohtml/exhibit/aopart7.html
The Bisbee Deportation of 1917, University of Arizona
   http://digital.library.arizona.edu/bisbee/
*The Duluth Lynchings Online Resource: Historical Documents Relating to the
Tragic Events of June 15, 1920,* Minnesota Historical Society
   http://collections.mnhs.org/duluthlynchings/
First World War.Com: The War to End All Wars, Michael Duffy, site editor
   http://www.firstworldwar.com
In Motion: The African-American Migration Experience, Schomburg Center for
Research in Black Culture
   http://www.inmotionaame.org/
Propaganda Postcards of the Great War, Jerry Kosanovich and Paul Hageman
   http://www.ww1-propaganda-cards.com/home.html
A Soldier's Diary and Views of War, Marv Cruzan
   http://www.kancoll.org/articles/cruzan/c_diary2.htm
The World War I Document Archive, World War I Military History List
   http://www.lib.byu.edu/~rdh/wwi/index.html
1919: Race Riots, Chicago Historical Society
   http://www.chipublib.org/004chicago/disasters/riots_race.html

ANSWERS TO OBJECTIVE QUESTIONS

Multiple Choice

1-B, 2-C, 3-D, 4-B, 5-C, 6-A, 7-D, 8-C, 9-A, 10-B, 11-B, 12-D, 13-B, 14-B,
15-C, 16-C, 17-A, 18-D, 19-D, 20-D, 21-B, 22-A, 23-B, 24-D, 25-B, 26-D,
27-C, 28-D, 29-B, 30-A, 31-B, 32-D

True or False

1-F, 2-T, 3-T, 4-F, 5-F, 6-T, 7-T, 8-F, 9-T, 10-F, 11-F, 12-F, 13-T, 14-T, 15-T, 16-T, 17-T, 18-F, 19-T, 20-F, 21-T, 22-F, 23-T, 24-F, 25-T, 26-F, 27-F, 28-F, 29-T, 30-T, 31-T, 32-F, 33-T, 34-F, 35-T, 36-F, 37-F, 38-T, 39-T, 40-T, 41-F, 42-T, 43-T

CHAPTER 20

From Business Culture to Great Depression: The Twenties, 1920–1932

CHAPTER OBJECTIVES

- In which ways can the 1920s be seen as a "modern" period; in which ways, as a "conservative" period?
- What were the sources and limits of the economic prosperity of the 1920s?
- What were key lines of cultural tension in 1920s America?
- What were the defining programs and philosophies of Republican Presidents Harding, Coolidge, and Hoover?
- What were the causes of the stock market crash of 1929 and the Great Depression that followed?
- How did Americans experience, explain, and respond to the Great Depression?

CHAPTER OUTLINE

I. Decade of prosperity
   A. Prevalence of business values
   B. Industrial boom
      1. Surging productivity and output
      2. Emergence of new industries
      3. Central role of automobile
   C. Consumer society
      1. Consumer goods
         a. Proliferation
         b. Marketing
         c. Impact on daily life
            i. Telephone
            ii. Household appliances

  2. Leisure activities
   a. Vacations
   b. Movies
    i. Popularity of
    ii. Hollywood's rising dominance of global film industry
   c. Sporting events
   d. Radio and phonograph
   e. Celebrity culture
  3. New values
   a. Growing acceptance of consumer debt
   b. Shifting ideas of purpose and value of work
 D. Limits of prosperity
  1. Unequal distribution of wealth, income
  2. Ongoing concentration of industry
  3. Scale of poverty, unemployment
  4. Deindustrialization in the North
  5. Rural depression
   a. Passing of wartime "golden age" for agriculture
   b. Drop in farm incomes, rise in foreclosures
   c. Decline in number of farms and farmers
   d. Rural outmigration
 E. Celebration of business
  1. Themes
   a. "American way of life"
   b. Permanent prosperity
   c. Christ as business prototype
  2. Promoters
   a. Hollywood
   b. Photographers and painters
   c. Writers
   d. Corporate public relations departments
  3. Signs of impact
   a. Idolization of business figures
   b. Growing trust for business, stock market
 F. Decline of labor
  1. Postwar business campaign against unions
   a. Appropriation of "Americanism," "industrial freedom"
   b. "Welfare capitalism"
   c. American Plan
    i. Open shop
    ii. Rejection of collective bargaining
    iii. Depiction of unionism and socialism as sinister, alien
   d. Use of strikebreakers, spies, blacklists

      2. Ebbing of labor movement
        a. Decline in numbers organized
        b. Union concessions to employers
        c. Fading of union strongholds
        d. Diminishing prospects of labor strikes

  G. Fragmentation of feminism
      1. Aftermath of suffrage amendment
      2. Social and ideological fault lines
      3. Debate over Equal Rights Amendment (ERA)
        a. Terms of ERA
        b. Feminist support
          i. Alice Paul, National Women's Party
          ii. Commitment to individual autonomy, equal opportunity
        c. Feminist opposition
          i. Other leading women's organizations
          ii. Commitment to motherhood, protective legislation for women
        d. Defeat of ERA

  H. "Women's freedom" in the Twenties
      1. Mixed legacy of prewar feminism
        a. Fading of links to political and economic radicalism, social reform
        b. Survival and recasting of call for personal freedom
      2. Themes and images
        a. Consumer lifestyle
        b. Sexual freedom as individual autonomy, rebellion
        c. Youthful "flapper"; Clara Bow
        d. "Modernizing Mothers"
      3. Continued stress on marriage, homemaking as ultimate goals

II. Business and government
  A. Decline of Progressive-era faith in mass democracy
      1. Themes of disillusionment
        a. Popular ignorance, irrationality, disengagement
        b. Shift from public concerns to private (leisure, consumption)
      2. Voices of disillusionment
        a. Walter Lippmann (*Public Opinion, The Phantom Public*)
        b. Robert and Helen Lynd (*Middletown*)

  B. Republican era
      1. Pro-business agenda
        a. Content of
          i. Low income and business taxes
          ii. High tariffs
          iii. Support for employer antiunionism
          iv. Business-friendly appointees to regulatory agencies

        b. Support for in Washington
            i. Presidents Warren G. Harding and Calvin Coolidge
            ii. Supreme Court
    2. Harding administration
        a. Harding's indifference, lack of dignity
        b. Rampant corruption; Teapot Dome
    3. Election of 1924
        a. Coolidge victory over divided Democrats
        b. Robert La Follette's third-party Progressive campaign
  C. Economic diplomacy
    1. Retreat from Wilson's foreign policy principles
        a. Internationalism
        b. Free trade
    2. Close interlinking of business interests and foreign policy
        a. Government initiatives
            i. Diplomatic pressure for access to foreign markets
            ii. Increased tariffs; Fordney-McCumber Act
            iii. Military interventions to protect U.S. business interests
        b. Private initiatives
            i. Loans to foreign governments
            ii. Expansion of industrial production overseas
            iii. Acquisition of raw materials overseas

III. Birth of civil liberties
  A. Persistence of WWI-era repression, censorship into 1920s
    1. Targets of
        a. Political dissent
        b. Sexual themes in the arts
    2. Agents of
        a. Mob violence
        b. Government agencies
        c. Local crusades
        d. Self-censorship; Hollywood's Hays code
    3. Disaffection of Lost Generation
  B. Wartime formation of Civil Liberties Bureau
    1. Reaction to Espionage and Sedition Acts
    2. Predecessor to American Civil Liberties Union
  C. Evolving position of Supreme Court
    1. Initial blows to civil liberties
        a. Upholding of Espionage Act (*Schenck* case); Oliver Wendell Holmes's "clear and present danger" doctrine
        b. Upholding of Eugene V. Debs conviction
        c. Further cases

     2. Signs of a shift
       a. Defenses of free speech by individual justices
         i. Holmes: marketplace of ideas doctrine
         ii. Louis Brandeis: democratic citizenship doctrine
       b. Pro–civil liberties rulings

IV. Culture wars
   A. Fundamentalist reaction against modern urban culture
     1. Sources of alarm
       a. Religious and ethnic pluralism
       b. Urban vice
         i. Mass entertainment
         ii. Alcohol
         iii. New sexual mores
       c. Entry of "modernist" outlook into Protestant mainstream
     2. Manifestations
       a. Billy Sunday
       b. Nationwide presence
       c. Prohibition
   B. Scopes trial
     1. Clash of traditional and modern perspectives
       a. Fundamentalism vs. secularism
       b. Darwinian science vs. scripture
       c. "Moral" liberty vs. freedom of thought
     2. Face-off of Clarence Darrow and William Jennings Bryan
     3. Outcome and aftermath
   C. Resurgence of Ku Klux Klan
     1. Roots in wartime "Americanism" obsession
     2. Profile and influence
       a. Rapid growth
       b. Wide following among white, native-born Protestants
       c. Nationwide presence
     3. Diverse range of targets
   D. Immigration restriction
     1. Earlier legislative precedents
     2. 1921 temporary restriction measure
     3. 1924 permanent restriction measure
       a. National quotas for Europeans
       b. Exclusion of Asians (exception for Filipinos)
       c. Admittance and curtailing of Mexicans
       d. Emergence of "illegal alien" classification
     4. Ideological underpinnings
       a. Conservative nativism
       b. Progressive assumptions about "race"

    E. Pluralism
- 1. Scholarly challenges to prevailing racial thought
  - a. Pioneering voices
    - i. Horace Kallen; "cultural pluralism"
    - ii. Anthropologists Franz Boas, Alfred Kroeber, Ruth Benedict
  - b. Minimal immediate impact
- 2. New immigrants and the pluralist impulse
  - a. Urban ethnic enclaves, community institutions
  - b. Self-reinvention as "ethnic" Americans
  - c. Resentment of cultural hostility and coercion
  - d. Claims to equal rights, mainstream acceptance, cultural autonomy
  - e. Antidiscriminatory campaigns
- 3. Antidiscriminatory rulings by Supreme Court, federal courts

    F. Black urban life and Harlem Renaissance
- 1. Ongoing migration from South, West Indies
- 2. Emergence of Harlem; "capital" of black America
- 3. "Exotic" Harlem vs. real Harlem
- 4. Harlem Renaissance
  - a. Poets, novelists
  - b. Actors, dancers, musicians
  - c. "New Negro"
    - i. In politics
    - ii. In art
- 5. New black assertiveness; Henry O. Sweet case

    G. Election of 1928
- 1. Republican candidate Herbert Hoover
  - a. Background and career
  - b. Embodiment of "new era" of American capitalism
- 2. Democratic candidate Alfred E. Smith
  - a. Background and career
  - b. Embodiment of urban, Catholic, Progressive outlook
- 3. Outcome and significance
  - a. Hoover victory
  - b. Reflection of "culture wars"
  - c. Preview of new Democratic coalition

V. The Great Depression
    A. Stock market crash of 1929
- 1. Black Thursday
- 2. Onset of Great Depression

B. Precursors of Depression
   1. Frenzied speculation
   2. Unequal distribution of income, wealth
   3. Rural depression
   4. Stagnating demand for consumer goods
C. Repercussions of crash
   1. Magnitude
   2. Scope of devastation
      a. Business and consumer confidence
      b. Solvency of investment companies, businesses, banks
      c. Gross national product
      d. Life savings
      e. Employment
      f. Wages
   3. Persistence of downward slide
D. Americans and the Depression
   1. Material hardship
      a. Hunger; breadlines
      b. Homelessness; Hoovervilles
      c. Meagerness of public relief
      d. Reversal of movement from farm to city
   2. Patterns of popular response
      a. Collapse of faith in big business
      b. Personal resignation, self-blame
      c. Stirrings of protest
         i. Spontaneous incidents
         ii. Bonus March
         iii. Rallies for jobs and relief, against evictions
         iv. Farmers' Holiday campaign
         v. Communist party
E. Hoover and the Depression
   1. Hoover's approach
      a. Acceptance of business cycle
      b. Aversion to government relief
      c. Preference for voluntary, "associational" initiatives
      d. Regular forecasts of recovery
   2. Perception of Hoover as indifferent, out of touch
   3. Ill-fated remedies
      a. Hawley-Smoot tariff
      b. Tax increase
   4. Eventual turn to recovery measures
      a. Reconstruction Finance Corporation
      b. Federal Home Loan Bank System

CHRONOLOGY

1915	Rebirth of Ku Klux Klan
1917	Founding of Civil Liberties Bureau (later American Civil Liberties Union)
1919	Supreme Court upholds Espionage Act, conviction of Eugene V. Debs
	Claude McKay publishes poem, "If We Must Die"
1920	Election of Warren G. Harding to presidency; "return to normalcy"
1921	Congress passes temporary immigration quotas
1922	Adoption of Hays code by film industry
	Herbert Hoover publishes *American Individualism*
1923	Equal Rights Amendment introduced in Congress
	Meyer v. Nebraska
1924	Congress passes permanent immigration quotas
	Horace Kallen coins phrase "cultural pluralism"
	Calvin Coolidge wins presidential election
1925	Bruce Barton publishes *The Man Nobody Knows*
	Scopes trial
	Henry O. Sweet trial
1927	Execution of Nicola Sacco and Bartolomeo Vanzetti
	Charles Lindbergh's transatlantic flight
1928	Claude McKay publishes *Home to Harlem*
	Herbert Hoover defeats Alfred E. Smith in presidential election
1929	Robert and Helen Lynd publish *Middletown*
	Stock market crash
1930	Hawley-Smoot tariff
1932	Bonus March
	Creation of Reconstruction Finance Corporation, Federal Home Loan Bank System

KEY TERMS

productivity and wage gap: The decade of the 1920s witnessed impressive increases in productivity, or the amount of goods that a single worker could produce. The use of new technologies and methods of organization, such as the assembly line, enabled workers to produce a greater volume of goods. For example, between 1900 and 1926, productivity in the automobile industry increased by 1300 percent. Rising productivity increased profits and made possible wage increases; however, workers' real wages did not increase at nearly the same pace as did their ability to produce goods. Real wages in the automotive industry rose only 44 percent between 1900 and 1926. In addition, the real wages of unskilled workers remained flat for most of the 1920s. The gap between productivity and wages spelled trouble for an economy that increasingly relied upon consumers for growth. Without rising incomes, Americans could not purchase the automobiles, washing machines, and radios that had become an integral part of the manufacturing sector of the economy.

farming in the 1920s: World War I had been a boon for American farmers. Demand for agricultural products soared as both the U.S. government and European powers bought farmers' harvests. Prices for farm commodities rose 82 percent between 1913 and 1917, dramatically raising the incomes of some farmers. With the war's end, however, the boom turned to bust. European farmers returned from battle to plow their fields, ending demand for American agricultural products. In 1920, with the end of post-war government controls wheat prices dropped from over $2.00 a bushel to under $1.00. Prices for goods such as corn and cotton fell, too. As a consequence, farmers saw their real wages decline by some 25 percent over the course of the 1920s.

rise of the stock market: The phenomenal growth of the stock market in the 1920s led to a practice called "buying on margin." Investors took out loans from stock brokers, enabling them to purchase large amounts of stock with very little money down. As the share price rose, investors would sell, pay off their broker's loan, and still make a profit. Not only individuals bought on margin; banks and major corporations spent billions on brokers' loans. For example, Bethlehem Steel had $157 million in such loans in 1929. When the market crashed, many people and companies were unable to repay their outstanding loans, leading to a series of bank and business failures that worsened the economic crisis.

Teapot Dome Scandal: One of the most famous scandals in American political history, Teapot Dome took its name from a naval oil reserve in Wyoming. In 1922, interior secretary Albert Fall leased the reserves to Harry F. Sinclair, an oilman. Fall made a similar lease of oil reserves in California to Edward L. Doheny. Suspicions regarding the leases led to a senate investigation and, later, the appointment of special counsels. Investigators learned that Doherty and Sinclair had made large personal loans to the interior secretary. The leases were cancelled, and in 1929 Fall was sentenced to a year in prison for accepting bribes. While sensational, the scandal had a limited impact on the fortunes of the Republican Party, which remained in power throughout the 1920s.

McNary-Haugen Bill: As declining crop prices pushed many American farmers into poverty, members of Congress from agricultural states advocated legislation to aid their constituents. The McNary-Haugen Bill was one such effort. The legislation called for a government corporation that would purchase agricultural products at a price that would allow farmers to make a profit. The corporation would then sell the surplus crops on overseas markets. Critics noted that the plan would only stimulate more production because it guaranteed that farmers could sell their produce. In addition, dumping farm surpluses abroad at low prices would lead other countries to erect tariff barriers. These objections led President Coolidge to veto the McNary-Haugen Bill twice.

Tennessee and the teaching of evolution: The Tennessee law that prohibited the teaching of evolution in public schools remained on the books after the Scopes trial. Two efforts to repeal it, first in 1935 and again seventeen years later, failed. In 1967, a third effort generated national media attention. John Scopes, by then a 67-year-old retiree, supported the repeal movement. The Tennessee legislature voted to repeal the 1925 act; nonetheless, the state still required teachers to pledge that they would not teach evolution in their classrooms.

American Indians and citizenship: In the 1884 case of *Elk v. Wilkins*, the U.S. Supreme Court ruled that American Indians were not automatically U.S. citizens. By 1919, acts of Congress and treaty provisions ensured that about half of the nation's native population had citizenship, leaving some 125,000 people without that status. That year New York representative Homer Snyder introduced legislation extending citizenship to all Indians who had served honorably in World War I. Snyder's bill failed, but five years later Congress passed legislation that conferred citizenship upon all American Indians.

defining whiteness: During the 1920s, the U.S. Supreme Court issued rulings in two cases that defined whiteness as a racial category. The first case involved a Japanese immigrant, Takao Ozawa, who had migrated to California in 1894. In 1916, Ozawa filed a petition to become a naturalized citizen. At that time, U.S. naturalization laws permitted only "free white persons" and individuals of African descent to apply for citizenship. As a result, a court rejected Ozawa's petition on the grounds that as an Asian he did not meet the racial qualifications for citizenship. Six years later, the U.S. Supreme Court rejected Ozawa's appeal, declaring that the term "white persons" applied only to Caucasians. The court deemed Ozawa to be a Mongolian, and thus ineligible for citizenship. The following year Bhagat Singh Thind, an Asian Indian, claimed that he was Caucasian and should be eligible for citizenship. The U.S. Supreme Court rejected his argument by narrowing the definition of whiteness—a white person was not only Caucasian but also an individual that the common man would recognize as white. Thind did not meet the new standard of whiteness, and his application for citizenship was rejected.

Bonus Army: Veterans who returned home after World War I received a $60 severance bonus, a small sum given the high wages that many workers had enjoyed during the wartime economic boom. In 1924 Congress approved a bonus payment, which veterans would receive in 1945. The onset of the Great Depression led many veterans to demand early payment of the bonus, a request that prompted Representative Wright Patman of Texas to introduce legislation allowing for such a payment. The Patman bill drew thousands of veterans to Washington, D.C. in an effort to pressure Congress to enact the legislation. After the measure failed, most veterans left the city, but some 2,000 remained. After a conflict in which police killed two members of the Bonus Army, President Herbert Hoover authorized the use of federal troops. General Douglas MacArthur used force to drive the veterans from the nation's capital. The incident reflected poorly on Hoover, who appeared unsympathetic to the economic hardships caused by the Depression, and contributed to his loss in the presidential election of 1932.

Hawley-Smoot Tariff: The Republican Party of the late-nineteenth and early-twentieth centuries favored high tariffs as a means of protecting American producers from foreign competition. During his presidential campaign, Herbert Hoover called for an increase in agricultural tariffs as a means to raise the incomes of farmers. Congress obliged, but included high tariffs on industrial products in its legislation as well. The advent of the Great Depression altered the tariff debate, as many economists and some business leaders such as Henry Ford maintained that the new tariff, called Hawley-Smoot after its congressional authors, would hurt the U.S. economy. They argued that foreign governments would erect their own tariff barriers, weakening U.S. export sales. Despite these concerns, Hoover signed the tariff bill into law. Canada, Great Britain, and other U.S. trading partners soon enacted their own tariff measures, and world trade slowed considerably.

OBJECTIVE QUESTIONS

Multiple Choice

1. 1920 presidential candidate Warren G. Harding rode to victory on the slogan:
   A. "Sweet land of liberty."
   B. "Torches of freedom."
   C. "The tide has turned."
   D. "Return to normalcy."

2. An attorney renowned for his contributions to the causes of labor, racial equality, and civil liberties was:
   A. Jack Dempsey.
   B. Billy Sunday.
   C. Clarence Darrow.
   D. Walter Lippmann.

3. Which of the following series of events is listed in proper sequence?
   A. Scopes trial; rebirth of Ku Klux Klan; election of Calvin Coolidge; passage of temporary immigration quotas
   B. Herbert Hoover victory over Alfred E. Smith; stock market crash; Hawley-Smoot tariff; creation of Reconstruction Finance Corporation
   C. Execution of Sacco and Vanzetti; upholding of Espionage Act by Supreme Court; election of Warren G. Harding; founding of Civil Liberties Bureau
   D. Bonus March; passage of permanent immigration quotas; introduction of Equal Rights Amendment; Teapot Dome scandal

4. Which of the following was *not* an important cultural trend in 1920s America?
   A. a more open expression of sexuality
   B. a flowering of urban black culture
   C. the rise of a new generation of writers, disaffected by the bland materialism of American culture
   D. a growing respect for newly arrived immigrants

5. Which of the following groups was *not* singled out as a threat to traditional American values by the Ku Klux Klan?
   A. Texans
   B. radicals
   C. blacks
   D. Jews

6. Which of the following was *not* a part of the Republican political perspective during the 1920s?
   A. Taxes on business profits and personal income should be lowered.
   B. Government regulation of the economy does more harm than good.
   C. Government regulation of personal behavior does more harm than good.
   D. The labor movement should not expect any support or protection from the federal government.

7. Which of the following was *not* an underlying cause of the stock market crash of 1929?
   A. Speculation on the stock market had spun out of control.
   B. The distribution of wealth had grown perilously uneven.
   C. Industry had begun producing more than Americans could consume.
   D. Runaway inflation triggered by high union wages had undermined prosperity.

8. Which of the following was *not* a common means of survival for out-of-work Americans during the opening years of the Great Depression?
   A. drawing federal unemployment benefits
   B. hitting the road or riding the rails in search of work
   C. selling everyday items, such as apples or pencils, on the street
   D. turning to community charities for whatever relief they could offer

9. Who were the two immigrants whose case became a cause célèbre, arrested for their participation in a robbery in which a security guard was killed?
   A. Nicola Sacco and Bartholomeo Vanzetti
   B. Enrico Caruso and Andre Siegfried
   C. Reinhold Niebuhr and Stewart Poyntz
   D. Stanton Blanche and Jacob Abrams

10. Who said, "the chief business of the American people is business"?
   A. Warren G. Harding
   B. Henry Ford
   C. John D. Rockefeller
   D. Calvin Coolidge

11. Production of the automobile in the 1920s:
   A. tripled.
   B. struggled in the face of foreign competition.
   C. increased by 50 percent.
   D. caused a surge of migration into rural America.

12. Which was not a consumer good in the 1920s?
   A. vacuum cleaners
   B. washing machines
   C. refrigerators
   D. televisions

13. In early 1929, the income of the wealthiest five percent of American families was greater than that of the bottom:
   A. 60 percent
   B. 40 percent
   C. 10 percent
   D. 5 percent

14. The West's leading industrial center, a producer of oil, automobiles, aircraft, and Hollywood movies, was:
   A. San Diego, California
   B. San Francisco, California
   C. Seattle, Washington
   D. Los Angeles, California

15. The open shop—a workplace free of unions (except, in some cases, "company unions") and free of government regulation—was part of the employer-backed:
   A. American Plan.
   B. Equal Rights Amendment.
   C. Federal law 10983.
   D. law declared unconstitutional by the United States Supreme Court.

16. The proposed constitutional amendment to eliminate all legal distinctions "on account of sex" promoted by Alice Paul was:
    A. the Fifteenth Amendment.
    B. the Equal Rights Amendment.
    C. the National Women's Amendment.
    D. the Equal Suffrage Amendment.

17. Upon taking office in 1921, Warren G. Harding promised a return to:
    A. Progressivism.
    B. one man-one vote.
    C. normalcy.
    D. the Gilded Age.

18. Who was the first cabinet member in American history to be convicted of a felony—for accepting nearly $500,000 from businessmen to whom he leased government oil reserves at Teapot Dome, Wyoming?
    A. Harry Daugherty
    B. Charles Forbes
    C. Albert Fall
    D. Charles Evans Hughes

19. The 1922 self-imposed guidelines in the film industry that prohibited depicting adultery, nudity, and long kisses, and barred scripts that portrayed clergymen in a negative light was called:
    A. "Banned in Boston."
    B. the Hays code.
    C. the Fortney-McCumber guidelines.
    D. the Diplomacy Guidelines.

20. What was the name of the principal organization to emerge in 1920 as a defender of American civil liberties?
    A. the American Civil Liberties Union
    B. the Federal Bureau of Investigation
    C. the Berkeley Free Speech Organization
    D. the Enterprise Institute

21. In what legal case did Justice Oliver Wendell Holmes, Jr. declare that the First Amendment did not prevent Congress from prohibiting speech that presented a "clear and present danger"?
    A. *Abramson v. U.S.*
    B. *Abrams v. U.S.*
    C. *Shenck v. U.S.*
    D. *Lopez v. U.S.*

22. During the 1920s, those who asserted their conviction in the literal truth of the Bible became known by this newly coined term (their most well-known leader was Billy Sunday):
    A. secularists
    B. fundamentalists
    C. mainstream Protestants
    D. Catholics

23. In 1925, what was the Tennessee trial in which a public school teacher faced charges of violating the state's law prohibiting the teaching of Charles Darwin's theory of evolution?
    A. the Darrow-Bryan Trial
    B. the Scopes trial
    C. the anti-evolution trial
    D. the creation science trial

24. The anti-black, anti-Catholic, and anti-Semitic organization that claimed over 3 million members by the mid-1920s was:
    A. the Anti-Immigration League.
    B. the American Party.
    C. the Ku Klux Klan.
    D. the Know Nothings.

25. The vibrant black culture in 1920s New York City that included poets and novelists Countee Cullen, Langston Hughes, and Claude McKay was called:
    A. the Harlem Renaissance.
    B. the Ashcan School.
    C. the Armory Show.
    D. the Bronx Revival.

26. Who won the presidential election of 1928?
    A. Calvin Coolidge
    B. Herbert Hoover
    C. Al Smith
    D. Franklin Delano Roosevelt

27. Which of the following was *not* a cause of the Great Depression that began in October 1929?
    A. collapse of real estate prices in southern California and Florida
    B. stock market crash
    C. highly unequal distribution of income and prolonged depression in farm regions
    D. drastic tariff reductions

28. President Herbert Hoover's 1932 Reconstruction Finance Corporation did all of the following, except:
    A. loan money to failing banks.
    B. offer aid to homeowners threatened by foreclosure.
    C. appropriate nearly $2 billion for local relief efforts in public-works projects.
    D. offer direct relief to the unemployed.

True or False

1. According to 1920s sociologists Robert and Helen Lynd, Americans had become more interested in leisure activities and material comforts than in public issues.

2. Presidents Harding and Coolidge were very similar in personality, but very different in political outlook.

3. American women overwhelmingly supported the Equal Rights Amendment; American men overwhelmingly opposed it.

4. American agriculture slid into economic depression years before the stock market crash of 1929.

5. Although suppression of free speech remained commonplace in the 1920s, a commitment to civil liberties was slowly finding its way into judicial doctrine.

6. During the 1920s, the United States government showed little interest in world affairs.

7. In 1928, Democratic candidate Alfred E. Smith was the first Catholic to be nominated for president by a major party.

8. Remarkably, the stock market crash and subsequent depression did little to diminish popular reverence for big business.

9. The 1920s was a decade of social tensions between rural and urban Americans, as well as traditional and "modern" Christianity.

10. The 1920s—prior to October 1929—saw a sharp decline in the American economy.

11. President Warren G. Harding died suddenly of a heart attack in 1923.

12. By 1929, the United States produced more than 40 percent of the world's manufactured goods.

13. By 1929, 80 million Americans went to the movies each week, and almost 5 million owned radios.

14. Over 100 million records were sold each year during the 1920s.

15. Jack Dempsey made the first solo flight across the Atlantic.

16. A consumer culture in which the purchase of consumer goods (even if this meant going into debt) came increasingly to replace thrift and self-denial, which had earlier characterized notions of good character.

17. As real workers' wages rose by 25 percent in the period between 1922 to 1929, the sharply unequal distribution of wealth that characterized the nineteenth-century United States gave way increasingly to an equal distribution of wealth.

18. By 1929 three-quarters of American households had washing machines.

19. Farmers experienced booming profits during the 1920s.

20. During the 1920s (up until 1929), while inflation and war reparations payments crippled the German economy, and unemployment remained high in Great Britain, the U.S. economy boomed.

21. Comparatively high wages and efficient mass production characterized the American economy of the 1920s.

22. Business leaders like Henry Ford, and engineers like Herbert Hoover were cultural heroes in the 1920s.

23. Women's freedom in the 1920s was characterized by unapologetic use of birth control methods such as the diaphragm.

24. In marriage, according to advertisements in the 1920s, women were expected to find happiness and freedom within the home, especially in the use of new labor-saving appliances.

25. During the 1920s, as sociologists Robert and Helen Lyndon found in *Middletown,* elections were lively centers of public attention, much as they had been in the 19th century.

26. Consumerism was a principal component of the American character in the 1920s.

27. The politics of the 1920s was principally dominated by the Republican Party.

28. Florence Kelley was ecstatic when the United States Supreme Court repudiated *Mueller v. Oregon* in 1923.

29. The rights an individual may assert even against Democratic majorities—including freedom of speech—are called "civil liberties."

30. Oliver Wendell Holmes, Jr. and Louis D. Brandeis were proponents of civil liberties.

31. In 1925, John Scopes, a public school teacher in Tennessee, was convicted of violating the state's law against the teaching of Charles Darwin's theory of evolution.

32. In 1917, 1921, and again in 1924, European immigration was increasingly curtailed by federal law.

33. Nearly a million African-Americans migrated from the American South during the 1920s.

34. Herbert Hoover preferred "associational action" to government intervention in directing regulatory and welfare policies.

35. Al Smith, the Catholic governor of New York, ran as the Democratic Party's presidential nominee in 1928, but lost the election.

36. On October 24, 1929, Black Thursday, more than $10 billion in market value vanished in a sharp stock market downturn.

37. Quick action by President Hoover's administration kept millions of American families from losing their life savings, when, in the early 1930s, hundreds of banks across the United States failed.

38. In the three years after 1929, gross domestic production fell by one third in the U.S.

39. By 1932 a quarter of the U.S. labor force could not find work.

40. President Hoover and his secretary of the treasury Andrew Mellon took quick, decisive action to curtail the economic downturn that began in October 1929.

ESSAY QUESTIONS

1. The 1920s are remembered as a time of great economic prosperity. What were the indicators of this prosperity? How equally did Americans share in it?

2. Consider the following two statements:

   A) "The 1920s was a time of modernity and change."

   B) "The 1920s was a time of tradition and conservatism."

   In what ways (politically, culturally, economically) do you find statement "A" more persuasive as a description of 1920s America? In what ways do you find statement "B" more persuasive? Illustrate your analysis with examples from the text.

3. "It was a carefree, affluent, adventurous era." How well does this statement capture the America of the 1920s? Where does it fall short? Illustrate your analysis with examples from the text.

4. Assess the significance of the 1925 Scopes trial. What does the trial, and the controversy it generated, reveal about the "culture wars" of the 1920s?

5. How did Americans respond—as individuals, families, or communities—to the material and psychological ravages of the Great Depression?

6. How did Americans debate the causes of, and remedies for, the Great Depression? What kinds of protest movements arose during the first few years after the crash?

7. How was the Progressive belief in a socially conscious state challenged in the 1920s?

8. Write an essay on civil liberties and cultural pluralism during the 1920s.

9. Describe the Christian fundamentalism of the 1920s and explain the issues of the 1925 Scopes trial.

10. Describe the consumer culture of the 1920s.

11. What challenges, successes, and setbacks did the Republican Party face in the 1920s?

SOURCES FOR FURTHER RESEARCH

Books

GENERAL OVERVIEWS

Dumenil, Lynn, *The Modern Temper: American Culture and Society in the Twenties* (1995)
Garraty, John A., *The Great Depression* (1986)
Goldberg, David J., *Discontented America: The United States in the 1920s* (1999)

PARTICULAR ASPECTS

Boyle, Kevin, *Arc of Justice: A Saga of Race, Civil Rights, and Murder in the Jazz Age* (2004)
Cohen, Lizabeth, *Making a New Deal: Industrial Workers in Chicago, 1919–1939* (1990)
Cohen, Warren I., *Empire Without Tears: America's Foreign Relations, 1921–1933* (1987)

Cott, Nancy, *The Grounding of American Feminism* (1987)

Douglas, Ann, *Terrible Honesty: Mongrel Manhattan in the 1920s* (1995)

Dumenil, Lynn, *The Modern Temper: America in the Twenties* (1995)

Frank, Dana, *Purchasing Power: Consumer Organizing, Gender, and the Seattle Labor Movement* (1994)

Galbraith, John Kenneth, *The Great Crash, 1929* (1954)

Garrity, John A., *The Great Depression* (1986)

Gerstle, Gary, *American Crucible: Race and Nation in the Twentieth Century* (2002)

Gordon, Colin, *New Deals: Business, Labor, and Politics in America, 1920–1935* (1994)

Hall, Jacquelyn Dowd et al., *Like a Family: The Making of a Southern Cotton Mill World* (1987)

Higham, John, *Strangers in the Land: Patterns of American Nativism, 1865–1925* (1955)

Larson, Edward J., *Summer for the Gods: The Scopes Trial and America's Continuing Debate Over Science and Religion* (1998)

Lewis, David L., *When Harlem Was in Vogue* (1981)

Maclean, Nancy, *Behind the Mask of Chivalry: The Making of the Second Ku Klux Klan* (1994)

Marchand, Roland, *Advertising the American Dream: Making Way for Modernity, 1920–1940* (1985)

Marsden, George M., *Fundamentalism and American Culture: The Shaping of Twentieth-Century Evangelicism, 1870–1925* (1980)

Murphy, Paul L., *World War I and the Origin of Civil Liberties in the United States* (1979)

Ngai, Mae, *Impossible Subjects: Illegal Aliens and the Making of Modern America* (2004)

Ross, William G., *Forging New Freedoms: Nativism, Education, and the Constitution, 1917–1927* (1994)

Schneider, Mark Robert, *"We Return Fighting": The Civil Rights Movement in the Jazz Age* (2002)

Videos

A. Philip Randolph: For Jobs and Freedom (87 minutes, California Newsreel, 1996)

Demon Rum (58 minutes, PBS Video, 1990)

Eugene O'Neill: A Documentary Film (120 minutes, PBS Video, 2006)

The Great Depression: Episodes 1–2 (60 minutes each, PBS Home Video, 1993)

Langston Hughes: Working toward Salvation (57 minutes, Films for the Humanities and Sciences, 2003)

Mary Pickford (90 minutes, Ambrica Productions, 2005)

Miss America (90 minutes, PBS Video, 2001)

Monkey Trial: An All-out Duel between Science and Religion (90 minutes, PBS
   Home Video, 2002)
New York: A Documentary Film: Episode 5, Cosmopolis, 1919–1931 (120
   minutes, PBS Home Video, 1999)
The Twenties (55 minutes, PBS Video, 1983)

Web Resources

The African American Odyssey, Volume VII: World War I and Postwar Society,
Library of Congress
   http://memory.loc.gov/ammem/aaohtml/exhibit/aopart7.html

"Like a Family: The Making of a Southern Cotton Mill World," James Leloudis
and Kathryn Walbert, University of North Carolina, Chapel Hill
   http://www.ibiblio.org/sohp

Prosperity and Thrift: The Coolidge Era and the Consumer Economy,
1921–1929, Library of Congress
   http://memory.loc.gov/ammem/coolhtml/coolhome.html

The Red Hot Jazz Archive: A History of Jazz before 1930, Scott Alexander
   http://www.redhotjazz.com

The Sweet Trials, 1925 and 1926, Douglas Linder
   http://www.law.umkc.edu/faculty/projects/ftrials/sweet/sweet.html

Tennessee vs. John Scopes: The "Monkey Trial," Douglas Linder, University of
Missouri-Kansas City
   http://www.law.umkc.edu/faculty/projects/ftrials/scopes/scopes.htm

The Trial of Sacco and Vanzetti, Douglas Linder
   http://www.law.umkc.edu/faculty/projects/ftrials/SaccoV/SaccoV.htm

ANSWERS TO OBJECTIVE QUESTIONS

Multiple Choice

1-D, 2-C, 3-B, 4-D, 5-A, 6-C, 7-D, 8-A, 9-A, 10-D, 11-A, 12-D, 13-A, 14-D,
15-A, 16-B, 17-C, 18-C, 19-B, 20-A, 21-C, 22-B, 23-B, 24-C, 25-A, 26-B,
27-D, 28-D

True or False

1-T, 2-F, 3-F, 4-T, 5-T, 6-F, 7-T, 8-F, 9-T, 10-F, 11-T, 12-T, 13-T, 14-T, 15-F,
16-T, 17-F, 18-F, 19-F, 20-T, 21-T, 22-T, 23-T, 24-T, 25-F, 26-T, 27-T, 28-F,
29-T, 30-T, 31-T, 32-T, 33-T, 34-T, 35-T, 36-T, 37-F, 38-T, 39-F

CHAPTER 21 | The New Deal, 1932–1940

CHAPTER OBJECTIVES

- What were the key programs, aims, and underlying motivations of the New Deal?
- How did the New Deal evolve over the course of the 1930s?
- In what ways did the New Deal affect (or leave unaffected) the lives of Americans?
- What kinds of Americans rallied to the New Deal?
- What kinds of popular movements arose during the 1930s? How did they help to shape the New Deal?
- What types of controversy did the New Deal generate, and what kinds of opposition did it encounter?
- What explains the winding down of New Deal reform by the late 1930s?
- How were notions of American freedom transformed during the 1930s?

CHAPTER OUTLINE

I. First New Deal (the "Hundred Days")
   A. Franklin D. Roosevelt (FDR) and election of 1932
      1. Roosevelt background
      2. "New deal" promise
         a. Vagueness
         b. Popular reception
      3. Outcome
         a. FDR landslide victory over Herbert Hoover
         b. Strong Democratic gains in Congress

B. Initial approach to economic crisis
   1. New Deal as alternative to socialist, Nazi, and laissez-faire solutions
   2. Lack of initial blueprint
   3. Circle of advisors
      a. Leading figures
      b. Outlooks
         i. Roots in Progressive reform
         ii. Dominant preference for regulated "bigness"
C. FDR inaugural
D. Financial program
   1. Initiatives
      a. "Bank holiday"
      b. Emergency Banking Act
      c. Glass-Steagall Act
      d. Removal of United States from gold standard
   2. Aim: reversal of banking crisis
   3. Outcome: rescue of financial system
E. National Recovery Administration (NRA)
   1. Elements
      a. Business-government cooperation
      b. Industry codes for output, prices, working conditions
      c. Recognition of labor's right to organize
      d. Blue Eagle campaign
   2. Aims
      a. Restoration of economic vitality, stability
      b. Labor-management peace
   3. Outcomes
      a. Ebbing of public enthusiasm; growth of controversy
      b. Corporate domination
      c. Weak enforcement
      d. Minimal effectiveness
F. Relief and jobs programs
   1. Initiatives
      a. Federal Emergency Relief Administration (FERA)
      b. Civilian Conservation Corps (CCC)
      c. Public Works Administration (PWA)
      d. Civil Works Administration (CWA)
      e. Tennessee Valley Authority (TVA)
   2. Aims
      a. Direct relief for needy (FERA)
      b. Public employment (CCC, PWA, CWA, TVA)

      c. Improvement of nation's infrastructure (CCC, PWA, CWA, TVA)

      d. Expansion of electric power (TVA)

   3. Outcomes

      a. Mass participation

      b. Widespread relief

      c. Emerging opposition

      d. Long-term effects

G. Agricultural Adjustment Act (AAA)

   1. Elements

      a. Production quotas

      b. Subsidies for removal of land from cultivation

      c. Destruction of crops, livestock

   2. Aims: revival of farm prices and incomes

   3. Outcomes

      a. Revival of farm prices and incomes

      b. Uneven impact on farmers

         i. Gains for landowning farmers

         ii. Exclusion and displacement of tenants, sharecroppers

   4. Worsening of rural hardship

      a. Dust Bowl and mass displacement of farmers

      b. John Steinbeck's *The Grapes of Wrath*

H. Housing program

   1. Initiatives

      a. Home Owners Loan Corporation (HOLC)

      b. Federal Housing Administration (FHA)

      c. Federal construction of low-rent housing

   2. Aims

      a. Protection of homeowners from foreclosure

      b. Expanded access to home ownership

      c. Inexpensive rental housing

      d. New construction

   3. Outcomes

      a. Preservation or attainment of home ownership for millions

      b. Affirmation of "security of the home" as fundamental right

I. Further initiatives

   1. Repeal of Prohibition

   2. Federal Communications Commission

   3. Securities and Exchange Commission

J. Overall impact

   1. Transformation of role of federal government

   2. Scale of relief, public projects

   3. Failure to end Depression

K. Gathering Supreme Court assault
   1. Invalidation of NRA; Schecter Poultry case
   2. Invalidation of AAA; *United States v. Butler*

II. Grassroots revolt
   A. Reawakening of American labor movement
      1. Preconditions
         a. Encouraging signals from federal government
            i. Election of FDR
            ii. Section 7a of National Industrial Recovery Act
            iii. Wagner Act
         b. Receding of ethnic differences
         c. Militant leadership
      2. Aspirations
         a. Better wages
         b. Check on employer power
         c. Labor rights
         d. Union recognition
      3. Labor upheaval of 1934
         a. Nationwide wave of strikes
         b. Major strikes
            i. Toledo auto workers
            ii. Minneapolis truck drivers
            iii. San Francisco dockworkers
            iv. Textile workers (New England to Deep South)
   B. Rise of Congress of Industrial Organizations (CIO)
      1. Origins
         a. Split within American Federation of Labor (AFL)
         b. Walkout of insurgent AFL leaders; John L. Lewis
      2. Agenda
         a. Organization of industrial bastions
         b. "Economic freedom and industrial democracy"
      3. Landmark struggles
         a. United Auto Workers sit-down strikes (Cleveland, Flint)
            i. Spirit of militancy, unity
            ii. Victory, recognition by General Motors
         b. Steel Workers Organizing Committee
            i. Recognition by U.S. Steel
            ii. Continued resistance from small firms; Republic strike bloodshed
      4. Overall progress
         a. Explosion of union membership
         b. Achievement of workplace power, dignity
         c. Impact on politics

   5. Political vision
    a. Activist federal government
    b. Economic and social security
    c. Redistribution of wealth
  C. Other crusaders for economic justice
   1. Upton Sinclair; End Poverty in California movement
   2. Huey Long; Share Our Wealth movement
   3. Father Charles E. Coughlin
   4. Dr. Francis Townsend; Townsend Clubs

III. Second New Deal
  A. Triggering factors
   1. Persistence of Depression
   2. Popular unrest
   3. Democratic gains of 1934
  B. Underlying aims
   1. Economic security
   2. Redistribution of income; broadening of purchasing power
  C. Central initiatives
   1. Tax on wealth, corporate profits
   2. Rural Electrification Agency
    a. Electric power to farmers
    b. Soil conservation
    c. Minimal benefits for non-landholders
   3. Works Projects Administration (WPA)
    a. Mass participation
    b. Impact on national life
     i. Infrastructure
     ii. The arts
   4. Wagner Act (National Labor Relations Act)
    a. Provisions
     i. Rights to organize, union representation, collective bargaining
     ii. Federal enforcement; National Labor Relations Board
    b. Democratization of workplace; "Labor's Magna Carta"
   5. Social Security Act
    a. Provisions
     i. Unemployment insurance
     ii. Old-age pensions
     iii. Aid to disabled, elderly poor, and families with dependent children
    b. Key features
     i. System of taxes on employers and workers
     ii. Mix of national and local funding, control, and eligibility standards

  c. Significance: launching of American welfare state
  d. In comparison with European versions

IV. Reckoning with liberty
 A. Contested meanings of freedom
  1. New Deal version
   a. Expanded power of national state
   b. Social and industrial freedom
   c. Economic security over liberty of contract
   d. FDR and modern liberalism
  2. Anti-New Deal version
   a. Freedom from government regulation, fiscal responsibility
   b. Individual freedom
   c. American Liberty League
   d. Hoover's *The Challenge to Liberty*
 B. Election of 1936
  1. FDR vs. Republican Alfred Landon
  2. Sharp divisions between classes, conceptions of freedom
  3. Outcome: Roosevelt landslide
  4. Significance
   a. Seeds of anti-government conservatism
   b. "New Deal coalition"
  5. FDR's second inaugural
 C. FDR's court-packing plan
  1. Motivations
  2. Widespread alarm over
  3. Ultimate success
   a. New receptiveness of Supreme Court to New Deal regulation
   b. Chief Justice Charles Evans Hughes conversion
 D. Winding down of Second New Deal
  1. Last major New Deal measures
   a. United States Housing Act
   b. Fair Labor Standards Act
  2. 1937 economic downturn
  3. Shift in New Deal approach to economic crisis
   a. Adoption of Keynesian, public spending tool
   b. Discontinuation of economic planning, redistribution

V. Limits of change
 A. New Deal and American women
  1. Expanded presence of women in federal government
  2. Political decline of feminism
  3. Depression-era resistance to women's employment
   a. From government
   b. From labor movement

        4. Uneven access to New Deal benefits

  B. Exclusion of blacks from key entitlements of welfare state

      1. Reflection of southern Democrats' power

      2. Confinement to public assistance portion of Social Security Act

         a. Dismal provisions

         b. Stigma of welfare dependency

  C. "Indian New Deal"

      1. Commissioner of Indian Affairs John Collier

      2. Transformation of Indian policy

         a. Shift from forced assimilation to cultural autonomy

         b. Indian Reorganization Act

      3. Limits of progress

         a. Legal

         b. Material

  D. Hardships for Mexican-Americans

      1. Meager opportunity for work

      2. Mass departure for Mexico (voluntary and forced)

      3. Situation of California farmworkers

         a. Grim conditions

         b. Exclusion from Social Security and Wagner Acts

         c. Suppression of unionism

  E. Hardships for African-Americans

      1. "Last hired and first fired"

      2. Disproportionate rates of unemployment

      3. Growing black focus on economic survival

  F. New Deal for blacks

      1. Egalitarian current in New Deal

      2. Shift of black voters to Democratic party

      3. Preservation/reinforcement of racial order by New Deal

         a. FDR failure to support federal antilynching law

         b. Discriminatory aspects of New Deal

VI. New conception of America

  A. Absorption of new immigrants into public mainstream

      1. Prominence among framers and supporters of New Deal

      2. "Little New Deals"; Fiorello LaGuardia

      3. Cultural assimilation

      4. Americanization via labor and political activism

  B. Ascendancy of American left

      1. Elements

         a. Communists

         b. Socialists

         c. Labor radicals, CIO

         d. New Deal liberals

2. Growth
   a. In numbers
   b. In impact on political culture, conceptions of freedom
3. Activities and appeal of Communist Party
   a. Range of causes
      i. The unemployed
      ii. Industrial unionism; CIO
      iii. Civil rights; Scottsboro case
      iv. Civil liberties
   b. Popular Front vision
      i. Coalition with wider left
      ii. Broadening and energizing of New Deal liberalism
      iii. Promotion of social and economic radicalism, ethnic and racial diversity, unionism and social citizenship
   c. Growing size, respectability
4. Breadth of Popular Front vision
   a. FDR and the "common man"
   b. Manifestations in the arts
   c. Militant, inclusive unionism of CIO
   d. Spreading condemnations of racial, ethnic, religious intolerance
   e. Widening commitment to civil liberties, labor rights
      i. American Civil Liberties Union
      ii. Robert M. La Follette, Jr. committee exposés
      iii. Department of Justice's Civil Liberties Unit
      iv. Supreme Court decisions
C. End of New Deal
   1. Mounting opposition of southern Democrats
      a. Reasons: alarm over specters of unionization, racial equality, radicalism
      b. Key provocations
         i. "Report on Economic Conditions in the South"
         ii. Southern Conference for Human Welfare
         iii. FDR's crusade to liberalize southern Democratic party
   2. Consolidation of southern Democrat-northern Republican coalition
   3. Exhaustion of New Deal momentum
   4. Shifting focus from domestic to foreign affairs
D. Historical significance of New Deal
   1. Limits of
   2. Extent of

CHRONOLOGY

1932	Franklin D. Roosevelt defeats Herbert Hoover to win presidency
1933	Roosevelt inaugurated Peak of banking crisis "Hundred Days" legislation; First New Deal Repeal of Prohibition
1934	Nationwide strike wave End Poverty in California movement Launching of Huey Long's Share-Our-Wealth movement Establishment of American Liberty League Indian Reorganization Act Drought sweeps Great Plains; coming of Dust Bowl Democratic gains in midterm elections
1935	Founding of Congress of Industrial Organizations Second New Deal Supreme Court invalidates National Recovery Administration Assassination of Huey Long
1936	Supreme Court invalidates Agricultural Adjustment Act Roosevelt wins landslide reelection victory over Alfred Landon
1936–37	United Auto Workers sit-down strikes at Cleveland, Flint; recognition by General Motors
1937	Defeat of Roosevelt's "court packing" plan; subsequent Supreme Court acceptance of New Deal U.S. Steel recognizes Steel Workers Organizing Committee Economic downturn
1938	Fair Labor Standards Act Establishment of House Un-American Activities Committee Release of "Report on Economic Conditions in the South" Founding of Southern Conference for Human Welfare Southern Democrats' rebuff of Roosevelt in midterm elections John Steinbeck publishes *The Grapes of Wrath*
1939	Marian Anderson controversy
1940	Smith Act

KEY TERMS

bank holiday: When a bank failed, its depositors lost their savings. As a result of the wave of failures in the early years of the Great Depression, Americans were unwilling to put their money in banks. The lack of capital made it difficult to secure loans, which further slowed economic growth. President Roosevelt's bank holiday was an effort to restore confidence in the nation's banking system. The president's promise that any bank that reopened after the holiday was sound satisfied millions of Americans. Bank deposits exceeded withdrawals within days after the holiday ended; within a month, Americans had deposited nearly $1 billion.

Agricultural Adjustment Act: The Agricultural Adjustment Act (AAA) sought to increase prices for agricultural commodities. Because a decline in the supply of farm products available on the market would lead to higher prices, administration officials created programs to limit production. For example, in 1934 and 1935 producers were to decrease acreage devoted to cotton by 40 percent. However, at the time that Congress approved the AAA, the 1933 crop already had been planted, with farmers having increased cotton acreage by 4 million acres beyond the 1932 crop. The Roosevelt administration paid the cotton farmers to plow their young plants under, destroying some 10.5 million acres of cotton. Prices rose 10 cents a pound, increasing the sale value of the 1933 harvest by $114 million.

Townsend Plan: Like many Americans, Dr. Francis Townsend suffered hardship during the Great Depression. Disturbed by the effects of the crisis on older Americans, Townsend conceived a plan to help the aged and to speed economic recovery. He called for a two percent value-added tax (a tax that increased in value on an item at every step in the production process). Estimating that the tax would generate more than $20 billion, Townsend claimed that it could fund a $200 pension for every American over sixty years of age. He argued that the elderly would leave the labor pool, which would drive up wages. Because recipients had to spend their check within 30 days, consumption would increase. Economists immediately dismissed the Townsend Plan, noting that it would drive up taxes and consume half the national income. Despite these objections, Townsend claimed some 2 million followers. The popularity of Francis Townsend and others like him forced President Roosevelt to reevaluate the effectiveness of the New Deal.

court packing: The Constitution is silent on the number of justices that may serve on the United States Supreme Court. The first court had six members; during Lincoln's tenure the number rose to ten. The Judiciary Act of 1869 fixed the number of justices at nine, where it has remained ever since. Roosevelt's effort in 1937 to increase the number of justices so as to protect New Deal legislation proved to be a major political blunder. The public perceived it as an attack on the independence of the judiciary, thereby damaging Roosevelt's reputation.

minimum wage law: In its 1905 ruling in the case of *Lochner v. New York,* the U.S. Supreme Court overturned a New York law limiting the number of hours that bakery employees could work. This ruling was based on the notion of freedom of contract. In a 1923 ruling, the court declared that minimum wage laws also violated freedom of contract, a view reaffirmed in a 1936 case. However, in the 1937 case of *West Coast Hotel v. Parrish,* the court changed its position. Upon leaving her job as a hotel chambermaid, Elsie Parrish had received a check from her employer, West Coast Hotels. Parrish claimed that she had not received the full pay she merited under the terms of a Washington law that mandated a minimum wage for women. In a 5–4 ruling, the Supreme Court referred to the 1908 ruling in *Muller v. Oregon,* which allowed states to set maximum work hours for women. Chief Justice Charles Evans Hughes wrote that setting a minimum wage to protect women's interests was no different from setting maximum work hours. The *West Coast Hotel* ruling, which was based on the notion that women were unequal to men and needed protective legislation, made possible the establishment of federal minimum wage laws.

recession of 1937: By 1937, the economy showed significant signs of improvement. Unemployment was down, wages had increased, and corporate profits had more than doubled since the worst days of the Depression. Some of President Roosevelt's advisors, particularly Treasury Secretary Henry Morgenthau, argued that it was time to balance the federal budget. Morgenthau maintained that doing so would increase confidence in the business sector, leading to increased private investment. Roosevelt agreed, and slashed federal spending from $10.3 billion to $9.6 billion. The move cut hundreds of thousands of jobs from programs such as the Civilian Conservation Corps. To make matters worse, Social Security deductions from paychecks began at that time, removing some $2 billion from consumers' pockets. As a result, spending dropped dramatically and corporate profits immediately plunged, as did the stock market. Roosevelt changed course, abandoning efforts to balance the budget and requesting additional funds for jobs programs from Congress.

Indian New Deal: John Collier, commissioner of Indian affairs in the Roosevelt Administration, hoped the Indian Reorganization Act (IRA) would allow Indians more control over their lives. The act allowed for the creation of tribal governments and permitted tribes to form corporations to oversee the use of tribal resources. Opposition to the measure proved intense. Western congressmen and businesses feared the act would limit access to valuable resources in the region. Critics charged that Collier was creating communist or socialist societies on the reservations. Some tribes such as the Navajos linked the IRA to other administration measures they opposed. Still other tribes were bitterly divided, with some seeing the act as a threat to personal interests and others regarding it as a major improvement. As a consequence of the opposition to the law, many Indian tribes voted to not participate in the Indian Reorganization Act.

antilynching laws: Opponents of lynching hoped that a federal law would provide additional protections to African-Americans in southern states. In 1934, senators from Colorado and New York introduced legislation that would hold local law authorities responsible when prisoners in their custody fell victim to mob violence. However, a filibuster killed the bill in the Senate. After a particularly gruesome lynching in Florida received national press coverage, the National Association for the Advancement of Colored People initiated a nationwide campaign to raise public awareness regarding lynching. In this environment the senators again introduced their antilynching legislation. Forty senators publicly agreed to vote for the bill. However, administration officials, including the president, refused to offer their support, fearing that southern members of Congress would turn against the New Deal if the administration favored the legislation. Southerners mounted a filibuster that lasted seven weeks. When the bill was again introduced in 1938, southerners filibustered for another seven weeks, ensuring its failure.

Scottsboro boys: The Scottsboro incident began as a fight between black and white youths hitching a ride on a train. Law officials arrested nine black youths, ranging in age from twelve to twenty years, and charged them with raping two white women on the train. In the ensuing trial, which lasted two days, eight of the defendants received death sentences. Announcement of the verdict led to celebrations among the hundreds of white southerners outside the courthouse. However, the Scottsboro case was not yet over. While leaders of the National Association for the Advancement of Colored People debated how to react— some feared that the defendants actually might be guilty—the communist party acted. A nationwide campaign to draw attention to the incident prompted support from such figures as Albert Einstein and world leaders including Sun Yat Sen and Jomo Kenyatta. The national and international attention the Scottsboro case received revealed the grave injustices blacks endured in the American South, and contributed to the coming of the civil rights movement of the 1950s and 1960s.

Smith Act: The Smith Act resulted from the growing anxieties in the United States over the German conquest of Europe and the domestic rise of communist and other left-wing organizations. The legislation banned efforts to plan or advocate overthrow of the government and made it a crime to form or join any organization that supported such efforts. In a 1951 ruling in the case of *Dennis v. United States,* the U.S. Supreme Court upheld the constitutionality of the Smith Act. The majority opinion declared that free speech rights could be abridged in the face of "grave and probable danger," such as advocacy of revolution. In 1957, however, the Supreme Court distinguished between advocating revolution as an abstract doctrine and support for an actual plan to overthrow the government.

OBJECTIVE QUESTIONS

Multiple Choice

1. A major slogan of popular protest during the 1930s was
   A. "Freedom of contract."
   B. "Save the bald eagle."
   C. "Don't buy where you can't work."
   D. all of the above

2. Conservative critics of the New Deal regularly argued that
   A. the expansion of federal power posed a threat to American liberty.
   B. New Deal relief programs undermined individual self-reliance.
   C. excessive spending and regulation by Washington hurt the nation's economic prospects.
   D. all of the above

3. Which of the following series of events is listed in proper sequence?
   A. FDR's first inaugural; Social Security Act; assassination of Huey Long; "Bank holiday"
   B. National Industrial Recovery Act; labor upheaval of 1934; Wagner Act; Flint sit-down strike
   C. Fair Labor Standards Act; Agricultural Adjustment Act; End Poverty in California campaign; repeal of Prohibition
   D. FDR's court-packing plan; creation of Federal Emergency Relief Administration; FDR's second inaugural; Emergency Banking Act

4. Which of the following was *not* a key factor in Franklin Roosevelt's landslide victory over Herbert Hoover in 1932?
   A. Many felt that Hoover lacked an effective response to the economic crisis.
   B. Many felt that Hoover was too detached from the hardships of ordinary Americans.
   C. Voters were impressed by the elaborate blueprints for Roosevelt's New Deal program.
   D. Roosevelt's energy and optimism inspired confidence in his leadership potential.

5. Which of the following was *not* a significant motivation behind the New Deal?
   A. reviving America's commitment to family values at a time when they seemed to be in decline
   B. restoring the vitality of American agriculture, industry, and finance
   C. relieving the plight of the hungry, the homeless, and the jobless
   D. diminishing inequality and injustice in American society

6. Which of the following was *not* a key thrust of the Second New Deal?
   A. the right of workers to opt, by majority ballot, for union representation
   B. redistribution of national income through taxation
   C. financial assistance for the unemployed and the elderly
   D. guaranteed health care for every American citizen

7. Which of the following was *not* a theme of Popular Front radicalism?
   A. Ethnic, racial, and religious discrimination must be overcome.
   B. Organized labor must play a leading role in the struggle for social justice.
   C. The denial of civil liberties must be challenged wherever it arises—from capitalist America to communist Russia.
   D. America should celebrate its heritage of cultural diversity.

8. Which of the following was *not* a contributing factor in the winding down of New Deal reform by the late 1930s?
   A. a belief that the New Deal, having vanquished the Great Depression, was no longer necessary
   B. a feeling that President Roosevelt had grown too arrogant and powerful
   C. mounting concern that the New Deal was encouraging racial equality and labor radicalism
   D. a shift in public attention from domestic issues to the gathering crisis in Europe

9. Which is *not* true of Franklin D. Roosevelt?
   A. He served as undersecretary of the Navy during World War I.
   B. He ran for vice president on the Democratic Party ticket in 1920.
   C. He contracted polio and loss the use of his legs in 1921.
   D. He served as governor of Massachusetts in the 1920s.

10. Who was *not* a member of Franklin Delano Roosevelt's "brains trust" at the outset of his presidency?
    A. Frances Perkins
    B. Harold Ickes
    C. Harry Hopkins
    D. Andrew Mellon

11. In addressing the sense of crisis in the nation, Franklin Delano Roosevelt sought to reassure the public in his inaugural address, declaring:
    A. "never in the course of human conflict, have so many owed so much to so few."
    B. "we shall fight them on the beaches . . . we shall never be defeated."
    C. "we must let the rot work itself out of the system."
    D. "the only thing we have to fear is fear itself."

12. The initial flurry of legislation during Roosevelt's first three months in office is called:
    A. the "Hundred Days."
    B. the "Push for Unity."
    C. the "Second New Deal."
    D. the "Reconstruction Finance Corporation."

13. The National Recovery Administration (NRA), headed by Hugh S. Johnson, set codes that set prices and wages in many American industries; the NRA's symbol, which stores and factories that abided by the code displayed, was:
    A. an image of an unemployed worker.
    B. the Rising Sun.
    C. the Blue Eagle.
    D. a Native American Indian.

14. In March 1933, Congress established the federal government as a direct employer of the unemployed when it authorized the hiring of young men to work on projects to improve national parks, forests, and flood control, called:
    A. the Federal Emergency Relief Administration.
    B. the Economy Act.
    C. the Civilian Conservation Corps.
    D. the Public Works Administration.

15. The Civil Works Administration (CWA), employed more than 4 million persons in:
    A. Civil Rights work, seeking to overcome racism.
    B. offering etiquette lessons to youngsters from impoverished urban and rural settings.
    C. post offices, hospitals, and government offices.
    D. construction of tunnels, highways, courthouses, and airports.

16. The effort undertaken on the part of the federal government to supply cheap electrical power for homes and factories in a seven-state region, preventing flooding, and putting the federal government in the business of selling electricity by building a series of dams was called:
    A. the Tennessee Valley Authority (TVA).
    B. the Public Works Administration (PWA).
    C. the National Industrial Recovery Administration (NIRA).
    D. the Glass-Steigal Act.

17. At a time of widespread hunger in the United States, the Agricultural Adjustment Act (AAA) did all of the following, except:
    A. ordered 6 million pigs destroyed.
    B. ordered destruction of many crops already planted.
    C. set production quotas for major crops and paid farmers not to plant some crops.

    D. ordered a vast expansion in the production of cotton, wheat, barley, and corn across the Midwest in an effort to stave off hunger and starvation.

18. Which was *not* a decision of the United States Supreme Court in 1934–36, vis-à-vis New Deal legislation?
    A. It declared the AAA an unconstitutional exercise of congressional power over local economic activity.
    B. It declared the NRA unconstitutional in a case brought by the Schechter Poultry Company of Brooklyn, New York.
    C. It declared the Civilian Conservation Corps constitutional, insofar as it abided the interstate commerce clause in the United States Constitution.
    D. It ruled that New York State could not establish a minimum wage for women and children.

19. Which was *not* the case with regard to American labor and workers in 1934?
    A. There were more than 2,000 strikes across the country.
    B. Farmers from California to Maine led a general strike for shorter hours, better pay, and improved working conditions.
    C. Ten thousand striking workers in the auto industry in Toledo, Ohio, battled with police in a seven-hour fight.
    D. A four-month strike by truck drivers in Minneapolis, Minnesota led the governor to declare martial law.

20. In the mid-1930s, Unions of industrial workers, led by John L. Lewis, founded a new labor organization, called:
    A. the American Federation of Labor.
    B. the Industrial Workers of the World.
    C. the Congress of Industrial Organizations.
    D. the Knights of Labor.

21. Which was *not* one of the "voices of protest" heard in the United States during the mid-1930s?
    A. Upton Sinclair's bid for the governorship of California as head of the End Poverty in California movement
    B. Huey Long's Share Our Wealth movement
    C. Mary Lease's "raise less corn, and more hell" movement
    D. Dr. Francis Townsend's Townsend clubs that sought monthly payments of $200 to elderly Americans

22. The emphasis of the Second New Deal was on:
    A. economic security, in an effort to protect Americans against poverty and unemployment.
    B. economic recovery, creating government programs to address the immediate needs of the unemployed.
    C. civil rights for African-Americans.
    D. protecting the rights of businesses, especially small businesses.

23. Which was *not* created by the Social Security Act of 1935, which launched the American welfare state?
    A. a system of unemployment insurance
    B. a system of old-age pensions
    C. a system of aid to families with dependent children
    D. minimum wage and child labor laws

24. What 1935 law outlawed "unfair labor practices," and was known at the time as "Labor's Magna Carta"?
    A. the Wagner Act
    B. the Social Security Act
    C. the Fair Labor Standards Act
    D. the Works Progress Act

25. Who was the author of *The General Theory of Employment, Interest, and Money,* who asserted that large-scale government deficit-spending was appropriate during economic downturns?
    A. John Maynard Keynes
    B. Alfred Landon
    C. Charles Evans Hughes
    D. Arthur Schlesinger

26. The Commissioner of Indian Affairs who launched an "Indian New Deal" that ended a policy of forced assimilation and allowed Indians unprecedented cultural autonomy, and who secured the passage of the Indian Reorganization Act of 1934, was:
    A. John Collier.
    B. Francis Perkins.
    C. Ernest Lundeen.
    D. Robert Wagner.

27. Franklin Roosevelt appointed this person, a prominent educator, special adviser on minority affairs:
    A. Mary McLeod Bethune
    B. W. E. B. Du Bois
    C. Booker T. Washington
    D. Harold Ickes

28. The House of Representatives' Un-American Activities Committee, established in 1938, set out to investigate disloyalty with an expansive definition of "un-American" that included all of the following groups, except:
    A. the left wing of the Democratic Party.
    B. the right wing of the Republican Party.
    C. communists.
    D. labor radicals.

True or False

1. The break-up of large corporations is essential to economic recovery—this was a core principle of the New Deal.

2. The National Industrial Recovery Act boosted the prospects for American unionism, but did little to restore economic prosperity.

3. The Tennessee Valley Authority brought electric power to many Americans for the first time.

4. The Congress of Industrial Organizations enjoyed broad appeal among skilled workers, but found little support among the nation's millions of unskilled workers.

5. Grassroots protest movements—such as those led by Upton Sinclair, Huey Long, Father Charles Coughlin, and Dr. Francis Townsend—did much to fuel the passage of the landmark Social Security Act.

6. The 1936 election saw the crystallizing of the "New Deal coalition."

7. While the status of Mexican-Americans improved markedly under the New Deal, that of American Indians grew substantially worse.

8. The New Deal continued to expand throughout Roosevelt's second term; only with the coming of World War II would its momentum expire.

9. Russia and Germany suffered under the tyrants Stalin and Hitler during the 1930s.

10. Franklin Delano Roosevelt entered the presidency in 1933 with a complex, detailed blueprint for dealing with the Great Depression.

11. After a decade of Republican domination, Democrats won both the presidency and both houses of Congress in the 1932 election.

12. Between 1929 and 1933, about 5,000 banks (one-third of the nation's total) had failed.

13. Roosevelt's declaration of a four-day "bank holiday," along with emergency banking legislation, shored up citizens' confidence in the nation's banks, and in 1936, no bank failures were recorded.

14. The first "hundred days" of Franklin Delano Roosevelt's presidency witnessed the greatest expansion in the role of the federal government in the nation's history.

15. The National Recovery Act was modeled on the government-business partnership of the War Industries Board of World War I.

16. The National Recovery Administration (NRA) exempted businesses from antitrust laws.

17. Section 7a of the National Recovery Administration recognized the rights of workers to organize unions.

18. In the 1930s, good rains and good weather meant bountiful crops in Oklahoma, Texas, Kansas, and Colorado.

19. The Federal Housing Authority (FHA) ensured millions of mortgages issued by private banks; and during the 1930s, the federal government set out, for the first time, to build thousands of units of low-rent housing for American citizens.

20. The broad-ranging federal legislation that transformed the federal government's role in the American economy during the first two years of Franklin D. Roosevelt's presidency brought the nation out of economic depression, and resulted in nearly full employment.

21. Beginning with a sit-down strike of 7,000 General Motors workers in Cleveland, Ohio, sit-down strikes spread to Flint, Michigan and elsewhere in the mid-1930s.

22. By 1940, union membership had more than doubled from that of 1930.

23. The original Social Security Bill included a national system of health insurance, but this provision was dropped after fierce opposition from the American Medical Association.

24. A person's Social Security benefits derive from contributions that they themselves make into the program, from each and every paycheck throughout their working lives.

25. When Franklin Roosevelt set out to appoint additional Justices of the United States Supreme Court in an effort to keep the Court from invalidating legislative measures of the Second New Deal, most Americans supported his initiative.

26. Eleanor Roosevelt's name before she married Franklin Delano Roosevelt was Eleanor Roosevelt—they were distant cousins.

27. Eleanor Roosevelt transformed the role of "first lady," making it a base for political action.

28. Women were considered critical to the success of America as workers in the cash-nexus economy, and significant and specific laws were passed during the New Deal to prioritize and protect women workers in high-paying, professional jobs.

29. In a blow to Mexican-Americans and many other agricultural workers, the Wagner and Social Security Acts did not apply to them.

30. In the 1934 and 1936 elections, black Americans abandoned their traditional allegiance to the Republican Party in favor of the Democrats and the New Deal.

31. Federal programs such as the Agricultural Adjustment Act helped nearly all sharecroppers live better, more productive, and more profitable lives.

32. The 1930s proved to be the heyday of American Communism through the Popular Front.

33. When nine young black men—the "Scottsboro boys"—were arrested for the rape of two white women in Alabama in 1931, the Communist-dominated International Labor Defense represented them in what became an international cause célèbre.

34. Black Americans were unwelcome as members of the Congress of Industrial Organizations.

35. By the end of the 1930s, civil liberties had achieved a central place in the New Deal understanding of freedom.

ESSAY QUESTIONS

1. What were the key motivations behind the New Deal? In what measures was it designed to 1) alleviate human hardship; 2) promote business recovery; 3) diminish social unrest and conflict; or 4) equalize the distribution of wealth and power in American society? Illustrate your analysis with examples from the text.

2. Consider the social and economic "cast of characters" in American society in the 1930s—farmers, workers, blacks, businessmen, native-born white Protestants, the elderly, the wealthy, the unemployed, and so forth. In what ways were each of these groups affected by the New Deal? What might they like about it? What might they dislike?

3. Imagine a debate in 1936 between a proponent and a conservative critic of the New Deal. Transcribe this debate. (*NB:* Over the course of their exchange, each individual invokes his or her notion of freedom.)

4. What accounts for the resurgence of American unionism in the 1930s? How did the newly formed Congress of Industrial Organizations differ from the American Federation of Labor?

5. Popular movements for economic justice, the author notes, "helped to spark the Second New Deal." Identify three important reforms implemented by the

Second New Deal, and discuss how social movements helped to inspire and shape them.

6. Franklin Delano Roosevelt, "had repudiated the older idea of liberty based on the idea that the best way to encourage economic activity and ensure a fair distribution of wealth was to allow market competition to operate, unrestrained by the government." Write an essay comparing and contrasting this "older idea of liberty" with the version of liberty articulated and acted upon during the New Deal.

7. Write an essay on the role of labor in the politics of the 1930s.

8. Compare and contrast The First New Deal with The Second New Deal.

9. Describe the American welfare state that issued from the New Deal—in your answer, describe the provisions of the 1935 Social Security Act and other pieces of new deal legislation.

10. Write an essay on the presidency of Franklin Delano Roosevelt from 1933 to 1939, and include a discussion of the opposition Roosevelt faced from the political right, the political left, and the United States Supreme Court.

SOURCES FOR FURTHER RESEARCH

Books

GENERAL OVERVIEWS

Badger, Anthony J., *The New Deal: The Depression Years, 1933–1940* (1989)
Edsforth, Ronald, *The New Deal: America's Response to the Great Depression* (2000)
Kennedy, David M., *Freedom from Fear: The American People in Depression and War* (1999)

PARTICULAR ASPECTS

Brinkley, Alan, *Voices of Protest: Huey Long, Father Coughlin, and the Great Depression* (1982)
Cohen, Lizabeth, *Making a New Deal: Industrial Workers in Chicago, 1919–1939* (1990)
Denning, Michael, *The Cultural Front: The Laboring of American Culture in the Twentieth Century* (1996)
Fraser, Steve, and Gary Gerstle, eds., *The Rise and Fall of the New Deal Order, 1930–1980* (1989)
Goodman, James, *Stories of Scottsboro* (1994)
Gordon, Colin, *New Deals: Business, Labor, and Politics in America, 1920–1935* (1994)

Hall, Jacquelyn Dowd, et al., *Like a Family: The Making of a Southern Cotton Mill World* (1987)

Hawley, Ellis W., *The New Deal and the Problem of Monopoly: A Study in Economic Ambivalence* (1966)

Kessler-Harris, Alice, *In Pursuit of Equity: Men, Women, and the Quest for Economic Citizenship in 20th-century America* (2001)

Kirby, Jack T., *Rural Worlds Lost: The American South, 1920–1960* (1987)

Leuchtenberg, William E., *Franklin D. Roosevelt and the New Deal, 1932–1940* (1963)

Naison, Mark, *Communists in Harlem During the Depression* (1983)

Phillips, Sarah T., *The Land, This Nation: Conservation, Rural America, and the New Deal* (2007)

Sanchez, George, *Becoming Mexican American: Ethnicity, Culture, and Identity in Chicano Los Angeles, 1900–1945* (1995)

Sitkoff, Harvard, *A New Deal for Blacks: The Emergence of Civil Rights as a National Issue* (1978)

Sullivan, Patricia, *Days of Hope: Race and Democracy in the New Deal Era* (1996)

Worster, Donald, *Dust Bowl: The Southern Plains in the 1930s* (1979)

Zieger, Robert H., *The CIO, 1935–1955* (1995)

Videos

FDR (260 minutes, PBS Video, 1994)

The Fight (90 minutes, PBS Video, 2004)

The Grapes of Wrath (51 minutes, Discovery Channel/Films for the Humanities and Sciences, 2001)

The Great Depression: Episodes 3–7 (60 minutes each, PBS Video, 1993)

The New Deal Documentaries (105 minutes, Critics' Choice Video, 1995)

Oh Freedom after While (56 minutes, California Newsreel, 1999)

Scottsboro: An American Tragedy (90 minutes, PBS Video, 2001)

Surviving the Dust Bowl (60 minutes, PBS Video, 1998)

Union Maids (48 minutes, New Day Films, 1976)

Web Resources

The African American Odyssey, Volume VIII: The Depression, The New Deal, and World War II, Library of Congress
http://memory.loc.gov/ammem/aaohtml/exhibit/aopart8.html

America from the Great Depression to World War II: Photographs from the FSA and OWI, ca. 1935–1945, Library of Congress
http://memory.loc.gov/ammem/fsahtml/fahome.html

America in the 1930s, American Studies Program, University of Virginia
http://xroads.virginia.edu/~1930s/home_1.html

American Life Histories: Manuscripts from the Federal Writers' Project, 1936–40, Library of Congress
  http://memory.loc.gov/ammem/wpahome.html

The Flint Sit-Down Strike Audio Gallery, Michigan State University
  http://www.historicalvoices.org/flint/

Franklin D. Roosevelt Digital Archives: On-Line Documents, The Franklin D. Roosevelt Presidential Library and Museum
  http://www.fdrlibrary.marist.edu/online14.html

New Deal Network, The Franklin and Eleanor Roosevelt Institute
  http://newdeal.feri.org/

The New Deal Stage: Selections from the Federal Theatre Project, 1935–1939, Library of Congress
  http://memory.loc.gov/ammem/fedtp/fthome.html

"The Scottsboro Boys" Trials 1931–1937, Douglas O. Linder, University of Missouri-Kansas City
  http://www.law.umkc.edu/faculty/projects/FTrials/scottsboro/scottsb.htm

Studs Terkel: Conversations with America—Hard Times, Chicago Historical Society in conjunction with the National Gallery of the Spoken Word
  www.studsterkel.org/htimes.php

ANSWERS TO OBJECTIVE QUESTIONS

Multiple Choice

1-C, 2-D, 3-B, 4-C, 5-A, 6-D, 7-C, 8-A, 9-D, 10-D, 11-D, 12-A, 13-C, 14-C, 15-D, 16-A, 17-D, 18-C, 19-B, 20-C, 21-C, 22-A, 23-D, 24-A, 25-A, 26-A, 27-A, 28-A

True or False

1-F, 2-T, 3-T, 4-F, 5-T, 6-T, 7-F, 8-F, 9-T, 10-F, 11-T, 12-T, 13-T, 14-T, 15-T, 16-T, 17-T, 18-F, 19-T, 20-F, 21-T, 22-T, 23-T, 24-T, 25-F, 26-T, 27-T, 28-F, 29-T, 30-T, 31-F, 32-T, 33-T, 34-F, 35-T

CHAPTER 22

Fighting for the Four Freedoms: World War II, 1941–1945

CHAPTER OBJECTIVES

- What triggered the mounting international tensions of the 1930s? How did these tensions culminate in the outbreak of a second world war?
- What were the essential differences—in motivation and outlook—between the Allied and the Axis powers?
- What were the leading factors behind the final victory of the Allies? What were the key turning points along the way?
- What did the battle against Hitler and his allies mean to Americans?
- How did wartime mobilization transform the place of government in American society?
- In what ways did wartime mobilization expand—or constrain—the rights and opportunities of Americans? How did the outcome vary along lines of race, ethnicity, sex, and class?
- What were the Four Freedoms promulgated by FDR, and how did Americans respond to them?
- How did the United States seek to shape the postwar international order?

CHAPTER OUTLINE

I. Fighting World War II (WWII)
    A. Prewar trends in U.S. foreign policy
        1. Recognition of Soviet Union
        2. Good Neighbor Policy toward Latin America
    B. Aggression and repression abroad
        1. Japanese invasions of Manchuria, China
        2. Adolf Hitler's Germany
            a. Nazism

  b. Rearmament
  c. Annexation of Austria, Czechoslovakia
  d. Persecution of Jews
  e. Policy of appeasement toward
   i. Adoption by Britain, France, United States
   ii. Munich conference; "peace in our time"
3. Benito Mussolini's Italy
  a. Fascism
  b. Invasion of Ethiopia
4. Francisco Franco's Spain
  a. Spanish Civil War
  b. Overthrow of democracy; establishment of fascist regime
  c. Support from Hitler
C. American isolationism; reluctance to confront overseas aggression
  1. Sources
    a. Pro-Nazi sentiment
    b. Business ties to Japan, Germany
    c. Memory of World War I
    d. Pacifism
    e. Ethnic allegiances
  2. Manifestations
    a. Neutrality Acts
    b. Even-handed arms embargo on Spanish belligerents
D. Outbreak of WWII
  1. Hitler-Stalin non-aggression pact
  2. German invasion of Poland
  3. British and French declarations of war on Germany
  4. German conquests across Europe, North Africa
  5. Formation of German-Italian-Japanese Axis
  6. Battle of Britain
E. America's shifting response
  1. Persisting popular ambivalence
  2. Steps toward involvement
    a. Arms sale to Britain
    b. Military rearmament
  3. Reelection of Franklin Roosevelt (FDR)
    a. Unprecedented quest for third term
    b. Victory over Wendell Willkie
  4. Toward intervention
    a. America as "arsenal of democracy"
    b. Lend Lease Act
    c. Interventionist mobilization efforts
F. Pearl Harbor; U.S. entry into war

    G. War in the Pacific
        1. Early setbacks for Allies
            a. Japanese conquests
            b. Bataan "death march"
        2. Turning of the tide
            a. Battles of Coral Sea, Midway
            b. Island campaigns
    H. War in Europe
        1. Allied advances
            a. North Africa
            b. The Atlantic
            c. Italy
            d. D-Day
        2. Eastern front
            a. German invasion of Russia
            b. Siege of Stalingrad
            c. German surrender
            d. Magnitude of bloodshed
        3. The Holocaust

II. Home front
    A. Government mobilization of economy
        1. Wartime federal agencies
        2. Areas of impact
            a. Allocation of labor
            b. Types and labels of production
            c. Wages, prices, rents
            d. Public revenue
            e. Employment rate
    B. Business in wartime
        1. New relationship with government
            a. Prominence of business leaders in federal bureaucracy
            b. Federal funding for large corporations
        2. Achievements of wartime manufacturing
            a. Scale of production
            b. Scientific advances
            c. Restoration of public esteem for business
        3. Geography of manufacturing boom
            a. Revival of old industrial centers
            b. Emergence of new industrial centers
                i. West
                ii. South
            c. Centrality of military-related production

    C. Organized labor in wartime
        1. Government-business-labor collaboration
            a. Terms and impact
                i. Surge in union membership
                ii. Spread of union recognition
                iii. No-strike pledge
                iv. Acceptance of employer "prerogatives," "fair profit"
            b. Junior position of labor
        2. Rolling back of New Deal programs
        3. Rise of labor walkouts
    D. The Four Freedoms
        1. "Freedom" as ideological focus of wartime mobilization
        2. Content and implications
            a. Freedoms of speech and religion
            b. Freedoms from fear and want
        3. Points of controversy
            a. "Freedom from want"
            b. Office of War Information (OWI)
                i. New Deal liberalism of
                ii. Conservative curtailment of
        4. Freedom as "free enterprise," material consumption (the "fifth freedom")
    E. Women in wartime labor force
        1. Entry into traditionally "male" jobs
            a. Industry
            b. Other professions
        2. "Rosie the Riveter"
        3. Steps toward workplace equality, entitlements
        4. Experience of wartime labor; "taste of freedom"
        5. Postwar reversals

III. Visions of postwar freedom
    A. Alternative outlooks
        1. Conservative: Henry Luce's *American Century*
            a. Free enterprise, material abundance
            b. America as world's dominant power
        2. New Deal liberal: Henry Wallace's "Price of Free World Victory"
            a. "Century of the common man"
            b. International cooperation
            c. Global New Deal
        3. Shared conception of America as world model
    B. Liberal economic program
        1. National Resources Planning Board (NRPB); wartime blueprints
            a. Goals and principles
                 i. Economic security, full employment

        ii.   Expanded welfare state

       iii. Mass consumption

       iv. Keynesian emphasis on government spending

    b. Strongholds of support

    c. Congressional opposition

  2. FDR's Economic Bill of Rights

    a. Goals and principles

    b. Failure to pass in Congress

  3. Servicemen's Readjustment Act (GI Bill of Rights)

    a. Provisions

    b. Impact and significance

  4. Full Employment Bill

    a. Goals and principles

    b. Passage of watered-down version

C. Renewal of economic conservatism: Friedrich A. Hayek's *The Road to Serfdom*

  1. Themes

    a. Economic planning as threat to liberty

    b. Superior effectiveness of free market

    c. Critiques of absolute laissez-faire dogma, social hierarchy, authoritarianism

  2. Basis for modern conservatism

IV. Race and ethnicity in wartime America

  A. Discrediting of ethnic and racial inequality, intolerance

  B. Broad assimilation of ethnic outsiders

    1. Diversity of army, industrial work force

    2. Shift from forced Americanization (WWI) to patriotic assimilation (WWII)

  C. Promotion of pluralism, group equality

    1. Government

      a. FDR

      b. OWI; other government agencies

    2. Scholars

      a. Ruth Benedict's *Races and Racism*

      b. Ashley Montagu's *Man's Most Dangerous Myth: The Fallacy of Race*

    3. Hollywood

  D. Ongoing barriers to assimilation

    1. Anti-Semitism

    2. Racism

  E. Mexican-Americans

    1. Bracero program

      a. Purposes

      b. Promise and reality

      2. New employment opportunities
      3. Emergence of Chicano culture
      4. Intolerance and discrimination
         a. Zoot Suit riots
         b. Discrimination
      5. Mexican-American response
         a. Heightened civil rights consciousness
         b. Challenges to workplace discrimination
  F. American Indians
      1. Participation in military, war industry
      2. Exposure to urban life
      3. Marginality of reservations
  G. Chinese-Americans
      1. Easing of traditional stereotypes
      2. Participation in military, war industry
  H. Japanese-Americans
      1. Dehumanizing portrayals
      2. Internment policy
         a. FDR's Executive Order 9066
         b. Expulsion to internment camps
         c. Negation of civil liberties
         d. Dearth of public protest
         e. Supreme Court affirmation: *Korematsu v. United States*
         f. Japanese-American response
         g. Eventual apology

I. African-Americans
      1. On the home front
         a. Accelerated migration to industrial heartland
         b. Hostile reception; Detroit race riot, "hate strike"
         c. Persistence of lynching
      2. In the military
         a. Scale of service
         b. Racial practices
            i. Discrimination
            ii. Abuse
      3. Birth of civil rights movement
         a. March on Washington initiative
            i. A. Philip Randolph
            ii. Demands
            iii. FDR's Executive Order 8802; establishment of Fair Employment Practices Commission (FEPC)
         b. Performance and impact of FEPC
         c. Growth of NAACP

        d. Congress of Racial Equality sit-ins
        e. Organized labor
        f. "Double-V" campaign
  J. Broadening opposition to racial inequality
      1. Black-Jewish collaboration
      2. Organized labor; CIO
      3. Growing dilemma for white southern moderates
      4. In government
        a. Federal agencies
        b. Supreme Court
        c. Armed forces
      5. Landmark publications
        a. *What the Negro Wants*
        b. Wendell Willkie's *One World*
        c. Gunnar Myrdal's *An American Dilemma*

V. Toward victory and beyond
  A. Winding down of war
      1. In Europe
        a. Battle of the Bulge
        b. Allied invasion of Germany
        c. Fall of Hitler; V-E Day
      2. In the Pacific: advance of U.S. forces toward Japan
  B. Changing of guard in Washington
      1. Replacement of Wallace by Harry S. Truman as FDR's running mate
      2. FDR reelection victory over Thomas E. Dewey
      3. Death of FDR; Truman succession to presidency
  C. The atomic bomb
      1. Development
        a. Albert Einstein's theory of relativity
        b. Manhattan Project
        c. Testing in New Mexico
      2. Use on Hiroshima, Nagasaki
        a. Devastating impact
          i. Immediate
          ii. Long-term
        b. Surrender of Japan
      3. Lasting controversy over use
        a. Justifications
        b. Criticism
      4. Context for decision to use
        a. WWII practice of targeting civilian populations
        b. Dehumanization of Japanese in wartime propaganda

    D. Postwar planning by Allied leaders (Britain, United States, Soviet Union)
      1. Summit meetings at Tehran, Yalta, Potsdam
      2. Emerging points of tension among Allies
        a. Timing of Allied invasion of France
        b. Soviet intentions in eastern Europe
        c. Prospects for dissolution of British empire
    E. New economic order: Bretton Woods conference
      1. Initiatives
        a. Eclipse of British pound by dollar in global trade
        b. Linking of dollar's value to price of gold
        c. Creation of World Bank, International Monetary Fund
      2. Significance for postwar capitalist economic system
        a. Trend toward removal of barriers to free trade
        b. Recognition of United States as world's financial leader
    F. The United Nations (UN)
      1. Founding
        a. Planning conference at Dumbarton Oaks
        b. Adoption of United Nations Charter at San Francisco
        c. Endorsement of United Nations Charter by U.S. Senate
      2. Structure and mission

CHRONOLOGY

1931	Japan invades Manchuria
1933	Hitler seizes power in Germany
1935	Mussolini invades Ethiopia
1935–37	Neutrality Acts
1936	Hitler sends troops into Rhineland
1936–39	Spanish Civil War; eventual victory of Franco's fascists
1937	Japan begins new invasion of China
1938	Hitler annexes Austria, Sudetenland Munich conference; "peace in our time"
1939	Hitler annexes remainder of Czechoslovakia Hitler-Stalin non-aggression pact Germany invades Poland; beginning of World War II

1940 German conquests across Europe, North Africa
     Formation of German-Italian-Japanese Axis
     Congress approves arms sale to Britain, military rearmament
     FDR defeats Wendell Willkie to win third term
     FDR authorizes Manhattan Project

1940–41 Battle of Britain

1941 FDR's "Four Freedoms" address
     A. Philip Randolph's March on Washington campaign
     FDR establishes Fair Employment Practices Commission
     Henry Luce publishes *The American Century*
     Lend-Lease Act
     Germany invades Russia
     Japanese attack on Pearl Harbor; U.S. entry into war

1942 FDR orders Japanese-American internment
     Henry Wallace delivers "Price of Free World Victory" address
     Wendell Willkie publishes *One World*
     Launching of "Double-V" campaign for racial equality
     Japanese conquests in the Pacific
     Bataan "death march"
     Battles of Coral Sea, Guadalcanal, Midway
     Battle of the Atlantic
     Launching of Bracero program

1942–43 National Resources Planning Board reports

1943 German defeats at Stalingrad, Kursk; subsequent retreat from Russia
     Allied victories in North Africa, Sicily, and the Atlantic
     Repeal of Chinese Exclusion Act
     Harlem race riot
     Anti-black violence and "hate strike" in Detroit
     Zoot Suit riots in Los Angeles

1944 Allies launch invasion of Normandy; D-Day
     Liberation of Paris
     Servicemen's Readjustment Act (GI Bill of Rights)
     Korematsu v. United States
     Friedrich A. Hayek publishes *The Road to Serfdom*
     Publication of *What the Negro Wants* and Gunnar Myrdal's
      An American Dilemma
     Bretton Woods conference
     United Nations planning conference at Dumbarton Oaks
     FDR replaces Wallace with Harry S. Truman as running mate
     FDR defeats Thomas E. Dewey to win fourth term

1944–45   Battle of the Bulge

1945   "Big Three" conference at Yalta
             Allied invasion of Germany; fire-bombing of Dresden
             Death of FDR; succession of Truman to presidency
             Fall of Hitler; V-E Day
             Founding of United Nations at San Francisco
             "Big Three" conference at Potsdam
             Atomic bombs dropped on Hiroshima and Nagasaki; Japanese
                surrender

KEY TERMS

Good Neighbor Policy: Franklin Roosevelt hoped to better U.S. relations with Latin American states, in part because improved relations might open new markets to U.S. goods, a desirable benefit during the Great Depression. By the late 1930s, his Good Neighbor Policy also aimed at limiting the influence of Nazi Germany in Latin America. In 1938, Mexico tested Roosevelt's commitment to the policy when it seized the property of several U.S. oil companies. Rather than invade, the president pursued a diplomatic resolution to the conflict, whereby Mexico offered compensation for U.S. losses.

Neutrality Acts: The Neutrality Act of 1935 prohibited the export of military goods to belligerents, or nations in armed conflict. Less than five weeks after President Roosevelt signed the bill into law, Italian forces invaded Ethiopia. Because the Neutrality Act did not differentiate between aggressors and victims, the United States could not provide assistance to the Ethiopians, who were virtually defenseless against the mechanized armies of Italy. The event revealed the weaknesses of neutrality in a world growing increasingly violent and dangerous.

Lend-Lease Act: Congressional approval of the Lend-Lease Act allowed the Allies to receive millions of tons of American goods without payment. Over the course of the war, the United States sent abroad some $48 billion worth of goods to 38 nations, with Great Britain, China, and the Soviet Union primary recipients of U.S. assistance. The Soviet Union alone received $10 billion of material, including 34 million uniforms, 3 million tons of gasoline, 15,000 airplanes and 7,000 tanks.

Pearl Harbor: The Japanese leadership hoped that the surprise attack on Pearl Harbor would cripple the United States Navy for months or even years. In that time, the Japanese could consolidate their hold on the western Pacific. Their plan, however, was flawed both tactically and strategically. In the attack on Pearl Harbor, the Japanese failed to sink any U.S. aircraft carriers. In addition, the

Japanese planes did not hit the fuel oil supplies at Pearl Harbor, a precious asset necessary for the United States to wage war in the Pacific. From a strategic perspective, Pearl Harbor was also a failure. The attack stunned Americans, but they quickly rallied and prepared for war with astonishing speed.

Holocaust: The United States did little when grim details of the Holocaust leaked out of Europe during World War II. Many Americans were unwilling or unable to grasp the magnitude of Hitler's "Final Solution." Administration officials rejected calls for bombing raids on Auschwitz, a major death concentration camp in Poland; instead, they focused on winning the war as the best means for ending the Holocaust.

saluting the flag: Lillian and William Gobitis, both Jehovah's Witnesses, were expelled from the public school in Minersville, Pennsylvania, for refusing to salute the American flag. Their father protested on the grounds that their refusal was based on their religious beliefs, which were protected under the First Amendment. In an 8-1 ruling in the 1940 case of *Minersville School District v. Gobitis,* the U.S. Supreme Court supported the school district. The majority ruled that the family's religious values paled in comparison to the need for national unity, which the flag salute promoted. In a similar case brought before the court in 1943, *West Virginia State Board of Education v. Barnette,* the U.S. Supreme Court reversed its ruling in the *Gobitis* case. Rather than view the debate from the perspective of religious freedom, the justices framed the flag salute controversy as a free speech issue. As a result, any American, not only those with religious objections, had the right to refuse to salute the flag.

Korematsu v. United States: Toyosaburo Korematsu was born to Japanese parents in Oakland, California, in 1919. Before the attack on Pearl Harbor, Korematsu, who went by the name Fred, tried to join the U.S. military, but was rejected because of his ancestry. Because he had a steady girlfriend and a good job, Korematsu decided to evade the military order to report for internment in May 1942. He underwent plastic surgery and tried to pass himself off as a Mexican-American, but was spotted by an old acquaintance and arrested. As a result of his arrest, he was sentenced to five years in prison, immediately placed on parole, and then sent to an internment camp. Forty years after losing his case, Korematsu was granted a new trial on the grounds that government lawyers had withheld evidence in his case. He won that trial. In 1998, Korematsu was awarded the Presidential Medal of Freedom.

Executive Order 8802: A. Philip Randolph first visited with President Roosevelt in an effort to end segregation in the armed forces. Believing that he had secured the president's agreement on that issue, Randolph was angry when the military's policies did not change. He planned the March on Washington to put pressure on Roosevelt, who in preparing the nation for war did not want a divisive battle over race issues. When the president personally demanded that the march be called off, Randolph stood his ground. The president acquiesced, issuing Executive Order 8802 a week before the planned march. Randolph's steadfastness revealed that mass protest, or its threat, could bring about change, a lesson put to good use during the civil rights protests of the 1950s and 1960s.

dropping the atomic bomb: As preparations to test the atomic bomb in New Mexico proceeded, officials in the Truman administration made plans to use the weapon against Japan. There was almost no debate as to whether it should be used; rather, the discussion focused on the most effective way to use it. There was a brief discussion about announcing a demonstration on an uninhabited island, allowing the Japanese to witness its destructiveness without having to kill civilians. However, that proposal was immediately rejected out of fear that the demonstration bomb might fail or that the Japanese would attack the plane delivering the weapon.

Yalta: President Franklin Roosevelt's willingness at Yalta to allow the Soviets to continue to control portions of Eastern Europe led to substantial criticism, especially from members of the Republican Party. They claimed that Roosevelt could have taken a tougher stand, and that his failure to do so was based on a misunderstanding of the Soviet threat that led to more provocative behavior from the communists in the years that followed. Roosevelt's supporters maintain that the president had few options at Yalta. Soviet troops occupied much of Eastern Europe and Roosevelt had to acknowledge that reality.

OBJECTIVE QUESTIONS

Multiple Choice

1. A key source of American reluctance to confront the rise of Nazism and fascism in Europe during the 1930s was:
   A. haunting memories of the First World War.
   B. widespread indifference to the persecution of European Jews.
   C. the ethnic allegiances of many Americans of Italian, German, or Irish descent.
   D. all of the above

2. A major success for Germany and its allies during World War II was:
   A. the Battle of Midway.
   B. the "blitzkrieg" campaign.
   C. the Battle of Stalingrad.
   D. the Battle of the Bulge.

3. Which of the following series of events is listed in proper sequence?
   A. German annexation of Austria; Hitler-Stalin non-aggression pact; Battle of Stalingrad; "Big Three" conference at Yalta
   B. publication of *What the Negro Wants;* Detroit "hate strike"; establishment of Fair Employment Practices Commission; A. Philip Randolph's call for March on Washington
   C. publication of John Hersey's *Hiroshima; Korematsu v. United States;* announcement of Japanese-American internment policy; testing of atomic bomb in New Mexico
   D. German invasion of Poland; Allied liberation of Paris; V-E Day; D-Day

4. Which of the following was *not* a major thrust of the Four Freedoms promoted by FDR?
   A. All people are entitled to express their views, whatever those views may be.
   B. Everyone—regardless of race or belief—has a right to freedom of speech, freedom of worship, freedom from want, and freedom from fear.
   C. The only thing Americans have to fear is fear itself.
   D. A decent standard of living is one of the bedrocks of freedom.

5. Which of the following was *not* a feature of American involvement in WWII?
   A. It took the Japanese attack on Pearl Harbor to shock a reluctant nation into entering the war.
   B. Only with the Allied invasion of Normandy did American troops assume a major presence in European combat.
   C. FDR agreed to a wartime alliance with the Soviet Union only after Stalin promised to rid his country of communism after the war.
   D. Truman's decision to drop the atomic bomb on Japan was based in part on a fear that hundreds of thousands of Americans might otherwise die in a land war.

6. Which of the following was *not* an effect of wartime mobilization on American society?
   A. Millions who had suffered underemployment or low pay in the 1930s suddenly found themselves in well-paying jobs.
   B. Americans of German descent were herded into internment camps, on the basis that their loyalties could not be trusted.
   C. Millions of women took industrial jobs traditionally reserved for men.
   D. Black leaders invoked the war against Hitler to promote racial equality at home.

7. Which of the following was *not* a significant difference between the conservative and liberal visions for postwar America?
   A. Conservatives emphasized the ideal of free enterprise; liberals, the ideal of social welfare.
   B. Conservatives envisioned America as the dominant power of the postwar world; liberals envisioned a world governed by international cooperation.
   C. Conservatives were more likely to present New Deal-style government as the chief threat to freedom; liberals, to present poverty as the chief threat to freedom.
   D. Conservatives regarded capitalism as essential to America's future; liberals regarded socialism as essential to America's future.

8. Which of the following gatherings did *not* play a major role in the planning of the postwar international order?
   A. the Bretton Woods conference
   B. the Munich conference
   C. the "Big Three" conference at Yalta
   D. the United Nations planning conference at Dumbarton Oaks

9. Which was *not* one of the Four Freedoms, President Roosevelt's shorthand for American purposes in World War II?
   A. Freedom from Fear
   B. Freedom of Liberty
   C. Freedom from Want
   D. Freedom of Speech

10. Franklin Delano Roosevelt "repudiated the right to intervene militarily in the internal affairs of Latin American countries," writes Eric Foner. Define "repudiated":
    A. to cast off or disown; to reject with disapproval
    B. to reassert; make clear by re-declaration
    C. to rework so as to improve or make better
    D. ambiguous

11. Franklin Delano Roosevelt's foreign policy with regard to Latin American countries was called:
    A. the Good Neighbor Policy.
    B. the Platt Amendment.
    C. the Roosevelt Corollary.
    D. appeasement.

12. What province of northern China did Japan invade in 1931?
    A. Canton
    B. Shanghai
    C. Beijing
    D. Manchuri

13. Which was *not* a goal or action of Adolf Hitler's?
    A. He sought to control the entire European continent.
    B. He violated the Versailles Treaty and pursued German rearmament.
    C. He sent troops to occupy the Rhineland.
    D. He seized control of the Philippines and Malaysia.

14. The founder of Italian fascism who sent troops to invade and conquer Ethiopia was:
    A. Francisco Franco.
    B. Charles de Gaulle.
    C. Benito Mussolini.
    D. Giovanni Berlusconi.

15. With the spread of this on college campuses, tens of thousands of students took part in a "strike for peace" in 1935.
    A. pacifism
    B. nativism
    C. interventionism
    D. globalization

16. During World War II, the Axis powers were:
    A. Great Britain, the United States, and the Soviet Union.
    B. France, Great Britain, and the Soviet Union.
    C. Germany, Italy, and Japan.
    D. Great Britain, the United States, and Italy.

17. On December 7, 1941, Japanese planes attacked the U.S. naval base at Pearl Harbor. Where is Pearl Harbor?
    A. Japan
    B. Hawaii
    C. Guam
    D. Cuba

18. June 6, 1944, the day on which nearly 200,000 American, British, and Canadian soldiers landed in northwestern France, in Normandy, is known as:
    A. V-E Day.
    B. V-J Day.
    C. D-Day.
    D. "a day that will live in infamy."

19. The mass extinction of "undesirable" peoples—Slavs, Gypsies, homosexuals, and, above all, Jews—that Hitler undertook in 1941, and that we now call the Holocaust, he called:
    A. the "final solution."
    B. the Reich.
    C. the Third Reich.
    D. Guadalcanal.

20. The branch of the federal government created in 1942 to mobilize public opinion, and that sought to make the conflict "a 'people's war' for freedom" was called:
    A. the Office of War Information.
    B. the Committee on Public Information.
    C. the Bureau of Municipal Defense.
    D. the Espionage Committee.

21. The self-confident woman, portrayed as fully capable of doing a man's job in posters and on magazine covers during World War II, was called:
    A. "Elsa the Alleviator."
    B. "Rosie the Riveter."
    C. "a svelte Miss Liberty."
    D. "Eleanor, First Lady."

22. The congressional legislation that extended an array of benefits, including unemployment pay, educational scholarships, low-cost mortgage loans, pensions, and job training to millions of returning veterans beginning in 1944, was called:
    A. the Economic Bill Of Rights.
    B. the Serviceman's Readjustment Act, or G.I. Bill of Rights.
    C. the New Republic.
    D. the National Resources Planning Act.

23. Executive Order 9066 led to Japanese-American internment during World War II. Define "internment":
    A. the act of confining someone during wartime
    B. burial
    C. hanging
    D. the act of offering someone an internship, so that they might improve themselves by learning a profession

24. The desire for both victory at home against segregation, and victory overseas against the Germans and the Japanese, came to be called this by African-Americans during World War II:
    A. antilynching
    B. the "double-V"
    C. the Fair Employment Practices Commission
    D. a new Emancipation Proclamation

True or False

1. The Roosevelt administration paid little attention to foreign affairs before the attack on Pearl Harbor.

2. Most of the bloodshed that occurred in Europe during World War II took place on the eastern front.

3. Following America's entry into the war, the federal government assumed vast powers to oversee the national economy.

4. War mobilization lifted the industrial Northeast out of the Depression, but left the economies of the South and the West virtually untouched.

5. With the coming of peace, women employed in war-related industries came under increasing pressure to leave their jobs and resume their role as homemakers.

6. President Roosevelt's Executive Order 9066 ordered the internment of all Japanese-Americans who refused to sign an oath of loyalty to the United States.

7. War mobilization greatly strengthened the size and stature of the American labor movement.

8. As the war drew to a close, tensions emerged among the Allied powers over Stalin's reluctance to allow self-rule in eastern Europe, and Churchill's reluctance to allow self-rule for Great Britain's colonies.

9. By the late 1930s, Americans were nearly universally in favor of intervening militarily in Germany to stop the horrors being perpetrated against Jews and others by Adolf Hitler and his followers.

10. The Ford Motor Company employed slave labor provided by the German government.

11. Eighty percent of Japan's oil came from the United States prior to 1941.

12. Senator Gerald P. Nye's 1934–1935 hearings demonstrated that bankers had suffered terrible economic setbacks during World War I.

13. The America First Committee sought to ensure that America would be one of the first nations to enter the conflict against Adolf Hitler.

14. The term "blitzkrieg" means "lightning war."

15. Josef Stalin and Adolf Hitler were bitter enemies who could agree upon nothing at the beginning of World War II.

16. In World War I the French had been successful at keeping the invading German army out of Paris; in World War II, the French also succeeded in keeping the Nazis from occupying Paris.

17. At Bataan in the Philippines, U.S. and Filipino forces captured 78,000 Japanese soldiers in the largest surrender in Japanese military history.

18. In May 1942, the United States Navy thwarted a Japanese attack against Australia in the Battle of the Coral Sea.

19. The United States inflicted severe losses on the Japanese Navy in the Battle of Midway Island.

20. As late as December 1944, more American military personnel were deployed in the Pacific theater of war than against Germany.

21. During Germany's effort to seize Stalingrad beginning in August 1942, 800,000 Germans and 1.2 million Russians died in the fighting.

22. Germany suffered far higher casualties among its soldiers on the Western Front than it did on the Russian Front.

23. At least 20 million Russians died during World War II, both soldiers and civilians.

24. By 1944, the United States produced a plane every five minutes, and a ship every day.

25. During World War II, the federal government spent twice the amount of money it had spent in all of the previous 150 years of American history.

26. Unions became firmly established in many sectors of the economy during World War II.

27. During World War II, 15 million American men served in the military, and 350,000 women served in auxiliary military units.

ESSAY QUESTIONS

1. Identify three leading factors that help account for the eventual victory of the Allies over the Axis powers in World War II. Explain the reasoning behind your selections, and illustrate your analysis with examples from the text.

2. How were the American people mobilized for a second world war? How did the strategies of mobilization compare with those of World War I?

3. How did World War II alter American thought, and debate, over the meanings of freedom?

4. World War II affected the freedoms and material circumstances of Americans in a variety of ways. Discuss the domestic impacts of the war, taking into account the areas of labor relations, gender, race, and ethnicity.

5. Imagine a spirited exchange in 1945 between two individuals—one a conservative, the other a New Deal liberal—in which each expresses his or

her vision for American society after the war, and the place of the United States in the postwar world. In the course of their discussion, divergent conceptions of American freedom come to light. Transcribe this conversation.

6. Imagine a chance meeting, in late 1945, among the following characters:

   - a labor organizer
   - a black advocate of racial equality
   - a women's rights activist
   - a Japanese-American community leader
   - a Mexican-American community leader
   - a son or daughter of European immigrants
   - an industrialist
   - a New Deal liberal
   - a laissez-faire conservative

   With passion and directness, they launch into a discussion of the recent war, its consequences for their lives, and its overall meanings for American society. Among the questions they debate: "In what ways were the freedoms, rights, and opportunities of Americans advanced over the course of the war? In what ways were they diminished?" Incorporating at least *four* of the characters above, transcribe this conversation.

7. Write an essay on the Four Freedoms, their meaning and importance, during World War II.

8. Describe the American military effort—strategies, deployments, casualties, and efforts on the home front—during World War II.

9. Discuss the differing roles that men, women, African-Americans, blacks, Japanese-Americans, Indians, and Mexican-Americans held, and the issues they confronted, during World War II.

10. Describe the reasons that the United States dropped two nuclear bombs on Japan in 1945.

11. Why was the United States so hesitant to enter World War II, and what events triggered its entry into the war?

SOURCES FOR FURTHER RESEARCH

Books

GENERAL OVERVIEWS

Blum, John M., *V Was for Victory: Politics and American Culture During World War II* (1976)

Keegan, John, *The Second World War* (1989)

Kennedy, David M., *Freedom from Fear: The American People in Depression and War, 1929–1945* (1999)

PARTICULAR ASPECTS

Ambrose, Stephen E., *Citizen Soldiers* (1997)

Anderson, Karen, *Wartime Women: Sex Roles, Family Relations, and the Status of Women During World War II* (1981)

Borgwardt, Elizabeth, *A New Deal for the World: America's Vision for Human Rights* (2005)

Brinkley, Alan, *The End of Reform: New Deal Liberalism in Recession and War* (1995)

Dalfiume, Richard M., *Desegregation of the U.S. Armed Forces: Fighting on Two Fronts, 1939–1953* (1969)

Daniels, Rogers, *Prisoners Without Trial: Japanese Americans in World War II* (1993)

Dower, John W., *War Without Mercy: Race and Power in the Pacific War* (1986)

Erenberg, Lewis A., and Susan E. Hirsch, eds., *The War in American Culture: Society and Consciousness During World War II* (1996)

Hayashi, Brian Masaru, *Democratizing the Enemy: The Japanese American Internment* (2004)

Isserman, Maurice, *Which Side Were You On? The American Communist Party During World War II* (1982)

Jeffries, John W., *Wartime America: The World War II Home Front* (1996)

Lichtenstein, Nelson, *Labor's War at Home: The CIO in World War II* (1982)

Linderman, Gerald F., *The World within War: America's Combat Experience in World War II* (1997)

Rhodes, Richard, *The Making of the Atomic Bomb* (1986)

Rosenberg, Emily S., *A Date Which Will Live: Pearl Harbor in American Memory* (2003)

Sullivan, Patricia, *Days of Hope: Race and Democracy in the New Deal Era* (1996)

Von Eschen, Penny, *Race Against Empire: Black Americans and Anticolonialism, 1937–1957* (1997)

Wyman, David S., *The Abandonment of the Jews: America and the Holocaust, 1941–1945* (1984)

Videos

Home Front USA: 1941–1945 (390 minutes, PBS Video, 1990)

Imaginary Witness: Hollywood and the Holocaust (92 minutes, Anker Productions, 2004)

The Invisible Soldiers: Unheard Voices (60 minutes, PBS Video, 2000)
The Life and Times of Rosie the Riveter (65 minutes, Direct Cinema, 1987)
The Nuremberg Trials (60 minutes, PBS Video, 2006)
Pearl Harbor: Surprise and Remembrance (58 minutes, PBS Video, 1991)
The Perilous Fight: America's World War II in Color (220 minutes, PBS Home
Video, 2003)
Victory in the Pacific (120 minutes, PBS Video, 2005)
Who Shall Live and Who Shall Die? (90 minutes, Kino International, 1982)
Without Due Process: Japanese Americans and World War II (52 minutes, New
Dimension Cinema, 1992)
World War II: The War Chronicles (490 minutes, International Video
Entertainment, 1983)
Zoot Suit Riots (60 minutes, PBS Video, 2001)

Web Resources

*The African American Odyssey, Volume VIII: The Depression, The New Deal,
and World War II,* Library of Congress
http://memory.loc.gov/ammem/aaohtml/exhibit/aopart8.html

*After the Day of Infamy: "Man-on-the-Street" Interviews Following the Attack
on Pearl Harbor,* Library of Congress
http://memory.loc.gov/ammem/afcphhtml/afcphhome.html

*America from the Great Depression to World War II: Photographs from the FSA
and OWI, ca. 1935–1945,* Library of Congress
http://memory.loc.gov/ammem/fsahtml/fahome.html

Franklin D. Roosevelt Digital Archives: On-Line Documents, The Franklin D.
Roosevelt Presidential Library and Museum
http://www.fdrlibrary.marist.edu/online14.html

Introduction to the Holocaust, United States Holocaust Memorial Museum
http://www ushmm.org

A People at War, National Archives and Records Administration
http://www.archives.gov/exhibits/a_people_at_war/a_people_at_war.html

Photos of World War II, Franklin D. Roosevelt Presidential Library and
Museum
http://www.fdrlibrary.marist.edu/wwphotos.html

Powers of Persuasion—Poster Art from World War II, National Archives and
Records Administration
http://www.archives.gov/exhibit_hall/powers_of_persuasion/powers_of_
persuasion_home.html

Studs Terkel: Conversations with America—The Good War, Chicago Historical
Society in conjunction with the National Gallery of the Spoken Word
www.studsterkel.org/gwar.php

"Suffering under a Great Injustice": Ansel Adams's Photographs of Japanese-American Internment at Manzanar, Library of Congress
http://memory.loc.gov/ammem/aamhtml/aamhome.html

ANSWERS TO OBJECTIVE QUESTIONS

Multiple Choice

1-D, 2-B, 3-A, 4-C, 5-C, 6-B, 7-D, 8-B, 9-B, 10-A, 11-A, 12-D, 13-D, 14-C, 15-A, 16-C, 17-B, 18-C, 19-A, 20-A, 21-B, 22-B, 23-A, 24-B

True or False

1-F, 2-T, 3-T, 4-F, 5-T, 6-F, 7-T, 8-T, 9-F, 10-T, 11-T, 12-F, 13-F, 14-T, 15-F, 16-F, 17-F, 18-T, 19-T, 20-T, 21-T, 22-F, 23-T, 24-T, 25-T, 26-T, 27-T

CHAPTER 23

The United States and the Cold War, 1945–1953

CHAPTER OBJECTIVES

- What were the causes of the Cold War? What were some of the pivotal moments in the escalating tensions between the United States and the Soviet Union?
- What was the role of the United States in international affairs following World War II? What were the guiding assumptions and objectives of American foreign policy?
- What were the essential features of the Truman Doctrine, the Marshall Plan, and the policy of "containment"?
- How did the Cold War reshape notions of American freedom and human rights?
- What were the central features of the Fair Deal program?
- What were the approaches of the labor and civil rights movements in the postwar years?
- What were the causes and significance of the Korean War?
- What were the causes and targets of McCarthyism? What were its impacts on American society?

CHAPTER OUTLINE

I. Origins of the Cold War
  A. Rival postwar powers
    1. United States
      a. Measures of power
      b. Global agenda

     2. Soviet Union
       a. Measures of power
       b. Global agenda
   B. Roots of "containment"
     1. Projection of Soviet dominance in eastern Europe
     2. George Kennan's Long Telegram
     3. Winston Churchill's "iron curtain" speech
   C. Truman Doctrine
     1. Background
       a. President Truman's perspective on world
         i. Lack of experience
         ii. Black-and-white outlook
       b. Greece and Turkey questions
         i. Internal conflicts
         ii. Strategic significance
         iii. Disengagement of Britain
       c. Unveiling by Truman
     2. Themes and significance
       a. Presidential embrace of containment policy
       b. Division of globe between "free" and "communist"
       c. America's ongoing mission to lead, defend "free world"
     3. Impact on popular conception of postwar world
     4. Broad bipartisan support
     5. Implementation
       a. Aid to anticommunist regimes
       b. Forging of global military alliances
       c. Founding of new national security bodies
         i. Atomic Energy Commission
         ii. National Security Council (NSC)
         iii. Central Intelligence Agency (CIA)
   D. Marshall Plan
     1. Provisions
     2. Underlying motivations and vision
     3. Achievements
   E. Berlin crisis
     1. Emerging East-West conflict over Berlin
     2. Soviet blockade
     3. Western airlift
     4. Lifting of blockade
   F. Escalation of Cold War
     1. Division of Germany into East Germany and West Germany
     2. Soviet acquisition of atomic bomb

        3. Establishment of North Atlantic Treaty Organization (NATO)
          a. Avowed mission
          b. Varied agendas
        4. Establishment of Warsaw Pact
        5. Communist revolution in China
          a. Mao Zedong
          b. Political repercussions in United States
          c. American response
        6. NSC-68
   G. Korean War
        1. Postwar division of Korea
        2. North Korean invasion of south
        3. Mobilization of U.S. military response
          a. Perception of Cold War test
          b. Obtainment of United Nations authorization
        4. Initial American military progress
        5. Intervention by China
        6. Removal of General Douglas MacArthur
        7. Protracted stalemate; eventual death toll
        8. Armistice and aftermath
   H. Concerns raised by Cold War critics
        1. Simplistic East-West dichotomies
        2. Inability to see foreign developments on case-by-case basis
        3. Continual intervention abroad
        4. Tendency to side with undemocratic regimes
        5. Aversion to colonial independence

II. Ideological mobilization for Cold War
   A. Effect on notions of freedom
   B. Realms
        1. Depictions of U.S. history
        2. The arts
          a. Areas
             i. Film
             ii. Painting
             iii. Music
             iv. Dance
          b. Secret involvement of national security agencies
        3. Political discourse
   C. Themes
        1. America as land of pluralism, tolerance, equality, free expression, individual liberty
        2. Communist regimes as "totalitarian"
        3. "Socialized" resources (medicine, housing) as communistic, negation of freedom

    D. Rise of "human rights"
        1. Background
            a. Historical origins of concept
            b. Impact of World War II
        2. Drafting of UN Universal Declaration of Human Rights
            a. Eleanor Roosevelt
            b. Range of rights identified
                i. Civil and political liberties
               ii. Social and economic entitlements
            c. Affirmation of global accountability of nations
        3. Cold War contest over
            a. U.S. emphasis on political rights
            b. Soviet emphasis on social, economic rights
            c. Compromise: two separate "covenants"

III. Truman presidency
    A. Postwar domestic situation
        1. Rapid demobilization; return of soldiers to civilian life
        2. Abolition of wartime regulatory agencies
    B. Fair Deal
        1. Aims
            a. Revive momentum of New Deal
            b. Improve social safety net and living standards
        2. Program
    C. Strike wave of 1946
        1. Contributing factors
        2. Scope and magnitude
            a. Range of industries affected
            b. Operation Dixie
        3. Truman response
            a. Concern over economic effect
            b. Threat to draft striking railroad workers
            c. Court order against striking miners
            d. Outcomes
    D. Republican congressional gains of 1946
        1. Causes
            a. Middle-class alarm over strike wave
            b. Labor disappointment over Truman
            c. Failure of Operation Dixie
        2. Consequences
            a. Rejection of Fair Deal program
            b. Tax cuts for wealthy
            c. Taft-Hartley Act
                i. Provisions
               ii. Impact on organized labor

E. Steps toward civil rights
   1. Anti-discrimination measures, state and local
   2. Vitality of civil rights coalition
   3. Growing response to lynching
   4. Integration of major league baseball; Jackie Robinson
   5. Commission on Civil Rights's *To Secure These Rights*
   6. Truman's civil rights initiatives
      a. Program presented to Congress
         i. Content
         ii. Defeat
      b. Desegregation of armed forces
      c. Underlying considerations
         i. Personal sentiments
         ii. Cold War implications
         iii. Political strategy
F. Election of 1948
   1. Truman and the Democrats
      a. Drive to revive and broaden New Deal coalition
      b. Progressive program
      c. Assault on "do-nothing Congress"
   2. Strom Thurmond and the States' Rights ("Dixiecrat") party
      a. Break from Democratic party
      b. Call for segregation, "states' rights"
   3. Henry A. Wallace and Progressive party
      a. Program
         i. Expansion of social welfare
         ii. Desegregation
         iii. De-escalation of Cold War
      b. Support from communists; abandonment by liberals
   4. Thomas A. Dewey and the Republicans
      a. Colorlessness of candidate
      b. Complacency and vagueness of campaign
   5. Truman's upset victory

IV. Anticommunist crusade
   A. Wide-ranging impact of Cold War on American life
      1. Permanent military-industrial establishment
      2. Federal projects
         a. Weapons development
         b. Military bases
         c. Higher education
         d. Interstate highway system
      3. Culture of secrecy, dishonesty
      4. Revised immigration policy

5. Dismantling of segregation
6. Assault on right to dissent
B. Emergence of anticommunist crusade
1. Truman's loyalty review system
2. House Un-American Activities Committee hearings on Hollywood
a. Pressure to testify about beliefs, "name names"
b. Cooperation and resistance
c. Hollywood Ten; blacklist
3. Legal cases
a. Trial, conviction, and imprisonment of Alger Hiss
b. Trial, conviction, and imprisonment of Communist Party leaders
c. Trial, conviction, and execution of Julius and Ethel Rosenberg
C. McCarthyism
1. Joseph R. McCarthy
a. Background
b. Emergence with sensational Wheeling speech
2. McCarthy's Senate committee hearings
a. Wild allegations regarding disloyalty, communist presence
b. Growing Republican ambivalence
3. McCarthy's downfall
a. Army-McCarthy hearings
i. Television exposure
ii. Scolding by Joseph Welch
b. Senate censure
4. Genesis of term "McCarthyism"
D. Breadth of anticommunist crusade around country
1. Initiatives of government (national, state, and local)
a. Investigative committees
b. Police department "red squads"
c. Laws to ban, monitor communist presence
d. Loyalty oaths
2. Initiatives of private organizations
3. Ideological "cleansing" of public libraries, universities
4. Acquiescence of judiciary: *Dennis v. United States*
5. Acquiescence of liberals
6. Cost to the persecuted
E. Anticommunism as popular mass movement
1. Strength among those of eastern European descent
2. Strength among Catholics
F. Multiple uses of anticommunism
1. Bureaucratic self-promotion

    2. Political self-preservation
    3. Discrediting of political, social targets
        a. New Deal legacy
        b. Economic regulation
        c. Organized labor
        d. Civil rights
        e. Feminism
        f. Homosexuality
G. Anticommunist politics
    1. Republican use of anticommunism to block Truman program
    2. McCarran Internal Security Act
    3. McCarran-Walter Act
    4. Operation Wetback
    5. Confinement of social welfare benefits to unionized workers
    6. Ideological taming of organized labor
        a. CIO expulsion of left-wing leaders and unions
        b. Labor's support for Cold War foreign policy
H. Response of civil rights movement to anticommunist crusade
    1. Outspoken opposition (Paul Robeson, W. E. B. Du Bois)
    2. Shifting approach of mainstream groups (NAACP, NUL)
        a. Initial resistance
        b. Growing accommodation
            i. Purges of Communist members
            ii. Silence about political persecution
            iii. Embrace of Cold War rhetoric
        c. Use of Cold War rhetoric to promote civil rights
    3. Demise of left-leaning organizations (Southern Conference for Human Welfare)
I. Lull in momentum for civil rights
    1. Dampening effect of Cold War
    2. Diminishing of efforts from Truman administration, Democrats
    3. Legacy for black postwar prospects

CHRONOLOGY

1944	President Roosevelt replaces Henry Wallace with Harry S. Truman as running mate
1945	Roosevelt's fourth reelection Death of Roosevelt; Truman becomes president
1946	George Kennan's Long Telegram Winston Churchill's "iron curtain" speech Atomic Energy Commission established

Philippine independence
Price controls ended
National strike wave
Launching of Operation Dixie
Republicans gain control of Congress in midterm elections

1947   Launching of Freedom Train
American aid to governments of Greece, Turkey
Announcement of Truman Doctrine
Announcement of Marshall Plan
Establishment of National Security Council, Central Intelligence
    Agency
Taft-Hartley Act
Jackie Robinson signs with Brooklyn Dodgers, breaks major league
    color line
President's Commission on Civil Rights issues *To Secure These
    Rights*
Truman establishes loyalty review system
House Un-American Activities Committee launches investigation of
    Hollywood

1948   Soviet blockade of Berlin; launching of airlift
United Nations General Assembly approves Universal Declaration
    of Human Rights
Truman orders desegregation of armed forces
Dixiecrat revolt
Truman wins surprise reelection in four-way contest

1949   Lifting of Soviet blockade
Soviet Union tests atomic bomb
Establishment of North Atlantic Treaty Organization
Communist revolution in China
CIO expulsion of left-wing leaders, unions

1950   NSC-68 approved
Outbreak of Korean War; subsequent entry of China
McCarran Internal Security Act
Joseph McCarthy's Wheeling speech
Alger Hiss convicted, sentenced to prison

1951   Truman relieves MacArthur of Korean command
Eleven Communist leaders convicted, sentenced to prison
Julius and Ethel Rosenberg convicted (executed in 1953)
Dennis v. United States

1952   Election of Dwight D. Eisenhower to presidency
         McCarran-Walter Act

1953   Armistice in Korea

1954   Army-McCarthy hearings; subsequent Senate censure of McCarthy
         Launching of Operation Wetback

1955   Establishment of Warsaw Pact

KEY TERMS

Long Telegram: The famous Long Telegram had its origins in an angry speech that Joseph Stalin delivered in February 1946. In the speech the Soviet leader argued that communism and capitalism were incompatible, and he called for the expansion of the Soviet military. That same month George Kennan, an American diplomat in Moscow, composed an 8,000 word telegram (it ran sixteen pages long when printed) offering his view of Stalin's motives. The Long Telegram quickly circulated among U.S. diplomats and politicians and—unbeknownst to the Americans—among Soviet officials, whose intelligence agents had acquired a copy. The Long Telegram became one of the most influential analyses of foreign affairs of the twentieth century, articulating the policy of containment that would guide U.S. foreign policy during the Cold War.

Marshall Plan: Immediately after World War II, the United States provided economic aid to Europe through the United Nations Relief and Rehabilitation Administration. However, when U.S. officials learned that communists in Eastern Europe used the aid to advance their political fortunes, the United States withdrew from the program. Europe, however, remained in crisis. A drought ruined the harvests of 1946 and severe winter weather later that year increased the misery the war had brought. The dire conditions raised the threat of political change—for example, communists won twenty percent of the vote in French elections. In response, Secretary of State George Marshall supported the European Recovery Program, more commonly known as the Marshall Plan. The secretary of state insisted that aid be made available to all European nations, even those with communist governments. While some Americans feared that Congress would refuse to fund the plan if communists participated, diplomats such as George Kennan realized that the Soviets would never allow their satellite states to accept U.S. assistance. As expected, the Soviets condemned the Marshall Plan. Nations in Western Europe quickly assembled requests for some $22 billion in aid.

The Soviet bomb: U.S. officials realized that the nation's nuclear monopoly would not last forever. They were certain that the Soviets were developing their own atomic weapons, and predicted a successful Soviet test sometime in the 1950s. In the immediate postwar period, however, nuclear monopoly played an important role in the nation's strategic thinking—the Soviet military buildup in Eastern Europe was offset by the United States's ability to use atomic bombs in the event of war. It came as a shock to the American people when President Harry Truman announced in September 1949 that the Soviets had successfully tested an atomic bomb. The United States had learned of the test by measuring radiation levels. After Truman's announcement, the Soviet government confirmed its achievement, and the nuclear arms race began.

the dismissal of Douglas MacArthur: His service during World War II and his command at the Inchon landing in Korea made General Douglas MacArthur a hero to the American people. However, President Truman was increasingly frustrated with MacArthur's public statements regarding the war. The general favored bombing sites in China, perhaps with atomic weapons. Truman dismissed MacArthur's proposals immediately, fearing that they might prompt Soviet intervention and another world war. When MacArthur continued to publicly condemn the president's conduct of the war, Truman fired the general for insubordination. Public outrage followed, and MacArthur was greeted with wild enthusiasm upon his return to the United States. In a speech delivered to Congress and broadcast on radio and television, MacArthur declared, "Old soldiers never die; they just fade away." The public initially seemed unwilling to let the general fade away, however, as millions of New Yorkers attended a tickertape parade held in his honor. MacArthur's popularity did wane, however, as many Americans agreed that military officers are subordinate to the president as commander-in-chief.

labor unrest: During World War II American workers saw their real incomes rise by as much as 53 percent. Most of the income increases resulted from working overtime, which was readily available because of the wartime demand for labor. At war's end opportunities for overtime declined, and many workers' incomes declined by as much as 30 percent. At that same time, the U.S. government removed price controls implemented during the war. Within two weeks of the end of the price controls, the cost of consumer goods rose by nearly 30 percent. Workers caught in the squeeze between lower incomes and rapidly rising prices were furious, and their outrage mounted with the realization that corporate profits were soaring. The anger resulted in a wave of strikes in 1946. One out of every fourteen workers went on strike during that year, leading to 120 million workdays of labor lost.

desegregating the armed forces: Several factors contributed to President Harry Truman's decision to issue Executive Order 9981, which required the desegregation of the U.S. military. Truman personally had mixed feelings about civil rights but was appalled by the abuse and violence that black veterans received in the South after the war. Politically, the president faced pressure from leading civil rights organizations such as the National Association for the Advancement of Colored People, which called for an end to racial discrimination. With a tough presidential election on the horizon, Truman could not afford to alienate black voters. Internationally, the United States was in a battle against communism, and segregation was becoming an issue that worked against the United States in the court of world opinion. These factors contributed to the president's decision to issue the executive order in July 1948.

loyalty review system: Less than two weeks after his speech outlining the Truman Doctrine, Harry Truman issued Executive Order 9835, creating the Federal Employee Loyalty Program. Under the program, federal agencies created boards to investigate the loyalty of government employees. Grounds for dismissal included reasonable doubts about a person's loyalty or suspected membership in any group listed by the Attorney General as "totalitarian, fascist, or subversive." Employees brought before the board could not confront anyone who accused them of disloyalty. In the end, the program resulted in 1,200 firings and some 6,000 resignations from the federal bureaucracy. The program never identified a single spy or discovered any acts of espionage against the United States.

Army-McCarthy hearings: A hero to many Americans, Joseph McCarthy was feared by many politicians who recognized his power to end their careers. McCarthy could not be stopped until public opinion regarding the Wisconsin senator shifted, an event that took place in 1954 and illustrated the growing influence of television in American life. The Army-McCarthy hearings stemmed from the senator's anger that the army had refused to extend preferential treatment to one of his friends. Claiming that military officials had given an honorable discharge to a left-wing dentist, McCarthy began hearings into the loyalty of several officers. Americans witnessed the senator's abusive and mean-spirited behavior—at one point he accused General Ralph Zwicker of having the brains of a small child—and public support for McCarthy rapidly waned. Later that year the U.S. Senate censured McCarthy by a vote of 67–22. After the vote McCarthy's alcoholism worsened, and he died in 1957.

McCarran-Walter Act: President Truman vetoed the McCarran-Walter Act because he opposed its quota provisions, which favored western European immigration. However, Truman favored some of the bill's provisions. The act ended the practice of prohibiting Asians from becoming naturalized citizens of the United States. In addition, it allowed the spouses and children of U.S. citizens to migrate without being counted as part of any nation's quota. The act thus had the effect of increasing immigration from Asia.

OBJECTIVE QUESTIONS

Multiple Choice

1. The United Nations committee which drafted the Universal Declaration of Human Rights was led by:
   A. George C. Marshall.
   B. Eleanor Roosevelt.
   C. Norman Rockwell.
   D. Alger Hiss.

2. Two outspoken critics of the domestic anticommunist crusade were:
   A. Thomas Dewey and Henry Luce.
   B. Strom Thurmond and Richard Nixon.
   C. Paul Robeson and W. E. B. Du Bois.
   D. Branch Rickey and Jackson Pollock.

3. Which of the following series of events is listed in proper sequence?
   A. George Kennan's Long Telegram; unveiling of Truman Doctrine; start of Korean War; founding of Warsaw Pact
   B. Joseph McCarthy's Wheeling speech; Taft-Hartley Act; reelection of Truman; launching of Operation Dixie
   C. Approval of NSC-68; Army-McCarthy hearings; Winston Churchill's "iron curtain" speech; announcement of Marshall Plan
   D. Dixiecrat revolt; signing of Jackie Robinson by Brooklyn Dodgers; HUAC investigation of Hollywood; trial of Julius and Ethel Rosenberg

4. Which of the following was *not* a contributing factor behind the rise of the Cold War?
   A. Soviet resentment over American intervention in parts of Europe
   B. American resentment over Soviet intervention in parts of Europe
   C. anxiety in both the United States and the Soviet Union over the nuclear capacity of each other
   D. Churchill's call for the construction of a great wall between East and West Germany

5. Which of the following was *not* a key provision of the 1947 Taft-Hartley Act?
   A. Workers cannot go on strike to support striking workers at other establishments.
   B. Union membership cannot be made a condition of employment.
   C. Unions cannot discriminate on the basis of race.
   D. Avowed communists cannot serve as union officials.

6. Which of the following was *not* a dramatic feature of the 1948 presidential election?
   A. lively debate between supporters and critics of the Korean War
   B. the "Dixiecrat" revolt of disaffected southern Democrats
   C. the left-wing Progressive party campaign of ex-vice president Henry Wallace
   D. the unexpected victory of President Truman over Republican challenger Thomas Dewey

7. Which of the following was *not* a step toward racial equality in postwar America?
   A. the signing of Jackie Robinson to the Brooklyn Dodgers
   B. the desegregation of the armed forces
   C. the defeat of Operation Dixie
   D. the release of the Commission on Civil Rights report, *To Secure These Rights*

8. Which of the following was *not* a common target of the anticommunist crusade?
   A. New Deal liberalism
   B. laissez-faire conservatism
   C. the labor movement
   D. civil rights efforts

9. Who was the person who sent the Long Telegram from Moscow in 1946 that lay the foundation for what became known as the policy of "containment"?
   A. Harry S. Truman
   B. George C. Marshall
   C. Douglas MacArthur
   D. George F. Kennan

10. "Containment" in the context of post-World War II international diplomacy on the part of the United States referred to:
    A. the policy by which the United States committed itself to preventing any further expansion of Soviet power.
    B. the policy by which the United States committed itself to containing its power principally to domestic issues; in this context containment is another word for isolationism.
    C. the policy by which the United States committed itself to containing the spread of disease, hunger, and extreme poverty.
    D. the policy by which the United States committed itself to containing the flow of illegal immigrants from Latin America.

11. The Truman Doctrine articulated in March 1947:
    A. asserted that the United States, as the leader of the "free world," must take up responsibility for supporting "freedom-loving peoples" wherever communism threatened them.
    B. asserted that an Iron Curtain had fallen across Europe, dividing free Western Europe from Communist Eastern Europe.
    C. established the Central Intelligence Agency (CIA).
    D. immediately challenged the Soviet blockade of West Berlin, with around-the-clock supply flights into West Berlin.

12. The June 1947 United States foreign-policy initiative that envisioned a New Deal for Europe, and pledged billions of dollars to finance European economic recovery was:
    A. the Truman Doctrine.
    B. the Marshall Plan.
    C. NATO.
    D. the Fair Deal.

13. In June 1948, when the United States, Britain, and France introduced a separate currency in their zones of control in the city of Berlin, the Soviet Union responded with:
    A. the development of the Warsaw Pact.
    B. the building of the Berlin wall.
    C. the Berlin Blockade.
    D. NATO.

14. Which was *not* a development of 1949?
    A. The Soviet Union tested its first atomic bomb, and Mao Zedong emerged victorious in the long Chinese Civil War.
    B. The North Atlantic Treaty Organization (NATO) was established.
    C. Truman's Berlin Airlift succeeded when Stalin lifted the blockade of West Berlin in May.
    D. The Soviets formalized their own eastern European alliance, the Warsaw Pact.

15. The 1950 National Security Council manifesto that called for a permanent military build-up to enable the United States to pursue a global crusade against communism, describing the Cold War as an epic struggle between "the idea of freedom" and the "idea of slavery under the grim oligarchy of the Kremlin" was:
    A. NSC-68.
    B. NATO.
    C. the OSC.
    D. the Marshall Plan.

16. The first hot war of the Cold War—beginning in June 1950—took place in:
    A. Greece and Turkey.
    B. Berlin.
    C. Korea.
    D. Yugoslavia.

17. Which is *not* true of the Korean War (1950–1953):
    A. Over 33,000 Americans died in Korea; an estimated one million Korean soldiers and 2 million civilians died, along with hundreds of thousands of Chinese troops.
    B. General Douglas McArthur launched a daring counterattack at Inchon, behind North Korean lines, in September 1950.
    C. In 1953, armistice was agreed to which restored the prewar status quo.
    D. President Truman acknowledged and accepted General MacArthur's push toward the Chinese border and his threat to use nuclear weapons against the Chinese.

18. The 1948 United Nations-approved document that called for a range of rights to be enjoyed by people everywhere, including freedom of speech and religion, as well as social and economic entitlements, including the right to an adequate standard of living, access to adequate housing, education, and medical care was called:
    A. the Universal Declaration of Human Rights.
    B. the Freedom House Manifesto.
    C. the Economic Bill Of Rights.
    D. the Fair Deal.

19. President Harry S. Truman's program that focused on improving the social safety net and raising the standard of living of ordinary Americans—calling on Congress to increase the middle wage, enact a program of national health insurance, and expand public housing, social security, and aid to education—was:
    A. the Square Deal.
    B. the Great Society.
    C. the Fair Deal.
    D. the New Frontier.

20. What was the name of the AFL and CIO campaign to bring unionization to the South, by which more than 200 labor organizations entered the region in an effort to organize workers?
    A. Operation Dixie
    B. Operation Mongoose
    C. Operation Organization
    D. Campaign to Victory

21. What was the 1947 law that sought to reverse gains made by organized labor in the preceding decade, and authorized the president to suspend strikes by ordering an 80-day cooling-off period, banned sympathy strikes and secondary boycotts, outlawed the closed shop, and authorized states to pass "right to work" laws?
    A. the Wagner Act
    B. the White Act
    C. the Taft-Hartley Act
    D. the Fair Labor Standards Act

22. In the context of postwar Civil Rights, what major league baseball player joined the Brooklyn Dodgers in 1947 and by so doing challenged the long-standing exclusion of black players from major league baseball?
    A. Paul Robeson
    B. Jim Thorpe
    C. Jackie Robinson
    D. James Farmer

23. Who was the United States senator from Wisconsin who announced in February 1950 that he had a list of 205 communists working for the State Department, and later entered the political vocabulary as a shorthand for character assassination, guilt by association, and abuse of power in the name of anticommunism?
    A. Julius Rosenberg
    B. George C. Marshall
    C. Joseph R. McCarthy
    D. Alger Hiss

True or False

1. George Kennan's Long Telegram provided an early formulation of the policy of "containment."

2. Under the Truman Doctrine, only those governments that respected the democratic rights of citizens and the sovereignty of other peoples could expect friendship and support from the United States.

3. The Central Intelligence Agency quietly subsidized artists it considered useful in the "cultural Cold War."

4. Comprised of the United States, Canada, and ten western European nations, the Warsaw Pact was launched as a collective deterrent against Soviet aggression.

5. The 1946 congressional elections marked a resounding triumph for Truman's Fair Deal program.

6. In the atmosphere of the Cold War, the United States tended to define "human rights" in terms of political liberty, while the Soviet Union emphasized social and economic entitlements.

7. While the anticommunist hysteria of the postwar years came to be known as "McCarthyism," it arose well before Senator Joseph McCarthy entered the scene.

8. In *Dennis v. United States,* the Supreme Court ruled that the imprisonment of communist leaders violated the right of free expression.

9. The United States emerged from World War II as the world's greatest power; it had the world's most powerful navy and air force, and accounted for half the world's manufacturing capacity.

10. By 1949, the world's largest country measured by land area (the Soviet Union), and the world's largest country by population (China) were both communist.

11. In the context of the Cold War, no matter how repressive a nation was, so long as it supported the United States it was counted as a member of the Free World.

12. As part of the cultural Cold War, the CIA secretly funded an array of overseas publications, conferences, publishing houses, concerts, art exhibits, and jazz performances.

13. Jackson Pollock's paintings were viewed as communistic by the CIA, and defunded.

14. The term totalitarianism originated in Europe between the world wars to describe aggressive, ideologically driven states that sought to subdue all civil society, including churches, unions, and other voluntary associations.

15. The words "under God" were added to the Pledge of Allegiance in the 1950s in response to Soviet opposition to organized religion and to "strengthen our national resistance to communism."

16. For the first time since the 1920s, the Republicans swept to power in both houses of Congress in the election of 1946.

17. The Democratic Party platform of 1948 was the most progressive in the party's history.

18. In July 1948, President Harry S. Truman issued an executive order desegregating the armed forces.

19. In 1947, the House Un-American Activities Committee (HUAC) launched hearings into communist influence in Hollywood, and, in consequence, actors, directors, and screenwriters were blacklisted or jailed.

20. Alger Hiss, an editor at *Time* magazine, accused Whittaker Chambers, a high-ranking State Department official, of giving him secret government documents to pass along to the Soviet Union.

ESSAY QUESTIONS

1. The second half of the 1940s witnessed a spiraling of tensions between the United States and the Soviet Union. Identify three episodes that contributed significantly to the escalation of the Cold War during these years, and describe how they did so.

2. Imagine a chance meeting during the 1948 election campaign between four individuals:

   • a supporter of Harry Truman (Democrat)
   • a supporter of Thomas Dewey (Republican)
   • a supporter of Henry Wallace (Progressive) and
   • a supporter of Strom Thurmond (States Rights)

   Before long, they enter into a spirited debate over the current state of affairs in the United States, and the nation's role in the wider world. Over the course of this discussion, each participant expresses his or her own conception of American freedom. Transcribe this exchange.

3. In what ways can the emergence of the Cold War during the late 1940s and early 1950s be attributed to the actions of the United States, and in what ways to those of the Soviet Union? Illustrate your analysis with examples from the text.

4. Consider the following two statements concerning the period 1945–1950:

   A. "It was a time of hope and progress for advocates of racial equality."
   B. "It was a time of disappointment and setbacks for advocates of racial equality."

   In what ways do the developments related in this chapter bear out Statement A? In what ways, Statement B?

5. Imagine a debate in 1954 between a defender and a critic of the following statement:

   "The anticommunist crusade has enhanced the heritage of freedom and democracy in America."

   Each participant supports his or her position with events from recent years. Transcribe this exchange.

6. In what ways did the decade after World War II in American society resemble the decade after World War I? In what ways did it look different?

7. Write an essay on how the Cold War helped reshape freedom's meaning, identifying freedom ever more closely with anticommunism, "free enterprise," and the defense of the social and economic status quo.

8. Write an essay on the cultural Cold War.

9. Write essay on Truman's Fair Deal and the Republican response to it.

10. Write an essay on the political conflicts between the United States and the Soviet Union in the late 1940s and early 1950s.

11. Write an essay on the Truman presidency. Be sure to include discussion both of Truman's domestic and foreign policies, as well as discussion of Truman's political proponents and antagonists.

12. Write an essay on how the Cold War shaped ideas of freedom in the United States.

13. Write an essay on how the anticommunism of the Cold War shaped American politics.

SOURCES FOR FURTHER RESEARCH

Books

GENERAL OVERVIEWS

Patterson, James T., *Grand Expectations: The United States, 1945–1974* (1996)

PARTICULAR ASPECTS

Biondi, Martha, *To Stand and Fight: The Struggle for Civil Rights in Postwar New York City* (2003)

Bird, Kai, and Martin J. Sherwin, *American Prometheus: The Triumph and Tragedy of J. Robert Oppenheimer* (2005)

Donovan, Robert, *Conflict and Crisis: The Presidency of Harry S. Truman, 1945–1948* (1977)

Dudziak, Mary L., *Cold War Civil Rights: Race and the Image of American Democracy* (2000)

Gaddis, John Lewis, *We Now Know: Rethinking Cold War History* (1997)

Gleason, Abbott, *Totalitarianism: The Inner History of the Cold War* (1995)

Glendon, Mary Ann, *A World Made New: Eleanor Roosevelt and the Universal Declaration of Human Rights* (2001)

Hogan, Michael, *The Marshall Plan* (1987)

Hunt, Michael, *Ideology and U.S. Foreign Policy* (1987)

LaFeber, Walter, *America, Russia, and the Cold War, 1945–1992* (1997)

Leffler, Melvyn P., *A Preponderance of Power: National Security, the Truman Administration, and the Cold War* (1992)

Lipsitz, George, *Rainbow at Midnight: Labor and Culture in the 1940s* (1994)

May, Lary, ed., *Recasting America: Culture and Politics in the Age of the Cold War* (1989)

Sandler, Stanley, *The Korean War: No Victors, No Vanquished* (1999)

Saunders, Frances S., *The Cultural Cold War: The CIA and the World of Arts and Letters* (2000)

Schrecker, Ellen, *Many Are the Crimes: McCarthyism in America* (1998)

Stueck, William, *The Korean War: An International History* (1995)

Sugrue, Thomas, *Origins of the Urban Crisis: Race and Inequality in Postwar Detroit* (1996)

Williams, William A., *The Tragedy of American Diplomacy* (1959)

Videos

Cold War (20 hours, PBS Video, 1998)

Korea: The Forgotten War (92 minutes, Fox Hills Video, 1987)

MacArthur (4 hours, PBS Video, 1999)

Point of Order (97 minutes, New Yorker Video, 1963)

The Rise and Fall of Jim Crow: Episode 4: Terror and Triumph (1940–1954) (60 minutes, Quest Productions, Videoline Productions, and Thirteen/ WNET, 2002)

Seeing Red: Stories of American Communism (100 minutes, Facets Video, 1984)

The Weapon of Choice (60 minutes, Annenberg/ CPB, 1998)

Web Resources

The Alger Hiss Trials, 1949–50, Douglas Linder, University of Missouri-Kansas City
http://www.law.umkc.edu/faculty/projects/ftrials/hiss/hiss.html

By Popular Demand: Jackie Robinson and Other Baseball Highlights, 1860s–1960s, Library of Congress
http://memory.loc.gov/ammem/jrhtml/jrhome.html

Cold War, Cable News Network, Inc.
http://www.cnn.com/SPECIALS/cold.war/

Foreign Relations of the United States, 1945–1950: Emergence of the Intelligence Establishment, U.S. State Department
http://www.state.gov/www/about_state/history/intel/index.html

The Rosenberg Trial, 1951, Douglas Linder, University of Missouri-Kansas City
http://www.law.umkc.edu/faculty/projects/ftrials/rosenb/ROSENB.HTM

ANSWERS TO OBJECTIVE QUESTIONS

Multiple Choice

1-B, 2-C, 3-A, 4-D, 5-C, 6-A, 7-C, 8-B, 9-D, 10-A, 11-A, 12-B, 13-C, 14-D, 15-A, 16-C, 17-D, 18-A, 19-C, 20-A, 21-C, 22-C, 23-C

True or False

1-T, 2-F, 3-T, 4-F, 5-F, 6-T, 7-T, 8-F, 9-T, 10-T, 11-T, 12-T, 13-F, 14-T, 15-T, 16-T, 17-T, 18-T, 19-T, 20-F

CHAPTER 24 | An Affluent Society, 1953–1960

CHAPTER OBJECTIVES

- What fueled the economic expansion of 1950s America?
- What were the defining features of suburban life during the Fifties?
- What was the "consumer culture" of the 1950s, and how did it transform the ideal of American freedom?
- What were the key policies and initiatives of the Eisenhower administration?
- How did the Cold War shape American foreign relations during the Fifties?
- How did contemporaries celebrate—or question—the direction of American society in the 1950s?
- What accounts for the awakening of civil rights protest in the South? What were the central philosophies of this emerging movement?

CHAPTER OUTLINE

I. Trends in postwar economy
  A. "Golden age" of American capitalism
    1. Economic expansion, growth
    2. Wide-ranging improvements in living standards
    3. Breadth of access to a better life
      a. Low unemployment
      b. Decline in poverty rate
    4. Industrial supremacy around world
  B. Emergence of West and South as centers of military production, mobilization
  C. Twilight of industrial age
    1. Gathering decline in manufacturing
    2. Shift toward white-collar occupations

    D. Transformations in agricultural America
      1. Acceleration of trend toward fewer and larger farms
      2. Mechanization of southern farming
      3. Expansion of corporate farming out West
        a. Fruits and vegetables
        b. Migrant labor

II. Suburbia
    A. Rise
      1. Pace and magnitude
      2. Central role in economic expansion
      3. Symbols and manifestations
        a. Levittown
        b. Malls
        c. California
          i. Los Angeles; "centerless city"
          ii. Freeways, cars
          iii. Shopping centers
          iv. Lawns
    B. Consumer culture
      1. Growth and spread
      2. Ideology of American consumerism
        a. As core of freedom
        b. As measure of American superiority
      3. Key elements
        a. Television
          i. Spreading presence
          ii. Growing prominence as leisure activity
          iii. Themes of programming, advertising
        b. Automobile
          i. Place in "standard consumer package"
          ii. Role in economic boom
          iii. Impact on American landscape, travel habits
          iv. Emergence as symbol of freedom
    C. Female sphere
      1. Place in labor force
        a. Rising numbers
        b. Limited aims
      2. Ideal of male as breadwinner, woman as homemaker
      3. Affirmation of family ideal
        a. Younger marriage age
        b. Fewer divorces
        c. Baby boom
      4. Separate spheres as Cold War weapon
      5. Receding of feminism

     D. Exclusion of blacks; racial wall between city and suburbs
        1. Pervasiveness
        2. Sources and mechanisms
           a. Federal government
           b. Banks and developers
           c. Residents
        3. Resulting patterns
           a. Suburbs for whites
              i. Fading of ethnic divisions
             ii. Fear of black encroachment
           b. Urban ghettoes for blacks, Puerto Ricans
              i. Bleakness of conditions and opportunities
             ii. Barriers to escape
           c. Self-reinforcing dynamic of racial exclusion

III. Celebratory perspectives on postwar America
     A. "End of ideology"; liberal consensus
     B. "Judeo-Christian" heritage
        1. Themes
           a. Group pluralism
           b. Freedom of religion
        2. Underlying trends
           a. Fading of religious bigotry
           b. Secularization of American life
     C. "Free enterprise" as essential part of freedom
        1. Marketing of "free enterprise"
        2. Varieties of "free enterprise" outlooks
           a. Conservative wing
           b. Liberal wing
     D. "People's capitalism"
        1. Receptiveness to big business
        2. Heralding of classless society
     E. Two strains of conservative renewal
        1. Libertarians
           a. Ideas
              i. Individual autonomy
             ii. Limited government
            iii. Unregulated capitalism
           b. Special appeal among businessmen of South and West
           c. Leading voice: Milton Friedman
        2. New conservatives
           a. Ideas
              i. Free World vs. communism
             ii. Absolute truth vs. toleration of difference

        iii. Christian values vs. moral decay
        iv. Community and tradition vs. excessive individualism
        v. Government as agent of moral regulation
     b. Leading voices: Russell Kirk, Richard Weaver
   3. Central points of divergence: "free man" vs. "good man"
   4. Common targets during the Fifties
     a. Soviet Union
     b. "Big government"

IV. Eisenhower era
  A. Election of 1952
    1. Republican ticket
      a. Dwight D. Eisenhower
        i. Political appeal
        ii. Decision to run as Republican
        iii. Nomination
      b. Richard M. Nixon
        i. Political rise
        ii. Anticommunist style
        iii. Reputation for opportunism, dishonesty
        iv. Populist brand of free-market conservatism
    2. Nixon scandal
      a. "Checkers speech"
      b. Demonstration of television's significance
    3. Eisenhower victory over Adlai Stevenson (first of two)
  B. Eisenhower's domestic policy: Modern Republicanism
    1. Pro-business administration
    2. Fiscal and budgetary conservatism
    3. Retention, expansion of New Deal programs
    4. Avoidance of European-style nationalization
    5. Use of government to spur productivity, employment
      a. Key examples
        i. Interstate highway system
        ii. National Defense Education Act
      b. Motivations
        i. Cold War
        ii. Economic prosperity
  C. Labor-management "social contract"
    1. Preconditions
      a. Taming of organized labor; Taft-Hartley Act
      b. Consolidation of organized labor; merger of AFL-CIO
    2. Terms
    3. Outcome for working-class America
      a. Prosperity for union workers

        b. Mixed outcome for nonunion workers
           i. Indirect benefits
           ii. Marginalization
    4. Fraying of social contract; 1959 steel strike

D. Ebb and flow of U.S.-Soviet tensions
    1. Acquisition by each side of hydrogen bomb; subsequent nuclear arms race
    2. Doctrine of "massive retaliation"; "mutually assured destruction (MAD)"
        a. Announcement by John Foster Dulles
        b. Themes
        c. Characterization by critics as "brinksmanship"
        d. Legacy
           i. Sobering effects on superpowers
           ii. Climate of fear
    3. Eisenhower-Khrushchev thaw
        a. First steps
           i. Korean armistice
           ii. Death of Stalin; succession by Nikita Khrushchev
           iii. Geneva summit
           iv. Khrushchev denunciation of Stalin, call for "coexistence"
        b. Setback: Hungary crisis
           i. Soviet repression of uprising
           ii. Eisenhower refusal to intervene
        c. Resumption of thaw
           i. Weapons testing halt
           ii. Khrushchev visit
        d. Setback: U-2 spy plane

E. Cold War in Third World
    1. Emergence of Third World
        a. Origins of term
        b. Impulse toward nonalignment with Cold War superpowers
        c. Bandung Conference
    2. Decolonization
        a. Pace
           i. India, Pakistan
           ii. British Gold Coast (Ghana)
           iii. Subsequent spread of independence
        b. Cold War context
           i. U.S. fear of communist influence
           ii. Participation of communists, socialists in independence struggles
           iii. Third World aversion to Cold War alignment

3. Cold War as determinant of U.S. alliances, interventions
   a. Covert subversion of sovereign governments
      i. Guatemala
      ii. Iran
   b. Extension of containment to Middle East
      i. Suez crisis
      ii. Eisenhower Doctrine
      iii. Lebanon intervention
   c. Vietnam
      i. Postwar support for French colonialism
      ii. Defeat of French by Ho Chi Minh's nationalists
      iii. Geneva agreement for 1956 elections
      iv. U.S.-backed scuttling of elections
      v. Support for unpopular Ngo Dinh Diem regime
   d. Long-term legacies of interventions
      i. Guatemala
      ii. Iran
      iii. Vietnam
F. Mass society and its critics
   1. Leading voices
      a. Hans J. Morgenthau, "new accumulations" of corporate power
      b. C. Wright Mills, "power elite"
      c. David Riesman's *The Lonely Crowd*
      d. John Kenneth Galbraith's *The Affluent Society*
      e. William Whyte's *The Organization Man*
      f. Vance Packard's *The Hidden Persuaders*
   2. Limited impact on popular consciousness
G. Cultural rebels
   1. Youth
      a. Themes
         i. Alienation from middle-class norms
         ii. Sexual provocativeness; rock and roll
      b. Leading examples
         i. J. D. Salinger's *The Catcher in the Rye*
         ii. *Blackboard Jungle, Rebel Without a Cause*
         iii. Elvis Presley
      c. Mainstream reaction
         i. "Juvenile delinquency" panic
         ii. Codes of conduct
   2. *Playboy* sensibility
   3. Gay and lesbian subcultures

4. The Beats
   a. Themes
      i. Rejection of materialism, conformity, Cold War militarization
      ii. Embrace of spontaneity, immediate pleasure, sexual experimentation
   b. Key works
      i. Jack Kerouac's *On the Road*
      ii. Allen Ginsberg's *Howl*

V. Emergence of civil rights movement
   A. Preconditions
      1. World War II challenge to racial system
      2. Black migration North
      3. Postwar global developments
         a. Cold War
         b. Decolonization
   B. Segregation and inequality in 1950s America
      1. Breadth of black poverty, barriers to opportunity
      2. Breadth of segregation
         a. In South
         b. In North, West
   C. Legal assault on segregation
      1. Main actors
         a. League of United Latin American Citizens (LULAC)
         b. National Association for the Advancement of Colored People (NAACP)
            i. Leadership of Thurgood Marshall
            ii. Step-by-step strategy
      2. Key steps (pre-*Brown* case)
         a. LULAC: *Méndez v. Westminster* in California
         b. NAACP
            i. 1938 University of Missouri Law School case
            ii. 1950 University of Texas Law School case
      3. *Brown v. Board of Education*
         a. Background
         b. NAACP legal argument
            i. Direct challenge to separate but equal doctrine
            ii. Emphasis on stigmatization, subversion of black self-esteem
         c. Earl Warren's desegregation decision
         d. Import of decision
            i. Limitations
            ii. Broader significance and impact

D. Montgomery bus boycott
  1. Rosa Parks
     a. Activist past
     b. Arrest on bus
  2. Year-long black boycott of segregated buses
  3. Supreme Court ruling against segregation in public transportation
  4. Victory
  5. Significance
     a. Launching of nonviolent southern crusade for racial justice
     b. Achievement of attention and support around country, world
     c. Emergence of Martin Luther King Jr.
E. Language of freedom
  1. Pervasiveness in movement
  2. Range of meanings
F. Leadership of King
  1. Themes
     a. Fusing of meanings of freedom
     b. Merging of black cause and experience with those of nation
     c. Capacity to reach both blacks and whites
     d. Philosophies of nonviolence, civil disobedience, Christian love, forgiveness
     e. Connections between struggles of African-Americans and non-whites overseas
  2. Formation of Southern Christian Leadership Conference
G. Southern white intransigence; "massive resistance"
  1. Contributing factor: lack of federal backing
     a. Supreme Court's "all deliberate speed" ruling
     b. Eisenhower's ambivalence, reluctance to act
  2. Forms
     a. Southern Manifesto
     b. Anti-desegregation laws
     c. Banning of NAACP
     d. Revival of Confederate flag
H. Little Rock crisis
  1. Governor Orville Faubus's obstruction of court-ordered integration
  2. Eisenhower's deployment of federal troops

VI. Toward the Sixties
A. Election of 1960
  1. Republican nominee: Nixon
  2. Democratic nominee: John F. Kennedy
     a. Background

      b. Choice of Lyndon B. Johnson as running mate
      c. Catholic issue
      d. Cold War outlook
      e. "Missile gap" claim
      f. Glamorous style
    3. Nixon-Kennedy debate
    4. Kennedy victory
  B. Eisenhower's farewell address; "military-industrial complex"
  C. Social problems on horizon

CHRONOLOGY

1946   *Méndez v. Westminster* in California

1948   Richard Weaver publishes *Ideas Have Consequences*

1949   Housing Act

1950   David Riesman publishes *The Lonely Crowd*

1951   J. D. Salinger publishes *The Catcher in the Rye*

1952   Richard Nixon's "Checkers speech"
       Dwight Eisenhower defeats Adlai Stevenson in presidential election
       United States acquires hydrogen bomb

1953   Soviet Union acquires hydrogen bomb
       John Foster Dulles announces "massive retaliation" doctrine
       Korean armistice
       Death of Stalin; succession by Nikita Khrushchev
       CIA deposes Iranian government of Mohammed Mossadegh, installs
         Shah
       Playboy begins publication
       Eisenhower appoints Earl Warren Chief Justice

1954   CIA deposes Guatemalan government of Jacobo Arbenz Guzmán
       France evacuates from Vietnam; recognizes Vietnamese
         independence
       Brown v. Board of Education

1955   Will Herberg publishes *Protestant-Catholic-Jew*
       AFL-CIO merger
       Geneva summit meeting between Eisenhower and Khrushchev
       Bandung Conference
       Release of *Blackboard Jungle, Rebel Without a Cause*
       Allen Ginsberg publishes *Howl*
       Arrest of Rosa Parks sparks Montgomery bus boycott

1956	Interstate Highway Act

1956   Interstate Highway Act
Khrushchev denunciation of Stalin, call for "peaceful coexistence"
Soviet invasion of Hungary
Eisenhower wins reelection over Stevenson
Suez crisis
William Whyte publishes *The Organization Man*
Southern Manifesto
Supreme Court strikes down segregation in public transportation
Autherine Lucy barred from attending University of Alabama

1957   Launching of *Sputnik*
Announcement of Eisenhower Doctrine
Jack Kerouac publishes *On the Road*
Founding of Southern Christian Leadership Conference
Civil Rights Act
Little Rock desegregation crisis begins

1958   National Defense Education Act
U.S.-Soviet suspension of weapons tests
U.S. intervention in Lebanon
John Kenneth Galbraith publishes *The Affluent Society*

1959   Nixon-Khrushchev "kitchen debate"
Khrushchev visits United States
Steel strike

1960   U-2 incident
Nixon-Kennedy debates
John F. Kennedy defeats Richard Nixon in presidential election

1961   Eisenhower's Farewell Address

1962   Milton Friedman publishes *Capitalism and Freedom*

KEY TERMS

television: The 1950s witnessed the rapid rise of television as an important part of American social and cultural life. During World War II the nation had six broadcasting stations, with only about 10,000 families owning television sets. By 1948 about 1 million sets were in use (many located in bars where viewers enjoyed sports programming), receiving broadcasts from 48 stations. By 1952, 15.3 million households had TV sets, a number that would more than double to 32 million households just three years later. By 1960, almost half of Americans polled said that watching television was their favorite leisure activity.

women at work: The increase in the number of working women in the 1950s included a dramatic rise in the number of married women in the workforce. In 1940, 36 percent of married women held jobs outside the home; in 1960, that number had risen to 60 percent. The number of double-income households increased by 330 percent between 1940 and 1960. Additional purchasing power allowed many families to become firmly entrenched in middle-class values. Polls revealed that households with working wives spent more on luxuries such as gifts, recreation, and eating out.

housing discrimination: In 1917, the United States Supreme Court struck down a city law that required racial segregation in housing, declaring it to be a violation of the Civil Rights Act of 1866 and the Fourteenth Amendment. Thereafter, many homeowners engaged in racial covenants, or agreements not to sell their houses to African-Americans. In 1948, the court heard a case involving racial covenants. J. D. Shelley, an African-American, had purchased land in St. Louis, unaware that the land was covered by a racial covenant agreed to in 1911. A nearby resident, Louis Kraemer, asked the court to declare the land sale null and void. After a court did so, Shelley appealed the ruling. In its 1948 ruling in *Shelley v. Kraemer,* the U.S. Supreme Court did not prohibit racial covenants, which it considered private agreements. Instead, it declared that the courts could not enforce such covenants because the process of enforcement violated the Fourteenth Amendment.

Sputnik: On October 4, 1957, the Soviet Union successfully launched a satellite into Earth orbit. Called *Sputnik,* Russian for "Fellow Traveler," the small device—it weighed only 184 pounds—shocked American leaders and the general public. (Horror author Stephen King later recalled a theater manager interrupting a science fiction movie to inform the audience about *Sputnik,* an announcement that shocked the audience into silence.) American confidence was further eroded when an American satellite launch that December exploded on the launch pad. *Sputnik* had its beneficial aspects—it prompted federal support for education in the sciences—but it also contributed to a sense of anxiety among the American people that was a prominent feature of Cold War life.

The U-2 incident: The United States began high-altitude reconnaissance missions over Soviet territory in 1956. The U-2 could fly at 80,000 feet, well above the range of Soviet anti-aircraft missiles. However, on May 1, 1960, the Soviets shot down a U-2 piloted by Francis Gary Powers, who worked for the Central Intelligence Agency. Powers had been unable to arm the aircraft's self-destruct mechanism, and the Soviets recovered parts of the U-2 as well as capturing Powers. After Khrushchev made the incident public (but did not reveal that he had captured Powers), President Eisenhower claimed that the plane was collecting weather data and had gone off course. Khrushchev then produced Powers, catching the president in a lie. Rather than condemn Eisenhower, most

Americans supported the spying program. Powers was released in a prisoner exchange in 1962; he died in a commercial helicopter accident in 1977.

The Iranian coup: Lacking the technology necessary to exploit oil resources, many Middle Eastern nations entered into contracts with western oil companies. One such company, the British-owned Anglo-Iranian Oil Company (AIOC) made tremendous profits from its activities in Iran. By the 1940s, AIOC paid more in taxes to the British government than it did in royalties to the government of Iran. This inequity fueled resentment that Mohammed Mossadegh used to become prime minister of Iran in 1951. Upon taking office, Mossadegh nationalized the Iranian oil industry, a move that earned him the wrath of Great Britain and its ally, the United States. American officials were especially alarmed when Mossadegh developed ties with the communist party in Iran. With assistance from the British, the United States orchestrated a coup to remove Mossadegh from power. The 1953 coup remains a source of tension between Iran and the United States in the twenty-first century.

rock and roll music: The popularity of rock 'n' roll music in the 1950s reflected several trends in American life. The music had its roots in black rhythm and blues, which received little airplay on southern radio stations but was familiar to people throughout the region. Its popularity with white southerners reflected the influence of African-American culture on mainstream society. In addition, rock 'n' roll revealed the growing economic power of American teenagers, a group that in the past had little spending money. The economic growth of the decade allowed many teens to work, not to support their families but to earn money to buy consumer goods such as rock 'n' roll records. Finally, rock 'n' roll illustrated the growing influence of the mass media on American life as the widespread availability of radios and television sets helped to create a national mass culture.

League of United Latin American Citizens (LULAC): Mexican-Americans faced racial discrimination similar to that experienced by African-Americans. In an effort to end segregation and secure better education for their children, a number of small Mexican-American organizations in Texas banded together to form the League of United Latin American Citizens (LULAC) in 1929. Because the group favored the assimilation of Mexican-Americans into the larger society, it adopted English as its official language. Following the lead of the National Association for the Advancement of Colored People, LULAC used the courts to achieve its goals.

Sweatt v. Painter: Heman Sweatt, an African-American mailman in Houston, Texas, first applied for admission to the University of Texas School of Law in 1946. Denied admission on the basis of race, Sweatt sued on the grounds that the state of Texas, which did not have a law school for black students, violated his Fourteenth Amendment rights. After Texas hastily opened a black law school in the basement of a building in Austin, Texas, a court dismissed Sweatt's suit. With the assistance of lawyers from the National Association for the Advancement of Colored People, Sweatt appealed his case. In its June 1950 ruling, the U.S. Supreme Court ordered the School of Law to admit Sweatt as a student. The court determined that the black law school did not meet the "separate but equal" standard set forth in the 1896 case of *Plessy v. Ferguson*. The ruling did not overturn *Plessy,* but it signaled that the courts would require states to meet the long-ignored standard of equality. Shrewd observers realized that the *Sweatt* ruling marked the beginning of the end of segregation in higher education because southern states could not afford the expense of maintaining a separate, quality educational system for blacks. As for Sweatt, persistent health problems stemming from the stress of his case led him to withdraw from law school.

OBJECTIVE QUESTIONS

Multiple Choice

1. A celebratory slogan for 1950s America was:
   A. "People's capitalism."
   B. "Classless society."
   C. "End of ideology."
   D. all of the above

2. A leading voice of the Beats was:
   A. Orville Faubus.
   B. William Levitt.
   C. Allen Ginsberg.
   D. Adlai Stevenson.

3. Which of the following series of events is listed in proper sequence?
   A. start of Montgomery bus boycott; Southern Manifesto; *Brown v. Board of Education;* appointment of Earl Warren as Chief Justice
   B. Nixon's "Checkers speech"; Eisenhower's Farewell Address; Nixon-Kennedy debates; Nixon-Khrushchev "kitchen debate"
   C. National Defense Education Act; launching of *Sputnik;* announcement of "massive retaliation" doctrine; end of Korean War
   D. Geneva summit between Eisenhower and Khrushchev; Soviet invasion of Hungary; Khrushchev visit to United States; U-2 incident

4. Which of the following was *not* a significant trend in 1950s America?
   A. the growing association of the automobile with individual freedom
   B. the emergence of TV as the nation's prevalent form of entertainment
   C. a surge of student radicalism on college campuses
   D. the rise of a youth culture that challenged the bland conformism of postwar America

5. Which of the following was *not* a key cause of the economic prosperity of the Fifties?
   A. large income tax reductions
   B. housing construction in the expanding suburbs
   C. Cold War-related military production
   D. the building of the interstate highway system

6. Which of the following was *not* a prominent feature of suburban married life during the Fifties?
   A. a rise in birth rates
   B. a decline in divorce rates
   C. a growing tendency of husbands and wives to share the roles of breadwinner and homemaker
   D. a growing desire among husbands and wives to find fulfillment through the shared enjoyment of material comforts, recreation, and sexual relations

7. Which of the following was *not* a key premise of American foreign policy during the Eisenhower years?
   A. Any Soviet attack on one of our allies will result in a nuclear assault on the Soviet Union.
   B. The United States will always respect the sovereignty of foreign democracies—even those whose policies we oppose.
   C. We must be prepared to negotiate with the Soviet Union.
   D. The United States will intervene in the Middle East—militarily, if necessary—to ward off the threats of communism or Arab nationalism in the region.

8. Which of the following was *not* a feature of Martin Luther King Jr.'s philosophy?
   A. Black Americans must not try for full racial equality too quickly; before they achieve that, they must first prove their worthiness to all America.
   B. Blacks and whites must work together to combat segregation.
   C. The civil rights movement should always fight racial injustice on a nonviolent basis.
   D. The civil rights movement is a crusade not merely to improve the lot of blacks, but, more broadly, to redeem the soul of America.

9. In 1953, Dwight Eisenhower brought to the presidency all of the following experiences, except:
   A. leading military general during World War II
   B. president of Columbia University
   C. supreme commander of NATO forces in Europe
   D. chief executive officer of the General Electric Corporation

10. In the 1950s, Richard Nixon pioneered efforts to transform the Republican Party's image:
   A. from defender of business to champion of the "forgotten man" for whom heavy taxation had become a burden.
   B. from defender of the small farmer to champion of the military-industrial complex.
   C. from defender of the military-industrial complex to champion of the small farmer.
   D. from defender of freedom-loving peoples and anticommunists to proponents of detente.

11. What did President Eisenhower call his domestic agenda, that embraced a "mixed economy" and in which the government played a major role in planning economic activity, and by which Eisenhower consolidated and legitimized the New Deal?
   A. the "New" New Deal
   B. Modern Republicanism
   C. the Great Society
   D. the New Frontier

12. The National Defense Education Act, which for the first time offered direct federal funding for higher education, was passed into law by Congress in 1957 in response to:
   A. the French defeat by Vietnamese forces at Dien Bien Phu.
   B. the Soviet launch of the first artificial Earth satellite, *Sputnik.*
   C. Soviet Premier Nikita Khrushchev's visit to the United States.
   D. inner city riots, and the rise of feminist activist endeavors across the Midwest.

13. In 1955, what percentage of non-agricultural workers were unionized?
   A. 10 percent
   B. 25 percent
   C. 35 percent
   D. 57 percent

14. Which was *not* part of the new "social contract" between organized labor and management in leading industries during the 1950s?
   A. Unions agreed to leave decisions regarding capital investment and plant location in management's hands.
   B. Employers ceased trying to eliminate existing unions.
   C. Employers granted benefits such as private pension plans, health insurance, and automatic cost-of-living pay adjustments to employees.
   D. Unions sponsored "wildcat" strikes in an effort to discipline management.

15. The 1954 update to the doctrine of containment, announced by Secretary of State John Foster Dulles, that declared a Soviet attack on any American ally would be countered by a nuclear attack on the Soviet Union, was called "brinksmanship" by its critics and this by supporters:
    A. SALT I
    B. Massive Retaliation
    C. Isolationism
    D. Nuclear Imperialism

16. The wave of decolonization that began when India and Pakistan achieved independence in 1947, and by which, in the decades following World War II, Europe's centuries-old empires collapsed, witnessed the newly created Third World nations:
    A. align with the Soviet Union.
    B. align with the United States.
    C. resist alignment with either major power bloc.
    D. align with Great Britain.

17. In 1957, the Eisenhower Doctrine:
    A. expanded the Marshall Plan to Southeast Asia.
    B. asserted American authority in Vietnam in the wake of the French defeat at Dien Bien Phu.
    C. pledged the United States to defend Middle Eastern governments threatened by communism or Arab nationalism.
    D. declared that the military-industrial complex must be reined in.

18. Eric Foner writes: "the either-or mentality of the Cold War obscured the extent to which the United States itself fell short of the ideal of freedom." In this context, to what does "the either-or mentality" refer?
    A. the notion that either you were for segregation, or against it
    B. the notion that, in a polarized world, you were either for the United States or for the Soviet Union
    C. the notion that you were either for the Democratic Party or for the Republican Party
    D. the notion that you were either for women's rights or against them

19. Which was *not* one of the elements of "the power elite"—the interlocking directorate that dominated government and society in the 1950s—in the view of sociologist C. Wright Mills?
    A. corporate leaders
    B. politicians
    C. labor leaders
    D. military men

20. The name for the small group of poets and writers who railed against
    mainstream culture, and that included Jack Kerouac and Allen Ginsberg
    was:
    A. Hippies.
    B. Yippies.
    C. Beats.
    D. Beatles.

21. During the 1950s, the mass movement for civil rights found principal
    support among:
    A. union leaders.
    B. corporate leaders.
    C. Democratic and Republican political leaders.
    D. the Southern black church.

22. The principal organization in the Southwest—the equivalent of the
    NAACP—that challenged restrictions on housing and employment, as well
    as the segregation of Latino students was named:
    A. the League of United Latin American Citizens (LULAC).
    B. the American Civil Liberties Union (ACLU).
    C. the National Urban League (NUL).
    D. the Congress on Racial Equality (CORE).

23. What was the landmark United States Supreme Court case decided on
    May 17, 1954, in which the Warren Court unanimously asserted that
    segregation in public education violated the equal protection of the laws
    guaranteed by the Fourteenth Amendment?
    A. *Menendez v. Westminster*
    B. *Loving v. Virginia*
    C. *Plessy v. Ferguson*
    D. *Brown v. Board of Education*

24. In the aftermath of Rosa Parks's arrest for refusing to give her bus seat to a
    white rider, a year-long bus boycott took place in what city?
    A. Memphis, Tennessee
    B. Birmingham, Alabama
    C. Montgomery, Alabama
    D. Little Rock, Arkansas

25. Which does *not* describe Rosa Parks in the years prior to her December 1,
    1955 arrest?
    A. She was a participant in meetings protesting the conviction of the
       Scottsboro Boys.
    B. She was for many years a secretary in her local NAACP chapter.

    C. She had attended a training session for political activists at the Highlander School in Tennessee.

    D. She was a housewife, with no previous experience as a political activist.

26. Which of the following did *not* inform Martin Luther King Jr.'s 1950s leadership of the civil rights movement?

    A. the writings of civil disobedience of Henry David Thoreau and Mahatma Gandhi

    B. the nonviolent protests of the Congress of Racial Equality

    C. a philosophy of struggle in which hate must be met with Christian love, and violence with peaceful demands for change

    D. the writings of Malcolm X, particularly his autobiography

27. What was the coalition of black ministers and civil rights activists formed in 1955 that pressed for desegregation and in whose organizing Martin Luther King Jr. took the lead?

    A. the Congress on Racial Equality

    B. the NAACP

    C. the Southern Christian Leadership Conference

    D. the Interfaith Council of Churches

True or False

1. Although it was a nationwide phenomenon, 1950s suburbanization gathered its greatest momentum in the West.

2. During the 1950s, material consumption came more and more to eclipse economic independence and democratic engagement as the hallmarks of American freedom.

3. The suburban explosion of the Fifties did much to diminish racial divisions in America.

4. Although Americans in the Fifties grew more intensely religious, fewer than ever were affiliated with religious institutions.

5. Richard Nixon's rise in politics was fueled in part by his ability to make free-market conservatism appealing to ordinary people.

6. Dwight Eisenhower entered the presidency determined to dismantle the New Deal.

7. Cultural dissent was more conspicuous than political dissent during the 1950s.

8. The *Brown* decision encouraged an awakening of civil rights protest—*and* segregationist protest—in the South.

9. World War II was followed in the United States by what has been called "a golden age" of capitalism; between 1946 and 1960, the nation's gross national product more than doubled.

10. For all of America's successes, by 1960 more than one in five Americans lived in poverty.

11. In the post-World War II United States, Americans' daily lives were transformed by the spread of televisions, air conditioning, dishwashers, long-distance telephone calls, and jet travel.

12. In the two decades following World War II, services—which had generally been enjoyed only by the rich or solidly middle-class in the years before the war—including central heating, indoor plumbing, and electricity now became features of common life.

13. In 1956, for the first time in American history, white-collar workers outnumbered blue-collar factory and manual laborers.

14. During the 1950s, the farm population rose from 15 million to 23 million, while agricultural production declined by 25 percent.

15. In the 1950s the number of houses in the United States doubled; most were built in the suburbs.

16. New York became the most prominent symbol of the postwar suburban boom; one fifth of the population growth of the 1950s occurred there.

17. In the consumer culture of the 1950s, the measure of freedom became the ability to gratify market desires.

18. By 1960, almost 90 percent of American families owned television sets, average daily television viewing time was five hours, and television had proven itself the most effective advertising medium ever invented.

19. In many ways, the economy and culture of the 1950s was dominated by the automobile.

20. In 1960, women earned, on average, 60 percent of the income of men.

21. During the 1950s, prominent psychologists insisted that women who were unhappy as housewives suffered from a failure to accept the "maternal instinct."

22. The economic abundance of the 1950s was shared equally by white and black Americans.

23. As part of the expansive and dynamic growth of the American economy, in the twenty years after 1950, about 7 million white Americans left cities for the suburbs, nearly 3 million blacks moved from South to North, and half a million Puerto Ricans moved to the mainland.

24. In the decades following World War II, pluralism reigned supreme, and the free exercise of religion was yet another way of differentiating the American way of life from that of life under communism.

25. Government policies and expenditures played a crucial role in the postwar economic boom.

26. By the mid-1960s, 25 million Americans owned shares of stock.

27. As president, Eisenhower sought to roll back the New Deal, abolish social security and unemployment insurance, and eliminate labor laws and farm programs.

28. It is a myth that children in the 1950s and 1960s were trained to hide under their desks in the event of an atomic attack.

29. In the 1950s, the National Security Council advised President Eisenhower to use nuclear weapons in Vietnam.

30. One strand of social analysis in the 1950s asserted that Americans were psychologically and culturally discontent, lonely and anxious, and yearned not so much for freedom, but for stability and authority.

31. One strand of social analysis in the 1950s criticized the monotony of modern work, the emptiness of suburban life, and the pervasive influence of advertising.

32. During the 1950s, gay men and lesbians increasingly created their own subcultures in major cities.

33. President Eisenhower hailed the Supreme Court decision in *Brown v. Board of Education* as a positive move toward a more equal and just America; when a federal court ordered that Autherine Lucy be admitted to the University of Alabama in 1956, Eisenhower authorized use of federal troops in her support.

ESSAY QUESTIONS

1. Identify three factors that helped bring about and sustain the economic expansion of the Fifties, and describe how each did so.

2. "The America of the 1950s resembled the America of the 1920s—culturally, economically, and politically." In what ways do you find this comparison persuasive? In what ways do the contrasts between the two decades seem greater than the similarities?

3. "The status of suburban women and the status of blacks in 1950s America were essentially the same—that of second-class citizens, denied the full

range of opportunities available to white men." In what ways do you find this comparison persuasive? In what ways do the contrasts between the positions of the two groups seem greater than the similarities?

4. Compare the policies (domestic and foreign) of Republican President Eisenhower with those of his Democratic predecessor Harry Truman. What stand out as the key continuities between the agendas of the two administrations? What stand out as the key differences?

5. On what grounds did the Supreme Court overturn segregation in the *Brown v. Board of Education* decision? (You might compare the court's reasoning with that of its 1896 *Plessy v. Ferguson* decision, which upheld segregation.) In what various ways did Americans respond to the *Brown* decision?

6. Imagine a chance meeting, in 1960, among the following characters:

   - a civil rights activist
   - a southern segregationist
   - an Eisenhower Republican
   - a representative of the Advertising Council
   - a union leader
   - a follower of the Beats
   - an intellectual critic of contemporary society
   - an advocate of the "women's sphere"
   - an opponent of the "women's sphere"

   With remarkable openness, they reflect on the various trends of American society over the past decade, and how they have experienced those trends. In the process, each offers a glimpse of his or her conception of American freedom. Incorporating at least *four* of the above characters, transcribe this conversation.

7. Describe the consumer culture of the 1950s and reflect on the ways it shaped Americans' conception of freedom.

8. Write an essay detailing the dynamic and expansive growth of the 1950s American economy; include discussion of advances in science and technology, growth in industrial and service sectors of the economy, and the impact this economic growth had on American culture and society.

9. Write an essay on U.S. foreign policy toward the Soviet Union during the 1950s. Include in your essay discussion of "mass retaliation," "brinkmanship," "mutual assured destruction," and President Eisenhower's and Nikita Khrushchev's views.

10. Write an essay on the history of the civil rights movement of the 1950s; include in your essay discussion of white race prejudice, legal precedent and

legal challenges, as well as the broader-ranging variety of efforts on the part of the African-American community and its white allies to end segregation.

11. While many Americans consider the 1950s a "golden age" of prosperity and freedom, among some intellectuals, the "mass society" had its critics. Write an essay describing the variety of cultural criticisms promoted by the Beats, C. Wright Mills, David Reisman, John Kenneth Galbraith, and others.

SOURCES FOR FURTHER RESEARCH

Books

GENERAL OVERVIEWS

Halberstam, David, *The Fifties* (1993)
Patterson, James T., *Grand Expectations: The United States, 1945–1974* (1996)

PARTICULAR ASPECTS

Altschuler, Glenn C., All *Shook Up: How Rock 'n' Roll Changed America* (2003)
Baxandall, Roslyn Fraad, and Elizabeth Ewen, *Picture Windows: How the Suburbs Changed America* (2000)
Belgrad, Daniel, *The Culture of Spontaneity: Improvisation and the Arts in Postwar America* (1998)
Branch, Taylor, *Parting the Waters: America in the King Years, 1954–1963* (1988)
Cohen, Lizabeth, *A Consumer's Republic: The Politics of Mass Consumption in Postwar America* (2003)
De Grazia, Victoria, *Irresistible Empire: America's Advance through Twentieth-Century Europe* (2005)
Engelhardt, Tom, *The Hearts of Men: American Dreams and the Flight from Commitment* (1998)
Fernlund, Kevin J., ed., *The Cold War American West, 1945–1989* (1998)
Fones-Wolf, Elizabeth A., *Selling Free Enterprise: The Business Assault on Labor and Liberalism, 1945–1960* (1994)
Freeman, Joshua B., *Working-Class New York: Life and Labor Since World War II* (2000)
Hirsch, Arnold R., *Making the Second Ghetto: Race and Housing in Chicago, 1940–1960* (1983)
Jackson, Kenneth T., *Crabgrass Frontier: The Suburbanization of the United States* (1985)

Jacobs, Meg., *Pocketbook Politics: Economic Citizenship in Twentieth-Century America* (2005)

Klarman, Michael J., *From Jim Crow to Civil Rights: The Supreme Court and the Struggle for Racial Equality* (2004)

LaFeber, Walter, *America, Russia, and the Cold War, 1945–1992* (1993)

Lipsitz, George, *Class and Culture in Cold War America* (1981)

May, Elaine T., *Homeward Bound: American Families in the Cold War Era* (1988)

May, Lary, ed., *Recasting America: Culture and Politics in the Age of the Cold War* (1989)

Nicolaides, Becky M., *My Blue Heaven: Life and Politics in the Working-Class Suburbs of Los Angeles, 1920–1965* (2002)

Pells, Richard, *The Liberal Mind in a Conservative Age: American Intellectuals in the 1940s and 1950s* (1984)

Self, Robert O., *American Babylon: Race and the Struggle for Postwar Oakland* (2003)

Tushnet, Mark, *Making Civil Rights Law: Thurgood Marshall and the Supreme Court, 1936–1961* (1994)

Westad, Odd Arne, *The Global Cold War* (2005)

Videos

The Atomic Cafe (86 minutes, First Run Features, 1993)

Building the American Dream (60 minutes, Cinema Guild, 1994)

Citizen King (120 minutes, PBS Video, 2004)

Cold War (20 hours, PBS Video, 1998)

David Halberstam's The Fifties (390 minutes, A&E Home Video, 1997)

Eyes on the Prize (14 hours, PBS Home Video, 1986)

Eisenhower (142 minutes, PBS Video, 1993)

The Great Debates: John F. Kennedy vs. Richard M. Nixon (60 minutes, MPI Home Video, 1989)

Hoxie: The First Stand (56 minutes, Cinema Guild, 2003)

Kinsey (90 minutes, PBS Video, 2005)

The Murder of Emmett Till (60 minutes, PBS Video, 2003)

The Quiz Show Scandal (58 minutes, PBS Video, 1991)

Ralph Ellison: An American Journey (87 minutes, California Newsreel, 2001)

Simple Justice (132 minutes, PBS Video, 1993)

Tupperware! (58 minutes, PBS Video, 2003)

When America Was Rocked (60 minutes, History Channel, A&E Home Video, 2006)

Web Resources

Brown v. Board of Education, University of Michigan Library Digital Archive
http://www.lib.umich.edu/exhibits/brownarchive/

Central High Crisis: Little Rock, 1957, Little Rock Newspapers, Inc.
http://www.ardemgaz.com/prev/central/

Cold War, Cable News Network, Inc.
http://www.cnn.com/SPECIALS/cold.war/

Levittown: Documents of an Ideal American Suburb, Peter Bacon Hales,
University of Illinois at Chicago
http://tigger.uic.edu/%7Epbhales/Levittown.html

The Literature & Culture of the American 1950s, Alan Filreis, University of
Pennsylvania
http://www.english.upenn.edu/%7eafilreis/50s/home.html

Separate Is Not Equal: *Brown v. Board of Education,* National Museum of
American History
http://americanhistory.si.edu/brown/

1952–1954, Guatemala, U.S. Department of State
http://www.state.gov/r/pa/ho/frus/ike/guat/

ANSWERS TO OBJECTIVE QUESTIONS

Multiple Choice

1-D, 2-C, 3-D, 4-C, 5-A, 6-C, 7-B, 8-A, 9-D, 10-A, 11-B, 12-B, 13-C, 14-D,
15-B, 16-C, 17-C, 18-B, 19-C, 20-C, 21-D, 22-A, 23-D, 24-C, 25-D, 26-D,
27-C

True or False

1-T, 2-T, 3-F, 4-F, 5-T, 6-F, 7-T, 8-T, 9-T, 10-T, 11-T, 12-T, 13-T, 14-F, 15-T,
16-F, 17-T, 18-T, 19-T, 20-T, 21-T, 22-F, 23-T, 24-T, 25-T, 26-T, 27-F, 28-F,
29-T, 30-T, 31-T, 32-T, 33-F

CHAPTER 25

The Sixties, 1960–1968

CHAPTER OBJECTIVES

- What made the Sixties such a tumultuous period in American history?
- How did the aims, attitudes, and strategies of the black freedom movement evolve over the course of the Sixties?
- What were the key factors behind the passage of the Civil Rights Act of 1964 and the Voting Rights Act of 1965, and how close did these measures come to fulfilling the mission of the civil rights movement?
- What was the Great Society, and how did it change America?
- What led the United States to intervene militarily in Vietnam, and how did Americans debate the merits of the war?
- What were the defining features of the New Left and of the "counterculture"?
- What sparked the reemergence of feminism in the late Sixties?
- What new lines of social protest and dissent arose during the late Sixties? What were the key features of the "rights revolution"?
- What gave rise to the conservative "backlash" of the 1960s?

CHAPTER OUTLINE

   I. Escalation of civil rights protest
      A. High points
          1. Sit-in campaigns
              a. Origins at Greensboro
              b. Spread across South
          2. Founding of Student Non-Violent Coordinating Committee (SNCC)

    3. Freedom Rides
       a. Congress of Racial Equality (CORE)
       b. Purpose
       c. Experience
       d. Outcome: desegregation of interstate bus travel
    4. Birmingham desegregation campaign
       a. Climax of region-wide demonstrations
       b. Leadership of Martin Luther King Jr.
          i. *Letter from Birmingham Jail*
          ii. Deployment of black school children
       c. Brutal response of "Bull" Connor; widespread revulsion over
       d. Impact on public opinion
          i. Growing sympathy for civil rights
          ii. Presidential endorsement of movement
       e. Outcome: adoption of desegregation plan
  B. Themes and characteristics
    1. Growing involvement of college students, youth
    2. Vision of empowerment of ordinary blacks
    3. Commitment to nonviolent resistance
    4. Multiplicity of organizations, settings, and strategies
  C. Escalation of violent response
    1. Perpetrators
       a. Ordinary citizens
       b. Local and state officials
    2. Targets, episodes
       a. Firebombing, beatings of Freedom Riders
       b. Mob violence against desegregation of University of
          Mississippi
       c. Use of fire hoses, dogs, beatings against Birmingham
          protesters
       d. Assassination of Medgar Evers
       e. Deadly bombing of Birmingham church
  D. March on Washington
    1. Magnitude
    2. As peak of nonviolent civil rights coalition
    3. Breadth of demands
    4. King's "I Have a Dream" speech
    5. Glimpses of movement's limitations and fault lines
       a. All-male roster of speakers
       b. Toning down of John Lewis's speech

II. The Kennedy presidency
  A. John F. Kennedy (JFK)
    1. Image of glamour, dynamism

        2. Inaugural themes

           a. ". . . new generation . . ."

           b. ". . . pay any price . . ."

           c. ". . . do for your country."

  B. JFK and the world

        1. New Cold War initiatives

           a. Peace Corps

           b. Space race; call for moon landing

           c. Alliance for Progress

        2. Bay of Pigs fiasco

        3. Berlin crisis; construction of Berlin Wall

        4. Cuban missile crisis

           a. Narrative

               i. Discovery of Soviet missiles in Cuba

              ii. U.S. "quarantine" of Cuba

             iii. Soviet withdrawal of missiles

           b. Significance and aftermath

               i. Imminence of nuclear war

              ii. Sobering effect on JFK; American University speech

             iii. Nuclear test ban treaty

  C. JFK and civil rights

        1. Initial disengagement

        2. Growing support

  D. Assassination of JFK

        1. Shock to nation

        2. Succession of Lyndon B. Johnson (LBJ) to presidency

III. The Johnson presidency

  A. LBJ

        1. Personal background

        2. New Deal outlook

  B. Civil rights under LBJ

        1. Civil Rights Act

           a. Support from LBJ

           b. Provisions

        2. Voter registration drive in Mississippi: Freedom Summer

           a. Concerted civil rights initiative

           b. Influx of white college students

           c. Violent reception

               i. Bombings, beatings

              ii. Murder of three activists

             iii. Widespread revulsion over

        3. Mississippi Freedom Democratic Party

           a. Crusade for representation at Democratic convention

        b. Fannie Lou Hamer
        c. Bitterness over Democrats' response
    4. Voting Rights Act
        a. Background
            i. Selma-to-Montgomery march
           ii. LBJ address to Congress
        b. Provisions
    5. Twenty-Fourth Amendment
    6. Immigration reform: Hart-Cellar Act
        a. Links to civil rights reform
        b. Provisions
        c. Long-term consequences
C. 1964 election
    1. Right-wing views of Republican Barry Goldwater
    2. Emergence of Sixties conservatism
        a. Young Americans for Freedom
            i. Sharon Statement
           ii. Ideas
          iii. Prominence in Barry Goldwater's 1964 campaign
        b. New conservative constituencies
            i. Expanding suburbs of southern California, Southwest
           ii. Sun Belt entrepreneurs
          iii. Deep South whites
        c. Racial overtones of conservative appeal
    3. LBJ's landslide reelection victory
    4. Seeds of conservative resurgence
D. Great Society
    1. Goals and philosophies
        a. Government action to promote general welfare
        b. Fulfillment and expansion of New Deal agenda
        c. Eradication of poverty
        d. Broadening of opportunity
        e. Lessening of inequality
        f. New conception of freedom
    2. Key measures
        a. Medicaid and Medicare
        b. Increased funding for education, urban development
        c. Increased funding for the arts, humanities, public broadcasting
    3. War on Poverty
        a. Outlook
            i. Influence of Michael Harrington's *The Other America*
           ii. Emphasis on fostering skills, work habits
          iii. De-emphasis on direct aid, structural remedies
          iv. Input of poor into local programs

        b. Key measures
           i. Food stamps
           ii. Office of Economic Opportunity initiatives
    4. Achievements
        a. Affirmation of social citizenship
        b. Substantial reduction of poverty
    5. Limitations
        a. Inadequate funding
        b. Long-term persistence of poverty, inequality

IV. Evolution of black movement
  A. Emerging challenges to civil rights movement
    1. Persistence of racial inequality and injustice, North and South
    2. Diverging perspectives of whites and blacks on racial issues
    3. Ghetto uprisings around nation
        a. Leading episodes: Harlem, Watts, Newark, Detroit
        b. Kerner Report
  B. Growing attention to economic issues
    1. King's "Bill of Rights for the Disadvantaged"
    2. A. Philip Randolph and Bayard Rustin's Freedom Budget
    3. King's Chicago Freedom Movement
        a. Demands
        b. Mayor Richard J. Daley's political machine
        c. Ineffectiveness of mass protest tactics
        d. Radicalization of King
  C. Malcolm X
    1. Background
    2. Black Muslims
    3. Message
        a. Black self-determination
        b. Rejection of integration, nonviolence
    4. Assassination
    5. Legacy
        a. Lack of consistent ideology or coherent movement
        b. Enduring appeal of call for black self-reliance
  D. Black Power
    1. Introduction by Stokely Carmichael
    2. Imprecision and multiplicity of meanings
    3. Resonance among militant youth
    4. Place in wider spirit of self-assertion; "black is beautiful"
    5. Militant directions of SNCC, CORE
    6. Black Panther Party
        a. Emergence
        b. Demands and programs

      c. Demise
         i. Internal divisions
        ii. Assault by government

V. Birth of New Left
    A. Arena: college campuses
    B. Following: white middle-class youth
    C. Spirit and ideology
      1. Departure from Old Left and New Deal liberal models
      2. Aspects of postwar society brought under challenge
        a. Personal alienation
        b. Social and political conformity
        c. Bureaucratization
        d. Corporate, Cold War outlook of American institutions
        e. Material acquisitiveness
        f. Social and economic inequality
        g. Gulfs between national values and realities
      3. Visions and inspirations
        a. "Authenticity"
        b. "Participatory democracy"
        c. Black freedom struggle
    D. Key moments
      1. Influential social critiques
        a. James Baldwin's *The Fire Next Time*
        b. Rachel Carson's *Silent Spring*
        c. Michael Harrington's *The Other America*
        d. Jane Jacobs's *The Death and Life of Great American Cities*
      2. Students for a Democratic Society (SDS)
        a. Emergence and growth
        b. Port Huron Statement
      3. Free Speech Movement at Berkeley

VI. War in Vietnam
    A. America's growing involvement (pre-LBJ)
      1. Outlook of policymakers
        a. Cold War assumptions
        b. Ignorance of Vietnamese history, culture
        c. Fear of "losing" Vietnam
      2. Key developments
        a. Defeat of French colonialism
        b. Fostering of Ngo Dinh Diem regime in South Vietnam
        c. Dispatch of counter-insurgency "advisers"
        d. Collapse of Diem regime; U.S.-backed coup
    B. Johnson's war
      1. LBJ's initial outlook

        2. Escalation
           a. Gulf of Tonkin resolution
           b. Initiation of air strikes
           c. Introduction of ground troops
           d. Increasing magnitude of troop presence, bombing
        3. Brutality
           a. Bombing
           b. Chemical defoliation, napalm
           c. "Search and destroy" missions; "body counts"
        4. Lack of progress
           a. Resilience of Viet Cong and North Vietnamese forces
           b. Failings of South Vietnamese government
    C. Opposition at home
        1. Emerging critiques
        2. Antiwar movement
           a. Early stirrings
               i. SDS rallies
              ii. Themes
           b. Growth
               i. Draft resistance
              ii. 1967 Washington rally

VII. Wider currents of dissent
    A. Counterculture
        1. Spread among youth
           a. College students
           b. Working class
        2. Spirit and vision
           a. Rejection of mainstream values
           b. Challenge to authority
           c. Community, creativity, pleasure over pursuit of wealth
           d. Cultural "liberation"
           e. "Sexual revolution"
        3. Symbols and manifestations
           a. Physical appearance, fashion
           b. "Sex, drugs, rock and roll"
           c. Be-Ins
               i. Timothy Leary; LSD
              ii. "Turn on, tune in, drop out"
           d. New forms of radical action
               i. Underground newspapers
              ii. Youth International Party ("Yippies")
           e. Communes
           f. Rock festivals; Woodstock
           g. *Hair*

B. Reawakening of feminism
    1. Status of women at outset of 1960s
        a. Legal subordination
        b. Barriers to power, opportunity
    2. Betty Friedan's *The Feminine Mystique*
    3. Steps toward equal rights
        a. Equal Pay Act
        b. Civil Rights Act of 1964
        c. Equal Employment Opportunity Commission
        d. Founding of National Organization for Women
            i. Range of demands
            ii. Middle-class character
    4. Rise of "women's liberation"
        a. Roots in civil rights and student movements
            i. Inspiration of movements' ideals
            ii. Indignation against movements' inequalities
        b. Key initiatives
            i. Protests within SNCC, SDS
            ii. "Consciousness-raising" groups
           iii. Miss America beauty pageant protest
        c. Impact on public consciousness
            i. Expansion of idea of freedom
            ii. Introduction of "sexism," "sexual politics," "the personal is political"
        d. Campaigns and demands
            i. Abortion rights; reproductive freedom
            ii. Wide-ranging issues; *Sisterhood Is Powerful*
    5. Growing acceptance of feminist ideas
C. Rise of gay liberation
    1. Traditional oppression of gay people
        a. Legal and cultural stigmatization
        b. Harassment of gay subcultures
    2. Stonewall revolt
    3. Emergence of militant movement
        a. "Out of the closet"
        b. Gay pride marches
D. Latino activism
    1. Chicano pride movement
    2. United Farm Workers
        a. Cesar Chavez
        b. Blend of civil rights and labor struggles
        c. Grape strike, boycott
    3. Young Lords Organization (New York)
    4. Feminist current

E. Indian militancy
    1. Background: shifting Indian policies of postwar administrations
    2. Demands
        a. Material aid
        b. Self-determination
    3. Initiatives
        a. Founding of American Indian Movement
        b. Occupation of Alcatraz; Red Power movement
    4. Impact
F. New environmentalism
    1. Themes
        a. Critique of prevailing notions of progress, social welfare
        b. Activist, youth-oriented style
        c. Language of citizen empowerment
    2. Initiatives
        a. Rachel Carson's *Silent Spring*
        b. Campaign to ban DDT
        c. Expanding range of causes, organizations
    3. Progress
        a. Bipartisan appeal
        b. Clean Air and Clean Water Acts
        c. Endangered Species Act
        d. Inauguration of Earth Day
G. Consumer activism
    1. Ralph Nader
        a. *Unsafe at Any Speed*
        b. Subsequent investigations
    2. Spread of consumer protection laws, regulations

VIII. Rights revolution under Warren Court
  A. Warren Court
  B. Reaffirmation of civil liberties
    1. Curtailing of McCarthyite persecution
    2. Intertwining of civil liberties and civil rights
        a. *NAACP v. Alabama*
        b. *New York Times v. Sullivan*
        c. *Loving v. Virginia*
        d. *Jones v. Alfred H. Mayer Co.*
    3. Imposition of Bill of Rights protections on states
        a. Bars on illegal search and seizure, cruel and unusual punishment
        b. Right of defendant to speedy trial, legal representation
        c. *Miranda v. Arizona*
  C. Political reapportionment: *Baker v. Carr*

    D. Reinforcement of separation of church and state
    E. Establishment of right to privacy
       1. *Griswold v. Connecticut*
       2. *Roe v. Wade*
         a. Implications for women's rights
         b. Source of ongoing controversy

IX. 1968: climax of Sixties turmoil
    A. Momentous events around nation
       1. Tet offensive; repercussions at home
       2. Eugene McCarthy's challenge to LBJ for nomination
         a. New Hampshire primary
         b. Withdrawal of LBJ
       3. Assassination of King; subsequent urban unrest
       4. Student revolt at Columbia University
       5. Assassination of Robert F. Kennedy
       6. Antiwar protests, police riot at Chicago Democratic convention
    B. Momentous events around the world
       1. Worker-student uprising in France
       2. Soviet invasion of Czechoslovakia
       3. Killing of student protesters at Mexico City Olympics
    C. Comeback of Richard Nixon
       1. Stages
         a. Attainment of Republican nomination
         b. Narrow election victory over Hubert Humphrey
         c. Independent campaign of George Wallace
       2. Sources
         a. Conservative backlash
         b. Resonance of appeals to "silent majority," "law and order"

CHRONOLOGY

1960   Lunch counter sit-in at Greensboro
        Founding of Student Non-Violent Coordinating Committee
        Founding of Young Americans for Freedom
        John F. Kennedy defeats Richard Nixon for presidency

1961   Congress of Racial Equality launches Freedom Rides
        Kennedy establishes Peace Corps
        Alliance for Progress launched
        Bay of Pigs invasion
        Construction of Berlin Wall

1962 Desegregation of University of Mississippi met with violence
Michael Harrington publishes *The Other America*
Rachel Carson publishes *Silent Spring*
Students for a Democratic Society adopts Port Huron Statement
Cuban missile crisis
Baker v. Carr

1963 Birmingham desegregation campaign; Martin Luther King Jr.'s
  Letter from Birmingham Jail
Assassination of Medgar Evers
March on Washington; Martin Luther King Jr.'s "I Have a Dream"
  speech
Fatal bombing of black Birmingham church
Betty Friedan publishes *The Feminine Mystique*
Equal Pay Act
Nuclear test ban treaty
Fall of South Vietnamese leader Ngo Dinh Diem in U.S.-backed
  coup
Assassination of Kennedy; succession of Lyndon B. Johnson to
  presidency

1964 Johnson declares War on Poverty
Civil Rights Act
Ratification of Twenty-Fourth Amendment
Harlem riot
New York Times v. Sullivan
Freedom Summer
Murder of civil rights activists Michael Schwerner, Andrew
  Goodman, and James Chaney
Mississippi Freedom Democratic Party campaign at Democratic
  convention
Gulf of Tonkin resolution
Free Speech Movement at Berkeley
Johnson wins landslide victory over Barry Goldwater in presidential
  election

1965 Selma-to-Montgomery voting rights march
Voting Rights Act
Assassination of Malcolm X
Watts riot
Initiation of U.S. air strikes on North Vietnam
Introduction of U.S. ground troops in South Vietnam
First demonstrations against Vietnam war

Hart-Cellar Act
United Farm Workers (UFW) launches grape boycott
Griswold v. Connecticut
Ralph Nader publishes *Unsafe at Any Speed*

1965–67   Johnson's Great Society initiatives

1966   *Miranda v. Arizona*
          Martin Luther King Jr. launches Chicago Freedom Movement
          Stokely Carmichael introduces Black Power slogan
          Founding of Black Panther Party
          Founding of National Organization for Women

1967   Denunciation of Vietnam War by Martin Luther King Jr.
          Antiwar protest at Pentagon
          Newark and Detroit riots
          Human Be-In in San Francisco
          Loving v. Virginia

1968   Tet offensive
          Kerner Report
          Eugene McCarthy campaign for Democratic nomination
          Withdrawal of Johnson from race for reelection
          Assassination of Martin Luther King Jr.
          Student protests at Columbia
          Worker-student uprising in France
          Assassination of Robert F. Kennedy
          Soviet invasion of Czechoslovakia
          Antiwar protests, police riot at Chicago Democratic convention
          Feminist protest at Miss America beauty pageant
          Killing of student protesters at Olympics in Mexico City
          Founding of American Indian Movement
          Nixon defeats Hubert Humphrey in presidential election

1969   First moon landing
          Stonewall revolt
          Woodstock rock festival

1969–71   Indian occupation of Alcatraz

1970   Publication of *Sisterhood is Powerful*
          Migrant farmworkers gain UFW contracts
          First Earth Day

1973   *Roe v. Wade*

KEY TERMS

Freedom Rides: In 1960, the United States Supreme Court ruled that segregation in bus stations that served interstate travelers was unconstitutional. Because most southern states ignored the order, members of the Congress of Racial Equality and, in time, the Student Nonviolent Coordinating Committee organized the Freedom Rides to bring about federal enforcement of the ruling. The Freedom Riders were both black and white civil rights activists who traveled on interstate bus routes in the South. The resulting violence was shocking in its intensity, as on several occasions the Riders were fortunate not to have been killed. Kennedy administration officials regarded the protests as a distraction from foreign policy concerns and asked that the Freedom Rides end, but CORE officials refused. Frustrated, Attorney General Robert Kennedy grudgingly ordered the Interstate Commerce Commission to end segregation in interstate travel. The Freedom Rides had served their purpose.

Bay of Pigs: In 1960, President Dwight Eisenhower authorized the Central Intelligence Agency to train Cuban refugees to invade Cuba and overthrow the communist government of Fidel Castro. When John Kennedy took office in January 1961, CIA officials assured them that the plan would work. Kennedy was doubtful but approved the invasion nonetheless. The invasion proved to be disastrous. The 1,400 refugees landed in a swamp, where they were met by Cuban forces. A United States rescue effort failed because its leaders did not realize that Cuba and Nicaragua, the launching point for air support, were in different time zones and so did not properly coordinate their efforts. The episode was an international embarrassment that made Kennedy look inept during his first months in office.

Voting Rights Act of 1965: In response to the violence at Selma, Alabama, in March 1965, Congress passed the Voting Rights Act of 1965. The legislation barred the use of literacy or other voter tests in any state in which less than 50 percent of eligible voters were registered or had voted in the 1964 presidential election, a provision that applied to the states of Alabama, Georgia, Louisiana, Mississippi, North Carolina, South Carolina, and Virginia. In those states federal officials would take charge of voter registration, and poll watchers would verify that elections were conducted without voter intimidation. As a result of the legislation, black voter participation increased markedly in the South. For example, the percentage of eligible African-Americans who registered in Mississippi rose from 7 percent to 60 percent.

Hart-Celler Act: The Immigration and Naturalization Act of 1965, also known as the Hart-Celler Act after its congressional sponsors, dramatically altered immigration patterns into the United States. Abolishing the quota system that had long favored migrants from western and northern Europe, the legislation created seven categories of immigrants. Preference was given to family members of U.S. citizens and individuals with skills such as medical training. One provision created a category for refugees. Because the law allowed for immigration beyond the annual cap of 290,000 in some instances, the actual number of immigrants into the United States each year soon rose to some 400,000 individuals. Interestingly, the legislation was intended to limit immigration from Mexico, but under its terms immigration from the nation's southern neighbor increased as Mexicans took up an increasingly large percentage of the 120,000 immigrants allowed to come from countries in the Western Hemisphere.

War on Poverty: The Economic Opportunity Act, the legislation that implemented Lyndon Johnson's War on Poverty, included a provision calling for "maximum feasible participation" of the residents of areas receiving assistance in fighting poverty. One war on poverty effort, the Community Action Program (CAP), allowed poor people to organize and operate anti-poverty programs in their neighborhoods. They could form Community Action Agencies, design programs to meet local needs, and apply for federal grant money to run their programs. This well-intentioned program often met with disastrous results as local government officials resented the influx of federal dollars that they could not control. For Johnson, the numerous complaints about the CAPs were a burden that diminished his enthusiasm for his own initiative. By the end of the 1960s most War on Poverty money was once again flowing into the offices of local authorities.

Chicago Freedom Movement: Dr. King's experiences in Chicago in 1966 revealed the depth of racism in northern cities and illustrated the difficulties of applying the lessons civil rights activists had learned in the South to other regions of the country. Efforts in the South had focused on rural areas and the small cities of the region. The system of black churches in the South had provided a pre-existing network for organizing protests and supporting activists. Chicago, an enormous city, proved much more difficult to deal with, especially because the churches did not wield the same level of influence that they did in the South. In addition, King discovered that many black politicians in Chicago owed their loyalty to the city's political machine and were not willing to support the movement.

Red Power: Indian reservations were one area in which Lyndon Johnson's War on Poverty scored successes. For decades, officials from the Bureau of Indian Affairs and other government agencies had made most of the major decisions regarding federal spending on reservations. As the 1960s began, American Indians began demanding greater control over their communities. Because the War on Poverty required community participation, Indians seized on its programs as a means to promote self-determination. Many prominent Indian leaders of the 1970s and 1980s praised War on Poverty initiatives for providing them with experience and skills needed to lead their communities.

Baker v. Carr: In 1959, residents of the cities of Knoxville, Memphis, and Nashville filed a lawsuit in federal court against Joseph Carr, the Tennessee secretary of state. Tennessee had not reapportioned its electoral districts since 1901, and the plaintiffs in the suit argued that rural districts had far more political clout than did the urban districts, which had grown dramatically in size over the preceding decades. A Tennessee judge dismissed the suit, deeming it a political matter outside the court's jurisdiction. Upon appeal, however, the United States Supreme Court ruled that the failure to reapportion the districts violated the right to equal protection guaranteed in the Fourteenth Amendment. Within a year of the ruling, similar suits were filed in thirty-six states, leading to redistricting throughout much of the nation.

Chicago Seven: The government's indictment of eight political radicals for conspiring to incite violence at the 1968 Democratic national convention led to a bizarre trial that gained national media attention. Angered at efforts by Bobby Seale to represent himself, Judge Julius Hoffman ordered the Black Panther leader bound and gagged while in the courtroom. Hoffman then sentenced Seale to four years in prison for contempt of court (thus, the Chicago Seven). The remaining defendants often mocked the proceedings. A jury found them not guilty of the conspiracy charge, but five were found guilty of inciting a riot. Hoffman sentenced those five to jail sentences, and then gave all seven time for contempt of court. In 1972, an appeals court overturned the convictions, noting over 100 errors on the judge's part and citing Hoffman's obvious bias.

George Wallace presidential candidacy: Former Alabama governor George C. Wallace entered the 1968 presidential race as the candidate for the American Independent Party. A champion of segregation as governor, Wallace appealed to working class Americans anxious over the effects of the rights revolution of the 1960s. He attacked feminism, the counterculture, and anti-war demonstrators with vigor and a cruel humor that attracted many voters in the South. Wallace knew he would not win, but hoped to secure enough votes to force the election into the House of Representatives. On Election Day he received 9.9 million votes, or almost 14 percent of the popular vote. In addition, he captured 46 electoral votes, all from states in the Deep South.

OBJECTIVE QUESTIONS

Multiple Choice

1. At the peak of the Vietnam war, the number of American troops in Vietnam was approximately:
   A. 17,000.
   B. 200,000.
   C. 500,000.
   D. 1,750,000.

2. A leading motto of the Women's Liberation movement was:
   A. "Pay any price, bear any burden."
   B. "Turn on, tune in, drop out."
   C. "We are the silent majority."
   D. "The personal is political."

3. Which of the following series of events is listed in proper sequence?
   A. Voting Rights Act; Greensboro student sit-in; founding of Black Panther Party; Martin Luther King Jr.'s *Letter from Birmingham Jail*
   B. Betty Friedan's *The Feminine Mystique;* founding of National Organization for Women; *Sisterhood Is Powerful; Roe v. Wade*
   C. Tet offensive; Gulf of Tonkin resolution; nuclear test ban treaty; Cuban missile crisis
   D. announcement of War on Poverty; assassination of John Kennedy; election of Nixon to White House; Michael Harrington's *The Other America*

4. Which of the following books was *not* an important influence on the New Left?
   A. Rachel Carson's *Silent Spring*
   B. James Baldwin's *The Fire Next Time*
   C. Michael Harrington's *The Other America*
   D. Barry Goldwater's *The Conscience of a Conservative*

5. Which of the following was *not* a central purpose of President Johnson's Great Society program?
   A. establishing a federally guaranteed annual income for every family
   B. enhancing the access of poor people to a good education
   C. providing food for the needy
   D. ending poverty in America

6. Which of the following was *not* a common theme of the antiwar movement?
   A. America's military venture abroad undermines our capacity to address pressing social problems at home.
   B. American forces are bringing needless death and destruction to millions of Vietnamese citizens.
   C. Communism is preferable to democracy, so why fight it?
   D. Thousands of young Americans are dying for an ill-conceived objective.

7. Which of the following was *not* one of the climactic moments of 1968?
   A. the assassination of Martin Luther King Jr.
   B. the Berkeley Free Speech Movement
   C. Eugene McCarthy's strong showing in the New Hampshire primary
   D. bloody clashes between police and protesters at the Chicago Democratic convention

8. Which of the following was *not* a target of the conservative "backlash" of the late Sixties?
   A. President Johnson's Great Society initiatives
   B. the rights revolution promoted by the liberal Warren Court
   C. the growing power and militancy of organized labor
   D. the civil rights and antiwar protest movements

9. The organizer of the Student Non-Violent Coordinating Committee (SNCC) in April 1960 was:
   A. John Lewis.
   B. Martin Luther King Jr.
   C. Stokely Carmichael.
   D. Ella Baker.

10. The Student Non-Violent Coordinating Committee's goals included:
    A. replacing the culture of segregation with a "beloved community" of racial justice
    B. replacing the culture of militarism, with a foreign policy of isolationism and disarmament.
    C. recontextualizing the Cold War and unilateral disarmament on the part of the United States.
    D. contrary to its name, seeking to coordinate the achievement of better schooling, "by any means necessary" including violence.

11. The organization that launched the Freedom Rides, by which integrated groups traveled by bus into the deep South to test compliance with court orders banning segregation on interstate buses and trains was called the:
    A. Student Non-Violent Coordinating Committee.
    B. Congress of Racial Equality (CORE).
    C. Southern Christian Leadership Conference.
    D. Democratic Party.

12. Which was *not* an event in the civil rights movement of 1963?
    A. A sniper killed Medgar Evers, field secretary of the NAACP in Mississippi.
    B. A bomb at a black Baptist church in Birmingham, killed four young girls.
    C. 250,000 people, black and white, marched in Washington, D.C. in support of civil rights.
    D. James Meredith, a black student, entered the University of Mississippi.

13. Which was *not* a goal of the August 28, 1963 March on Washington?
    A. passage of a civil rights bill
    B. legislation barring discrimination in employment

   C. a public works program to reduce unemployment
   D. an end to the use of the Grandfather Clause restricting suffrage

14. What was the principal concern of John F. Kennedy's presidency?
   A. the vigorous conduct of the Cold War
   B. civil rights
   C. an end to sexist discrimination against women
   D. expansion of the modern welfare state

15. What was the organization created by the Kennedy administration to aid the
    economic and educational progress of developing countries?
   A. Volunteers in Service of America
   B. The Peace Corps
   C. COINTELPRO
   D. Alliance for Progress

16. What was the April 1961 CIA-led invasion of Cuba to topple Fidel Castro
    that proved to be a total failure, when of the invading force of 1,400, 1,100
    were captured and more than 100 killed?
   A. Cuban Crisis
   B. Bay of Pigs
   C. Havana Filibustera
   D. Cuban Missile Crisis

17. In August 1961, the Berlin Wall was erected:
   A. to separate Berlin from East Germany—a decision mutually agreed
       upon by the United States and the Soviet Union.
   B. by the United States so that East Germans could not enter West Berlin.
   C. by the Soviet Union so that peoples from Eastern Bloc countries could
       not flee to West Berlin.
   D. by the United States in an effort to keep illegal immigrants from
       entering West Berlin and subsequently claiming freedom in Western
       Europe.

18. Which was *not* true of the Cuban missile crisis?
   A. President Kennedy imposed a "quarantine" of Cuba.
   B. Nikita Khrushchev agreed to withdraw the missiles from Cuba.
   C. President Kennedy secretly agreed to remove American missiles from
       Turkey.
   D. The crisis unfolded in the course of four months in the spring of 1963.

19. The 1964 Civil Rights Act prohibited all of the following, except:
   A. racial discrimination in employment.
   B. racial discrimination in privately owned public accommodations.
   C. discrimination on the grounds of sex.
   D. racial discrimination in housing rental or sale.

20. The 1964 voter registration drive in Mississippi in which hundreds of white college students from the North participated was known as:
    A. Mississippi Freedom.
    B. Mississippi Freedom Democratic Party.
    C. Freedom at Last.
    D. Freedom Summer.

21. In *The Conscience of a Conservative,* Barry Goldwater argued for all of the following, except:
    A. more aggressive conduct of the Cold War.
    B. abolition of the graduated income tax.
    C. substitution of private charity for public welfare programs.
    D. support for the Civil Rights Act of 1964.

22. What was the name for the 1965 immigration law that abandoned the national origins quota system, and established racially neutral criteria for immigration?
    A. Hart-Cellar Act
    B. The Dawes Act
    C. The Johnson-Hays Act
    D. The Turner-Whitfield Act

23. Which was *not* part of President Johnson's 1965–1967 "Great Society"?
    A. Medicare and Medicaid
    B. funds poured into urban development and education
    C. the establishment of the Equal Employment Opportunity Commission
    D. the overturned Taft-Hartley Act of 1947

24. Which was *not* an initiative undertaken as part of President Johnson's Great Society's War on Poverty?
    A. food stamps
    B. VISTA
    C. Head Start
    D. universal healthcare

25. The 1968 Kerner Report blamed the widespread inner-city riots—occurring across the country from Harlem to Watts—on:
    A. African-Americans
    B. the Democratic Party
    C. segregation, poverty, and "white racism"
    D. the Republican Party

26. Who was the leading African-American known for his fiery oratory, insistence that blacks control the political and economic resources of their communities, and who was assassinated by members of the Nation of Islam after he formed his own Organization of Afro-American Unity?
    A. Medgar Evers
    B. Bobby Seal

    C. Stokely Carmichael

    D. Malcolm X

27. Which was *not* embraced by the "Black Power" movement of the mid-1960s?
    A. expression of racial self-assertion, reflected in the slogan "black is beautiful"
    B. adoption of the word "Afro-American" in place of the term "Negro"
    C. the Black Panther Party advocating armed self-defense in response to police brutality
    D. expansion of interracial coalition-building in SNCC and CORE

28. What made the New Left new?
    A. It viewed the working class as the main agent of social change.
    B. It adopted the language of economic inequality and social citizenship.
    C. It called for a democracy of citizen participation.
    D. It saw the Soviet Union as a model of social change.

29. What was the organization that crafted The Port Huron Statement, criticized corporations, unions, and the military-industrial complex, and proclaimed "a democracy of individual participation"?
    A. Students for a Democratic Society (SDS)
    B. Congress for Racial Equality (CORE)
    C. the National Organization of Women (NOW)
    D. Student Non-Violent Coordinating Committee (SNCC)

30. The gelatinous form of gasoline that burns the skin of anyone exposed to it, that was dropped by American airplanes on enemy positions during the Vietnam War, was called:
    A. Agent Orange.
    B. deoxygen.
    C. napalm.
    D. petroline.

31. What was the title of the 1963 book by Betty Friedan that took as its theme the emptiness of consumer culture, and painted the suburban home as a "comfortable concentration camp" for women?
    A. *A Fierce Discontent*
    B. *The Flames of Discontent*
    C. *The Feminine Mystique*
    D. *Fear of Flying*

32. What was the first gay rights organization in the United States, founded in 1951 by Harry Hay?
    A. the Mattachine Society
    B. the Rainbow Association
    C. the Gay, Lesbian, Bi-Sexual, and Transgendered Association (GLBT)
    D. the Pink Triangle Group

33. Who was the leader of the United Farm Workers (UFW)—as much a movement for civil rights as a campaign for economic betterment—who, beginning in 1965, led nonviolent protests, including fasts, marches, and a national boycott of California grapes?
    A. Cesar Chavez
    B. Julian Nava
    C. Jaime Escalante
    D. Santos C. Vega

34. The organization demanding greater Indian tribal self-government and the restoration of economic resources guaranteed in treaties, founded in 1968 was called:
    A. the Indian Militancy Group.
    B. the American Indian Movement.
    C. the Wounded Knee Solidaritists.
    D. the American Indian Assimilationists.

35. Who was the marine biologist whose book, *Silent Spring,* spelled out how DDT kills birds, animals, and causes sickness among humans, and who launched the modern environmental movement:
    A. Ralph Nader.
    B. John Muir.
    C. Rachel Carson.
    D. Helen Caldicott.

36. The 1967 United States Supreme Court decision that declared unconstitutional the laws in sixteen states that prohibited interracial marriage was:
    A. *Lawrence & Garner v. State of Texas.*
    B. *Loving v. Virginia.*
    C. *Griswold v. Connecticut.*
    D. *New York Times v. Sullivan.*

37. The United States Supreme Court ruling that an individual in police custody must be informed of the right to remain silent was:
    A. *Baker v. Carr.*
    B. *Missouri v. Seibert.*
    C. *Miranda v. Arizona.*
    D. *Harris v. New York.*

True or False

1. The Greensboro lunch counter sit-in marked the first appearance of college students at the forefront of social protest in America.

2. President Kennedy entered office determined to rid American foreign policy of its Cold War assumptions.

3. President Johnson entered office determined to see a substantial civil rights bill passed by Congress.

4. Johnson's Great Society failed to reduce poverty in America to any significant degree.

5. A key slogan of the Students for a Democratic Society was "participatory democracy."

6. According to defenders of the Vietnam War, American military withdrawal would encourage the spread of communism elsewhere around the world.

7. In *Griswold v. Connecticut,* the Supreme Court struck down all laws discriminating against homosexuals as a violation of the right to privacy.

8. Richard Nixon won the 1968 presidential election by the largest landslide in American history.

9. By the end of 1960, some 70,000 demonstrators had taken part in sit-ins across the nation; the tactic had its 1960s origins in the initiative of four students from North Carolina Agricultural and Technical State University who, on February 1, 1960, sat down at a lunch counter in the local Woolworth's department store and asked to be served.

10. With the sit-ins, college students stepped onto the stage of American history as a leading force for social change.

11. In a single week in June 1963, more than 15,000 people were arrested in 186 cities across the United States in civil rights demonstrations.

12. While serving a nine-day jail term in 1963 for violating a ban on demonstrations, Martin Luther King Jr. wrote his eloquent plea for racial justice, *Letter from a Birmingham Jail.*

13. In his August 1963 speech on the steps of the Lincoln Memorial delivered to 250,000 black and white Americans, Martin Luther King Jr. declared: "I have a dream that one day this nation will rise up and live out the true meaning of its creed: 'we hold these truths to be self-evident, that all men are created equal.'"

14. President Kennedy's policy toward Latin America, the Alliance for Progress, failed because the money as distributed enriched military regimes and local elites.

15. President Lyndon Johnson grew up in one of the wealthiest sections of United States—the central Texas Hill country.

16. The Civil Rights Bill and program of domestic liberalism launched by President Lyndon B. Johnson were far less ambitious than President Kennedy's initiatives on these matters.

17. As president of the United States, Lyndon B. Johnson never forgot the poor Mexican and white children he had taught in a Texas school in the early 1930s.

18. In June 1964, three young voting rights activists were murdered in Mississippi—James Chaney, Andrew Goodman, and Michael Schwerner.

19. The Twenty-Fourth Amendment to the Constitution is the 1965 law that allowed federal officials to register voters.

20. The centerpiece of President Lyndon Johnson's Great Society was the endeavor to eradicate poverty.

21. The War on Poverty guaranteed an annual income to all Americans, created jobs for the unemployed, promoted unionization, and made it more difficult for businesses to shift production overseas.

22. President Lyndon Johnson's Great Society's War on Poverty required poor people to play a leading part in designing and implementing local policies.

23. In the weeks following passage of the 1965 Voting Rights Act, a joyful calm, mixed with a great celebratory jubilee that included parades, barbecues, and church prayer meetings characterized the principal response of inner city African-Americans to the new law.

24. "Black Power" was a highly precise idea that asserted that only through revolutionary struggle for self-determination could black Americans achieve their rightful ends.

25. The Free Speech movement was initiated at the University of Minnesota in 1964.

26. By 1968, the United States had more than a half million troops stationed in Vietnam.

27. The Vietnam War was the longest war in American history and the only war that the United States has lost.

28. In the "counterculture" of the 1960s there was, for the first time in American history, a rejection of respectable norms of clothing, language, and sexual behavior.

29. Although the media came to derisively label radical feminists "bra burners," no bras were ever actually burned.

30. Following a 1969 police raid on the Stonewall Bar, a gathering place for homosexuals in New York City's Greenwich Village, five days of rioting occurred and a militant gay rights movement was born.

ESSAY QUESTIONS

1. What were some of the main themes and approaches of the Black Freedom movement of the 1960s? What were the key lines of debate *within* this movement?

2. Compare the programs and agenda of the Great Society of the 1960s to those of the New Deal of the 1930s. In what ways was the Great Society simply an extension of the New Deal approach? In what ways did it represent something new?

3. Identify and analyze the key arguments raised both for and against the war in Vietnam during the mid- to late 1960s.

4. "The 1960s were like a return to the 1930s—both were turbulent, traumatic, conflictual times." In what ways do you find this comparison persuasive? In what ways do the contrasts between the two decades seem greater than the similarities?

5. Imagine a chance meeting, in 1968, among the following characters:

   - an advocate of black power
   - a proponent of women's liberation
   - a member of the New Left
   - a supporter of Richard Nixon
   - a supporter of Lyndon Johnson

   With candor and feeling, they exchange views on the tumultuous issues and events of the past decade. Among the questions they debate: "In what ways has American society been improved or uplifted over the course of the Sixties? In what ways has it been undermined or subverted?" Transcribe this conversation.

6. Write an essay on the New Left's definition of freedom.

7. Write an essay on the civil rights movement of the 1960s.

8. Write an essay on President Lyndon Johnson's Great Society and War on Poverty.

9. Write an essay on the principle organizations associated with the Rights Revolution of the 1960s.

10. Write an essay on the cultural and political elements of the youth movement of the 1960s.

SOURCES FOR FURTHER RESEARCH

Books

GENERAL OVERVIEWS

Bloom, Alexander, ed., *Long Time Gone: Sixties America Then and Now* (2001)
Brick, Howard, *Age of Contradiction: American Thought and Culture in the 1960s* (1995)
Gitlin, Todd, *The Sixties: Years of Hope, Days of Rage* (1987)
Isserman, Maurice, and Michael Kazin, *America Divided: The Civil War of the 1960s* (2000)
Patterson, James T., *Grand Expectations: The United States, 1945–1974* (1996)

PARTICULAR ASPECTS

Anderson, Terry H., *The Movement and the Sixties: Protest in America from Greensboro to Wounded Knee* (1995)
Andrew, John A., *The Other Side of the Sixties: Young Americans for Freedom and the Rise of Conservative Politics* (1997)
Appy, Christian G., *Working-Class War: American Combat Soldiers in Vietnam* (1993)
Branch, Taylor, *Parting the Waters: America in the King Years, 1954–1963* (1988)
_____. *Pillar of Fire: America in the King Years, 1963–1965* (1998)
Carson, Clayborne, *In Struggle: SNCC and the Black Awakening of the 1960s* (1981)
Carter, Dan T., *The Politics of Rage: George Wallace, the Origins of American Conservatism, and the Transformation of American Politics* (1996)
Dittmer, John, *Local People: The Struggle for Civil Rights in Mississippi* (1994)
D'Emilio, John, *Sexual Politics, Sexual Communities: The Making of a Homosexual Minority in the United States, 1940–1970* (1983)
Foley, Michael S., *Confronting the War Machine: Draft Resistance during the Vietnam War* (2003)
Goldman, Peter Louis, *The Death and Life of Malcolm X* (1979)
Herring, George C., *America's Longest War: The United States and Vietnam, 1950–1975* (2002)
Horwitz, Morton J., *The Warren Court and the Pursuit of Justice* (1998)
Matusow, Allen J., *The Unraveling of America: A History of Liberalism in the 1960s* (1984)
Porter, Gareth, *Perils of Dominance: Imbalance of Power and the Road to Vietnam* (2005)
Rosen, Ruth, *The World Split Open: How the Modern Women's Movement Changed America* (2000)

Rossinow, Douglas C., *The Politics of Authenticity: Liberalism, Christianity, and the New Left in America* (1998)

Sale, Kirkpatrick, *The Green Revolution: The American Environmental Movement, 1962–1992* (1993)

Skretny, John, *The Minority Rights Revolution* (2002)

Videos

After Stonewall (88 minutes, First Run Features, 1999)

America's War on Poverty (264 minutes, PBS Video, 1995)

Berkeley in the Sixties (117 minutes, PBS Home Video, 1993)

Chicago 1968 (57 minutes, PBS Video, 1996)

Citizen King (120 minutes, PBS Video, 2004)

Cold War (20 hours, PBS Video, 1998)

Eyes on the Prize (14 hours, PBS Home Video, 1986)

Eyes on the Prize II (8 hours, PBS Video, 1989)

February One: The Story of the Greensboro Four (61 minutes, California Newsreel, 2004)

The Fight in the Fields: Cesar Chavez and the Farmworkers' Struggle (115 minutes, Paradigm Productions, 1997)

The Fog of War: Eleven Lessons from the Life of Robert S. McNamara (106 minutes, Senart Films Production, in association with Globe Department Store, 2003)

Freedom Summer (60 minutes, History Channel, A&E Home Video, 2006)

LBJ (4 hours, PBS Video, 1991)

Making Sense of the Sixties (6 hours, PBS Video, 1991)

The Pill (60 minutes, PBS Video, 2003)

Rachel Carson's Silent Spring (60 minutes, WGBH Boston, 1993)

RFK (120 minutes, PBS Video, 2004)

Standing on My Sisters' Shoulders (61 minutes, Sadoff Productions, 2002)

Two Days in October (90 minutes, PBS Video, 2005)

Vietnam: A Television History (780 minutes, WGBH, 1987)

Vietnam: The War at Home (88 minutes, MPI Home Video, 1986)

The Weather Underground (92 minutes, The Free History Project, 2003)

Web Resources

Cold War, Cable News Network, Inc.
  http://www.cnn.com/SPECIALS/cold.war/

Documents from the Women's Liberation Movement, Special Collections Library, Duke University
  http://scriptorium.lib.duke.edu/wlm/

Exhibits/Gallery, National Civil Rights Museum
  http://www.civilrightsmuseum.org/

Free Speech Movement Digital Archive, Bancroft Library, University of
California, Berkeley
  http://bancroft.berkeley.edu/FSM

Mississippi Civil Rights Documentation Project, Charles Bolton, University of
Southern Mississippi
  http://www.usm.edu/crdp

The Sixties Project, Kalí Tal
  http://lists.village.virginia.edu/sixties/

The Vietnam Project, The Vietnam Center at Texas Tech University, Lubbock
  http://www.vietnam.ttu.edu/index.htm

The Wars for Viet Nam, 1945–1975, Robert K. Brigham, Vassar College
  http://vietnam.vassar.edu/

ANSWERS TO OBJECTIVE QUESTIONS

Multiple Choice

1-C, 2-D, 3-B, 4-D, 5-A, 6-C, 7-B, 8-C, 9-D, 10-A, 11-B, 12-D, 13-D, 14-A,
15-B, 16-B, 17-C, 18-D, 19-D, 20-D, 21-D, 22-A, 23-D, 24-D, 25-C, 26-D,
27-D, 28-C, 29-A, 30-C, 31-C, 32-A, 33-A, 34-B, 35-C, 36-B, 37-C

True or False

1-T, 2-F, 3-T, 4-F, 5-T, 6-T, 7-F, 8-F, 9-T, 10-T, 11-T, 12-T, 13-T, 14-T, 15-F,
16-F, 17-T, 18-T, 19-F, 20-T, 21-F, 22-T, 23-F, 24-F, 25-F, 26-T, 27-T, 28-T,
29-T, 30-T

CHAPTER 26

The Triumph of Conservatism, 1969–1988

CHAPTER OBJECTIVES

- What developments account for the growing sense of pessimism about American society during the 1970s?
- What explains the resurgence of American conservatism during the 1970s?
- What were the chief points of cultural conflict in 1970s America?
- What were the essential themes and features of the Reagan revolution of the 1980s? What factors gave rise to it?
- How did the Reagan revolution reshape American politics and society?
- What were the leading critiques of Reaganism during the 1980s?
- How did American foreign policy evolve over the course of the 1970s and 1980s?

CHAPTER OUTLINE

I. Nixon years
   A. Sporadic conservatism of President Richard Nixon
   B. Nixon's domestic policy
      1. Liberal side
         a. New regulatory agencies
            i. Environmental Protection Agency
            ii. Occupational Safety and Health Administration
            iii. National Transportation Safety Board
         b. Lavish spending on social services
         c. Environmental protection legislation
            i. Endangered Species Act
            ii. Clean Air Act

        d. Family Assistance Plan

        e. Promotion of affirmative action: Philadelphia Plan

    2. Conservative side

        a. New Federalism: "block grants" to states

        b. Nomination of jurists with segregationist pasts to Supreme Court

        c. Abandonment of Philadelphia Plan; courting of working-class whites

C. Racial policy and the Burger Court

    1. Burger Court

        a. Appointment of Chief Justice Warren Burger by Nixon

        b. Burger's surprisingly moderate tenure

    2. Rulings on school desegregation measures

        a. Approval

           i. *Swann v. Charlotte-Mecklenburg Board of Education*

           ii. Subsequent spread of court-ordered busing plans

           iii. Local controversies; Boston crisis

        b. Limits on extent: *Milliken v. Bradley*

    3. Rulings on affirmative action

        a. Background on affirmative action

        b. Approval

           i. *Griggs v. Duke Power Company*

           ii. *United Steelworkers of America v. Weber*

        c. Mixed: *Bakke v. University of California*

           i. Rejection of racial quotas, approval of consideration of race

           ii. Ambiguous legacy

D. Mainstream acceptance of sexual revolution

    1. Premarital sex

    2. Rising divorce rate

    3. Declining birth rate

E. Expanding opportunities for women

    1. Title IX

    2. Equal Credit Opportunity Act

    3. Influx of women into workforce

        a. Professional

        b. Pink collar

F. Strides of gay and lesbian movement

    1. Growing political presence

    2. Gay rights measures

    3. Coming out

G. The Seventies as "me decade"

H. Nixon's foreign policy
    1. Hard-line side
        a. Support for pro-U.S. dictatorships
        b. Chilean coup
            i. U.S. role
            ii. Brutal outcome
    2. "Realist" side
        a. New approach to communist powers
            i. Break from monolithic conception
            ii. Pursuit of "peaceful coexistence"; "détente"
        b. China initiative
            i. Nixon visit
            ii. Broadening of diplomatic and trade relations
        c. Soviet Union initiative
            i. Nixon visit
            ii. Trade agreements
            iii. Arms control treaties: SALT, Anti-Ballistic Missile Treaty
I. Vietnam
    1. Nixon initiatives
        a. "Secret plan"
        b. "Vietnamization"
        c. Invasion of Cambodia
    2. Swelling of antiwar sentiment
        a. Indications
            i. Magnitude of campus protest
            ii. Social breadth of protest
            iii. Spread of alienation among troops
            iv. War Powers Act
        b. Contributing factors
            i. Killings at Kent State, Jackson State
            ii. Revelations of My Lai massacre
            iii. Publication of Pentagon Papers
    3. Winding down of war
        a. Paris peace agreement
            i. Provisions
            ii. Unresolved issues
        b. Collapse of South Vietnam
J. Nixon's landslide reelection over George McGovern
K. Watergate and fall of Nixon
    1. Background: Nixon's obsession with secrecy, thwarting opposition
        a. "Enemies list"

          b. Pattern of illegal actions
             i. Wiretapping, break-ins, political sabotage
            ii. "Plumbers": Ellsberg break-in
    2. Watergate break-in
    3. White House cover-up
    4. Unraveling of cover-up
          a. Trial of burglars
          b. Investigative journalism
          c. Congressional hearings
          d. Special prosecutor
          e. Revelations of White House tapes
          f. Supreme Court ruling on tapes
    5. House Judiciary Committee call for impeachment
    6. Resignation of Nixon
    7. Significance and aftermath
          a. Convictions, imprisonment of top administration figures
          b. Measures to address government abuse of power
             i. Church Committee hearings
            ii. Congressional restrictions on FBI, CIA
           iii. Freedom of Information Act
          c. Corrosion of public faith in government, liberal outlook

  II. End of Golden Age
    A. Economic slowdown
      1. Indications
          a. Decline of manufacturing
          b. Slow growth rate
          c. Inflation
          d. Trade deficit
          e. Federal deficit
          f. Unemployment
          g. Interest rates
          h. "Stagflation"; "misery index"
      2. Causes
          a. Competition from foreign manufacture
          b. Cost of Vietnam War
          c. Surge in oil prices
             i. 1973 Middle East war
            ii. Oil embargo
           iii. "Oil shocks" in America
           iv. Growth of western energy production
      3. Nixon economic responses
          a. United States off gold standard
          b. Wage and price controls

B. Social impact on industrial areas
   1. New hardships
      a. Accelerated decline of manufacturing jobs; shift to lower-paying service jobs
      b. Decline of public services
      c. Rise in poverty rate
      d. Weakening and shrinking of labor movement
   2. New opportunities
      a. Growth of Sunbelt
      b. Remaking of city centers
C. Ford years
   1. Gerald Ford's ascension to presidency
   2. Domestic record
      a. Nixon pardon
      b. Anti-inflation campaign
      c. Economic recession; rise in unemployment
   3. Foreign policy record: Helsinki Accord
D. Carter years
   1. Jimmy Carter
      a. Background
      b. Reputation for honesty, piety; "outsider" status
      c. Political orientation
         i. Shades of old "Progressive" approach
         ii. Embrace of black aspirations
      d. Electoral victory over Ford
   2. Domestic record
      a. Conservative economic approach
         i. Elements: spending cuts, deregulation, higher interest rates
         ii. Conflict with Congress over persistence of inflation
      b. Call for expanded use of nuclear energy
         i. Argument for
         ii. Impact of Three Mile Island
      c. "Crisis of confidence" speech
   3. Foreign policy record
      a. Humanitarian philosophy
         i. De-emphasis of Cold War thinking
         ii. Emphasis on Third World poverty, nuclear proliferation, human rights
      b. Manifestations of humanitarian philosophy
         i. Camp David accord
         ii. Panama Canal treaty

           iii. Limits on support for Central American dictators (Nicaragua, El Salvador)

           iv. SALT II agreement

       c. Limits of humanitarian philosophy

           i. Continuation of international arms sales

           ii. Continued support for repressive allies

    4. Iran crisis

       a. Background

           i. Iran's strategic importance to United States

           ii. American support for repressive Shah

       b. Iranian revolution

           i. Islamic fundamentalism; Ayatollah Khomeini

           ii. Anti-American spirit

       c. Seizing of American hostages

       d. Plunging popularity of Carter

    5. Afghanistan crisis

       a. Soviet invasion

       b. Carter response

           i. Announcement of Carter Doctrine

           ii. Grain embargo

           iii. Olympic boycott

           iv. Withdrawal of SALT II treaty

           v. Boost in military spending

           vi. Aid to Afghan resistance

    6. Carter's conservative legacy

       a. Domestic policy

       b. Foreign policy

III. Rising tide of conservatism

    A. Context

       1. Economic problems

       2. International crises

       3. Civil rights and sexual revolutions

       4. Rising crime rates

    B. Currents

       1. "Neo-conservatives"

          a. Aims

            i. Curtailment of domestic programs

            ii. Renewal of Cold War foreign policy

          b. Think tanks

       2. Religious Right

          a. Popular base

          b. Aims

            i. Promotion of "Christian values"

            ii. Opposition to "sexual revolution"

       c. Mobilization
          i. Modern means of spreading message
          ii. Jerry Falwell, Moral Majority

C. Crusades
    1. Against gay rights
       a. Anita Bryant
       b. Save Our Children
    2. Against Equal Rights Amendment (ERA)
       a. Origins of ERA
       b. Approval by Congress
       c. Ratification battles
          i. Themes of opposition
          ii. Phyllis Schlafly
       d. Outcome: final defeat of ERA
    3. Against abortion rights
       a. Targeting of *Roe v. Wade*
       b. "Right to life" vs. "right to choose"
       c. Points of conflict
          i. *Roe v. Wade*
          ii. Judicial nominations
          iii. Public funding of abortions
          iv. Demonstrations, violence against abortion providers
       d. Outcomes
          i. Continuing legality of abortion
          ii. Impact of intimidation
    4. Against taxes
       a. Background: mounting resentment of government intervention, tax burden
       b. Proposition 13 (California)
          i. Passage
          ii. Material effects in California
          iii. Political repercussions around nation
    5. Against federal regulation of western lands; Sagebrush Rebellion

D. Election of 1980
    1. Backdrop: conservative tide across Western world
    2. Campaign of Ronald Reagan
       a. Breadth of conservative themes
       b. Ability to galvanize and broaden conservative base
    3. Reagan landslide victory
    4. Carter's historical reputation
       a. As president
       b. As former president

IV. Reagan revolution
    A. Background on Reagan
        1. Political evolution
        2. Political skills
    B. Impact on national agenda, discourse on "freedom"
    C. Economic program ("Reaganomics")
        1. Philosophy
            a. Theory of "supply side" ("trickle-down") economics
            b. Retreat from principle of progressive taxation
            c. Hostility to government regulation, union power
        2. Key initiatives
            a. Drastic reductions in federal taxes and top tax rates
            b. Dismantling of regulation
                i. Cutbacks on regulatory agencies
                ii. Appointment of pro-business regulators
            c. Dismissal of striking air traffic controllers (PATCO)
    D. Economic trends under Reagan
        1. Harsh recession, then prolonged expansion
        2. Strengths
            a. Robust stock market
            b. Low inflation
            c. High profits
            d. Technological advances
        3. Down-sides
            a. Weakening of labor movement
            b. Ongoing decline in manufacturing
            c. "Downsizing"
            d. Rising economic inequality
            e. Middle-class stagnation, hardships for working-class minorities and poor
            f. Emphasis on corporate deal making over production
            g. Reckless financial speculation; Savings and Loan scandal
            h. Ballooning of budget deficits, national debt
    E. Revival of "Gilded Age" values
        1. Affirmation of "greed"
        2. "Yuppies"
    F. Reagan reelection victory over Walter Mondale
    G. Conservatives' ambivalence over Reagan's domestic program
        1. Areas of approval
            a. Cuts in federal antipoverty efforts
            b. Curtailment of civil rights enforcement, affirmative action
            c. Verbal support for conservative social agenda
                i. Curtailment of abortion, gender equality
                ii. Prayer in schools
                iii. War on drugs

2. Areas of disappointment
   a. Unwillingness to undo core elements of welfare state
   b. Limited inclination or ability to advance conservative social agenda
H. Reinvigoration of Cold War
   1. Philosophy
      a. "Free World" vs. "evil empire"
      b. Commitment to military strength
      c. Impatience with "Vietnam syndrome"
      d. Distinction between "totalitarian" and "authoritarian" regimes
   2. Key initiatives
      a. Arms build-up
      b. Strategic Defense Initiative
      c. Nuclear deployment in Europe
      d. Interventions abroad
         i. Grenada
         ii. Libya
         iii. Lebanon
      e. Military aid
         i. To pro-U.S. dictators
         ii. To pro-U.S. insurgencies
I. Iran-Contra affair
   1. Features of scandal
      a. Secret sale of arms to Iran
      b. Illegal diversion of proceeds to Nicaraguan Contras
   2. Unraveling of scandal
      a. Press leaks
      b. Congressional hearings
   3. Political fallout
J. Reagan, Gorbachev, and easing of Cold War
   1. Mikhail Gorbachev
      a. Emergence as Soviet leader
      b. *Glasnost, perestroika*
   2. United States-Soviet negotiations
      a. Arms control talks, agreements
      b. Soviet withdrawal from Afghanistan
K. Reagan's mixed legacy
   1. Rhetoric of conservative values
   2. Undermining of conservative values
   3. Triumph of conservative assumptions; discrediting of liberalism
L. Election of 1988
   1. Mudslinging
   2. George H. W. Bush victory over Michael Dukakis

CHRONOLOGY

1966	Ronald Reagan elected governor of California
1968	Richard Nixon elected president
1970	U.S. invasion of Cambodia Killings at Kent State, Jackson State Revelations of 1968 My Lai massacre Founding of Environmental Protection Agency
1971	Publication of Pentagon Papers Nixon takes nation off gold standard, imposes wage and price controls *Swann v. Charlotte-Mecklenburg Board of Education*

1972	Passage of Title IX, Equal Credit Opportunity Act
	Nixon visits China, Soviet Union
	Signing of Strategic Arms Limitation Treaty and Anti-Ballistic
	    Missile Treaty
	Nixon's landslide reelection victory over George McGovern
	Watergate break-in; start of cover-up
	Congress approves Equal Rights Amendment; sends to states for
	    ratification

1972–74	Watergate scandal
1973	Paris peace agreement U.S.-backed coup in Chile War Powers Act *Roe v. Wade* Middle East war; start of oil embargo Resignation of Vice President Spiro T. Agnew
1974	*Milliken v. Bradley* House Judiciary Committee calls for impeachment Nixon resigns presidency; Gerald Ford assumes office Ford pardons Nixon
1975	Fall of South Vietnam regime; end of war New York City fiscal crisis Boston busing crisis Helsinki Accord
1976	Jimmy Carter defeats Ford in presidential election
1977	Anita Bryant leads anti-gay rights campaign

1978	*Bakke v. University of California* Ratification of Panama Canal treaty Camp David accord Proposition 13 in California
1979	Second "oil shock" Three Mile Island accident Carter's "crisis of confidence" speech Iranian revolution Soviet invasion of Afghanistan Founding of Moral Majority
1979–81	Iranian hostage crisis
1980	Carter imposes grain embargo, Olympic boycott Ronald Reagan defeats Carter in presidential election
1981	Congress passes major federal tax reduction Reagan fires striking air traffic controllers (PATCO)
1982	U.S. Marines dispatched to Lebanon
1983	Reagan announces Strategic Defense Initiative Withdrawal of Marines from Lebanon after bombing of barracks U.S. invasion of Grenada
1984	Reagan wins landslide reelection over Walter Mondale
1985	First summit meeting between Reagan and Gorbachev
1986	Tax Reform Act
1986–87	Iran-Contra scandal
1988	Soviet withdrawal from Afghanistan George Bush defeats Michael Dukakis in presidential election

KEY TERMS

Family Assistance Plan: Richard Nixon's proposal for eliminating the existing welfare program was the work of a Democrat, Daniel Moynihan. The Family Assistance Plan (FAP) guaranteed each adult in a poor family $1,600 a year, with an additional $300 granted for each child. Workers could keep part of their income without losing FAP benefits. In eight states, all in the South, the FAP would increase payments beyond the benefits received from Aid to Families with Dependent Children. Nixon saw the program as a way to streamline the federal bureaucracy and reduce costs, but was never fully committed to it. Opposition from liberals and conservatives doomed the measure in Congress.

San Antonio Independent School District v. Rodriguez: In Texas, each school district relied upon some state funding and property taxes levied within its district to meet expenses. Districts made up of poor neighborhoods had high tax rates yet did not raise as much money as districts that encompassed wealthier neighborhoods. Demetrio Rodriguez and other parents in a poor school district in San Antonio argued that the funding system created inequities in the state educational system that constituted a violation of the Fourteenth Amendment's guarantee of equal protection. In a 5–4 decision, the United States Supreme Court ruled that education was not a fundamental constitutional right. However, the ruling did not end battles over school funding in Texas and other states.

Title IX: Title IX of the Education Amendments Act of 1972 revolutionized women's athletics. Prior to passage of the act, most schools and universities spent little money or energy on women's sports activities. For example, in 1971 young women constituted only 7 percent of the athletes in high school programs. Because the act banned gender discrimination in education, the number of women involved in sports increased markedly—in 2001, women made up about 40 percent of the nation's high school athletes. Title IX had a similar impact on university athletic programs. Improvements in women's athletics programs in the decades following the act's passage increased U.S. women's participation in the Olympic Games and contributed to the formation of professional women's sports leagues.

Nixon and China: In the late 1960s, both China and the United States had concerns about the Soviet Union. Fighting broke out on the border between the two communist states, raising fears of a wider war. For the United States, the Soviet's iron grip on Eastern Europe and its large nuclear missile arsenal posed a threat to American interests. In addition to concerns about the Soviets, President Nixon sought an end to the Vietnam War and believed that China also desired an end to the conflict so near its own borders. These shared concerns and interests resulted in Nixon's historic visit to China in 1972, an event that historians regard as one of the president's major achievements.

oil crisis: The economic boom in the United States after World War II created an insatiable demand for oil. Through the 1960s the U.S. government placed quotas on oil imports, in part to protect domestic producers. In 1967, the nation imported 19 percent of the oil it consumed. However, ever-increasing demand made the quota unworkable, and Richard Nixon ended it in 1973. That year about one-third of the oil used in the United States was imported. The price for a barrel of oil was $3.00, which translated to about 27 cents for a gallon of gasoline at the pumps. The price hikes and oil embargo instituted in late 1973 had a devastating impact on the American economy. By January 1974 a barrel of oil cost $11.00, and a gallon of gas cost drivers 45 cents. The price hikes had a ripple effect, causing a round of inflation in the economy. Because the oil embargo of 1973 and the oil shock of 1979 gave way to cheap oil in the 1980s, the United States continued to rely on foreign sources of oil, importing some 60 percent of its oil in 2005.

The Nixon pardon: Gerald Ford entered the White House with broad support from the American people, who were relieved that the trauma of Watergate was coming to an end. One poll showed the new president's approval rating at 71 percent. However, his decision to offer former President Richard Nixon a "full, free, and absolute pardon" in September 1974 shocked the public, and his approval rating immediately dropped to 50 percent. By the following January only 37 percent of the public approved of Ford's job performance.

Iranian hostage crisis: The close alliance between the Shah of Iran and the United States contradicted President Carter's advocacy of human rights. The Shah relied upon repressive tactics, including the use of police violence and torture, to silence his critics. Some scholars estimate that his forces killed as many as 12,000 anti-regime protesters in 1978 and 1979. After a massacre in 1978, President Carter contacted the Shah with reassurances that he still had American support, a move that outraged Iranians. When revolutionaries overthrew the Shah in 1979, they focused their anger on the United States, seizing fifty-three hostages at the U.S. embassy that November. The hostage crisis lasted fourteen months, severely weakening Carter's presidency and contributing to his loss in the 1980 election.

Iran-Contra affair: The Iran-contra affairs involved two different Reagan administration initiatives. Dedicated to fighting communism in Central America, Reagan officials funneled aid to the contras, a Nicaraguan group battling that nation's leftist government. Despite a congressional ban on such assistance approved in 1982, the administration continued the flow of aid, prompting Congress to pass a more stringent ban in 1984. In an unrelated matter, President Reagan secretly approved the sale of arms to Iran (in violation of an arms embargo) in hopes that the Iranian government would help secure the release of seven American hostages held by a terrorist group in Lebanon. The two initiatives became linked when Oliver North, an assistant to the director of the National Security Council, used profits from the arms sales to fund the contras despite the 1984 ban on such efforts. Subsequent investigations criticized President Reagan for showing poor judgment but cleared him of any wrongdoing. The episode was an embarrassment to Reagan as it appeared that he did not have control over administration officials.

OBJECTIVE QUESTIONS

Multiple Choice

1. An indication of America's economic troubles during the 1970s was:
   A. the coming of a merchandise trade deficit.
   B. a decline in manufacturing.
   C. the advent of an urban fiscal crisis.
   D. all of the above

2. A major initiative of the Carter administration was the:
   A. Panama Canal treaty.
   B. Strategic Defense Initiative.
   C. Whip Inflation Now campaign.
   D. founding of the Environmental Protection Agency.

3. Which of the following series of events is listed in proper sequence?
   A. Jimmy Carter's election victory over Gerald Ford; Richard Nixon's election victory over George McGovern; George Bush's election victory over Michael Dukakis; Ronald Reagan's election victory over Walter Mondale
   B. announcement of President Nixon's "Vietnamization" policy; U.S. invasion of Cambodia; publication of Pentagon Papers; War Powers Act
   C. Three Mile Island accident; Helsinki Accord; Strategic Defense Initiative; Anti-Ballistic Missile Treaty
   D. U.S. invasion of Grenada; Proposition 13 in California; Soviet withdrawal from Afghanistan; Iran-Contra scandal

4. Which of the following developments did *not* help undermine public faith in the effectiveness of federal government?
   A. the Watergate scandal
   B. the economic downturn of the 1970s
   C. the Camp David agreement
   D. the outcome of the Vietnam War

5. Which of the following issues was *not* a focus of political conflict during the Seventies?
   A. federal programs addressing AIDS
   B. nuclear energy
   C. abortion
   D. affirmative action

6. Which of the following was *not* a key factor behind President Carter's 1980 reelection defeat?
   A. the Iranian hostage crisis
   B. high levels of inflation and unemployment

C. a general feeling that Carter was morally corrupt and hopelessly indifferent to the concerns of the people

D. a widespread belief that America had lost its way—both at home and abroad

7. Which of the following was *not* a central theme of the Reagan revolution?
   A. Federal regulation of the economy must be curtailed.
   B. Military spending has grown far too lavish, and must be reduced.
   C. Taxes are too high—in the name of American freedom, they must be cut back.
   D. America must lead the crusade against the evil of communism, wherever it may arise.

8. Which of the following was *not* a major theme raised by critics of Reagan's presidency?
   A. His policies have increased the hardships of America's have-nots.
   B. He appears more interested in safeguarding the environment than in safeguarding the nation from communism.
   C. His commitment to supporting the Nicaraguan Contras exceeds his commitment to obeying the law.
   D. His dramatic tax cuts, coupled with his equally dramatic military build-up, have fostered an alarming increase in the federal deficit.

9. Which was *not* one of the conservative ideas that informed Barry Goldwater's campaign for the presidency in 1964, and shaped conservatism for years thereafter?
   A. intense anti-Communism
   B. criticism of the welfare state for destroying "the dignity of the individual"
   C. a call for expansion of governmental regulations
   D. a call to reduce taxes

10. Which is *not* central to libertarian conservatism?
    A. limited government
    B. unregulated capitalism
    C. individual autonomy
    D. regulatory controls

11. Who was the author of the 1962 book *Capitalism and Freedom,* which held the capitalist free market to be the necessary foundation for individual liberty, and called for the repeal of the minimum wage and the Social Security system?
    A. Richard Weaver
    B. Russell Kirk
    C. Ayn Rand
    D. Milton Friedman

12. Who was the author of *Ideas Have Consequences* (1948)—a principal figure in the "new conservatism"—who asserted that the Free World needed to arm itself morally, and called for a return to a civilization based on values grounded in the Christian tradition?
    A. Milton Friedman
    B. Richard Weaver
    C. Anita Bryant
    D. Phyllis Schlafly

13. The 1960 statement drafted by young conservatives, members of Young Americans for Freedom (YAF), which asserted that the free market underpinned "personal freedom," and that international communism posed a grave menace to American liberty was called:
    A. The Port Huron Statement
    B. The Sharon Statement
    C. The Contract with America
    D. Morning in America

14. Which was *not* a reason that AFDC rolls expanded rapidly during the 1960s?
    A. The federal government quintupled AFDC payments to individual recipients.
    B. an increase in births to unmarried women
    C. a sharp rise in the number of poor female-headed households
    D. an aggressive campaign by welfare rights groups to encourage people to apply for benefits

15. Which was *not* one of President Nixon's apparent motivations in the context of his administration's Philadelphia Plan, and its promotion of "affirmative action"?
    A. He saw it as a way of fighting inflation by weakening the power of the building trades unions.
    B. If the plan caused tension between blacks and labor unions, Republicans could only benefit.
    C. Following May 1970, he abandoned the Philadelphia Plan because he decided he might be able to woo blue-collar workers' votes in doing so.
    D. He sought to garner the support of white working class voters for the Republican Party in initiating the Philadelphia Plan.

16. What was 1978 Supreme Court decision that rejected the idea of fixed affirmative action quotas, but allowed that institutions of higher learning could use race as one factor among many in admissions decisions?
    A. *Swan v. Charlotte-Mecklenberg Board of Education*
    B. *Regents of the University of California v. Bakke*
    C. *Griggs v. Duke Power*
    D. *San Antonio Independent School District v. Rodriguez*

17. Tom Wolfe dubbed the 1970s, a time in which "lifestyle" emerged in depoliticized form, the:
    A. "Me Decade."
    B. "Culture of Narcissism."
    C. "Conspicuous Consumption."
    D. "Morality Astray."

18. President Richard Nixon sought to replace the polarized and hostile relationship between the United States and the Soviet Union with a new era of "peaceful coexistence" called:
    A. détente.
    B. glasnost.
    C. perestroika.
    D. realism.

19. What was the name for the plan by which, beginning in 1969, President Nixon gradually drew down the number of American troops in Vietnam, saying they would be replaced by South Vietnamese soldiers?
    A. "Vietnamization"
    B. "Cut and Run"
    C. "Kissingerian Peace"
    D. "Operation Infinite Glory"

20. "Stagflation" refers to:
    A. men who burned the American flag in protest during the Vietnam War.
    B. environmentalists' concerns with falling deer populations in national parks.
    C. low inflation and high economic growth.
    D. stagnant economic growth and high inflation.

21. From 1973 to 1993, real wages:
    A. essentially did not rise.
    B. rose sharply for almost all American workers.
    C. fell gradually, then rose sharply.
    D. fell sharply.

22. Evangelical Christians of the Religious Right believe that, too often, American culture seems to trivialize religion and promote immorality, and demanded the Supreme Court reverse decisions in all of the following, except:
    A. the ban on prayer in public schools.
    B. the legalization of abortion in *Roe v. Wade*.
    C. the protection of pornography as free speech.
    D. the overly easy access to divorce.

23. What was the 1979 organization created by Virginia minister Jerry Falwell, devoted to waging a "war against sin" and electing "pro-life, pro-family, pro-America," candidates?
    A. America First
    B. Moral Majority
    C. Family First
    D. Save Our Children

24. The movement to reverse the 1973 *Roe v. Wade* decision was supported by all of the following except:
    A. the Roman Catholic Church.
    B. Evangelical Protestants.
    C. Feminists.
    D. Social Conservatives.

True or False

1. Upon entering office, President Nixon surprised many by retaining numerous aspects of Lyndon Johnson's Great Society program.

2. Upon entering office, President Nixon surprised many by calling a rapid halt to American military involvement in Vietnam.

3. Discredited by the Watergate scandal, the Republican party did not recover its momentum for another ten years.

4. The economic recession of the 1970s undercut the living standards and collective power of American labor.

5. Resentment over local initiatives to desegregate public schools was an important part of the conservative groundswell of the 1970s.

6. The Reagan administration conducted a massive expansion of military spending during the 1980s.

7. By the end of President Reagan's two terms in office, American conservatism was a spent force—its agenda, after all, had been completely fulfilled.

8. Although the Republicans held onto the White House in the election of 1988, "liberalism" regained its stature that year as the nation's dominant ideology.

9. Libertarians desire strong, activist national government.

10. "New conservatives" such as Russell Kirk wanted government expelled from the economy, but trusted government to regulate personal behavior to restore a Christian morality in a society they believed was growing weaker morally.

11. While libertarian conservatives spoke the language of progress and personal autonomy, the "new conservatives" emphasized tradition, community, and moral commitment; and herein lay the origins of the division in conservative ranks.

12. Conservatives in the Republican Party found Richard Nixon much to their liking.

13. As president, Richard Nixon expanded the welfare state, while also calling for law and order.

14. President Richard Nixon, a Republican, accepted and even expanded many elements of Lyndon Baines Johnson's Great Society.

15. By 1970, African-Americans, while about 12 percent of the population, accounted for nearly one-half of all welfare recipients.

16. By the 1990s, public schools in the North were considerably more segregated than those in the South.

17. During the 1970s, the divorce rate soared; by 1975 it was twice what it had been a decade earlier.

18. In 1960, only 20 percent of women with young children had been in the workforce; the figure reached 55 percent in 1990.

19. By 1979, there were thousands of local gay rights groups across the United States.

20. By the mid-1970s—in consequence of women's changing aspirations and the availability of birth control and legal abortions—the American birthrate declined dramatically.

21. In 1972 Congress approved Title IX, which banned gender discrimination in higher education.

22. President Nixon and Secretary of State Henry Kissinger continued President Lyndon Johnson's policy of attempting to undermine governments deemed dangerous to American strategic or economic interests.

23. In the spring of 1970 more than 350 colleges and universities experienced student strikes, and troops occupied 21 campuses in protest over the Vietnam War.

24. It is a myth that U.S. soldiers killed 350 South Vietnamese civilians in the My Lai massacre of 1968.

25. The Vietnam War was a military, political, and social disaster, and the only war the United States has ever lost.

26. President Nixon resigned the office of the presidency in 1974, in the wake of the Watergate scandal and cover up.

27. The Senate's Church Committee concluded that many of America's problems would be solved if people would attend church more frequently.

28. The number of workers employed in the manufacturing sector of the United States economy rose sharply during the 1970s.

29. The 1970s was one of only two decades (the other was the 1930s) in the twentieth century that ended with American workers on average poorer than when it began.

30. Both foreign-policy "realists" and conservative Cold Warriors applauded President Jimmy Carter's emphasis on human rights.

31. President Jimmy Carter's emphasis on human rights, and his continuation of the policies of détente, meant that, by the end of his presidency, relations with the Soviet Union were vastly improved, and the Salt II Treaty implemented.

32. By the end of the 1970s, the civil rights and sexual revolutions led to a nation overwhelmingly in favor of the Democratic Party's political agenda.

33. "Neoconservatives" came to believe that well-intentioned government social programs did more harm than good. In many cases, welfare, for example, not only did not alleviate poverty, but it encouraged single motherhood and undermined the work ethic.

34. Neoconservatives strongly supported America's efforts in the Cold War.

ESSAY QUESTIONS

1. Identify three episodes that helped propel the rise of American conservatism in the 1970s and describe how each did so.

2. "Although President Nixon was a Republican, his policies had more in common with those of President Carter, a Democrat, than with those of President Reagan, a Republican." In what ways do you agree with this statement? In what ways do you find it unpersuasive? Illustrate your discussion with examples from the text.

3. Lyndon Johnson is widely regarded as a symbol of postwar liberalism, and Ronald Reagan as a symbol of postwar conservatism. Compare and contrast their philosophies of government. What were the significant points of

difference between the two? What were the significant points of agreement? Consider both domestic and foreign affairs.

4. Consider the following thesis: "American freedom and prosperity have flourished under the presidency of Ronald Reagan." How might a defender of the Reagan administration make the case for this proposition? How might a critic make the case against it?

5. Imagine a chance meeting, in 1988, among the following characters:

   - a labor organizer
   - a civil rights activist
   - a women's rights activist
   - a gay rights activist
   - a wealthy entrepreneur
   - a middle-class professional
   - a poor person
   - a Great Society liberal
   - a laissez-faire conservative
   - a member of the religious Right

   With great fervor, they enter into an exchange over the key trends of American society during the past twenty years, focusing especially on the reemergence of conservatism and the Reagan revolution. Among the questions they debate: "In what ways have the freedoms, rights, and opportunities of Americans been advanced over this period? In what ways have they been diminished?" In the process, each discusses how his or her own life has been affected by these developments. Incorporating at least *four* of the above characters, transcribe this conversation.

6. Write an essay on Ronald Reagan's legacy.

7. Write an essay on conservative views regarding the virtues of the free market and the evils of "big government."

8. How did President Ronald Reagan's policies contribute to ending the Cold War?

9. Write an essay on the issues of the Iran-Contra Affair.

10. Write an essay on Reaganomics and the problem of economic inequality in the United States.

SOURCES FOR FURTHER RESEARCH

Books

GENERAL OVERVIEWS

Chafe, William H., *The Unfinished Journey: America since World War II* (2003)
Patterson, James T., *Grand Expectations: The United States, 1945–1974* (1996)

PARTICULAR ASPECTS

Adler, William M., *Mollie's Job: A Story of Life and Work on the Global Assembly Line* (2000)
Allitt, Patrick, *Religion in America Since 1945* (2003)
Anderson, Terry H., *The Pursuit of Fairness: A History of Affirmative Action* (2004)
Busch, Andrew E., *Ronald Reagan and the Politics of Freedom* (2001)
Carter, Dan T., *From George Wallace to Newt Gingrich: Race in the Conservative Counterrevolution, 1963–1994* (1996)
Coles, Robert, *Bruce Springsteen's America: The People Listening, A Poet Singing* (2003)
Dallek, Matthew, *The Right Moment: Ronald Reagan's First Victory and the Decisive Turning Point in American Politics* (2000)
Fink, Gary M., and Hugh Davis Graham, eds., *The Carter Presidency: Policy Choices in the Post–New Deal Era* (1998)
Fitzgerald, Frances, *Way Out There in the Blue: Reagan, Star Wars and the End of the Cold War* (2000)
Freedman, Samuel G., *The Inheritance: How Three Families and America Moved from Roosevelt to Reagan and Beyond* (1996)
Greenberg, David, *Nixon's Shadow: The History of an Image* (2003)
Harrison, Bennett, and Barry Bluestone, *The Great U-Turn: Corporate Restructuring and the Polarizing of America* (1988)
Herring, George C., *America's Longest War: The United States and Vietnam, 1950–1975* (2002)
Himmelstein, Jerome L., *To the Right: The Transformation of American Conservatism* (1990)
Kutler, Stanley I., *The Wars of Watergate: The Last Crisis of Richard Nixon* (1990)
Lukas, J. Anthony, *Common Ground: A Turbulent Decade in the Lives of Three American Families* (1985)
Luker, Kristin, *Abortion and the Politics of Motherhood* (1984)
Martin, William, *With God on Our Side: The Rise of the Religious Right in America* (1996)
Mathews, Donald G. and Jane S. De Hart, *Sex, Gender, and the Politics of ERA* (1990)

McGirr, Lisa, *Suburban Warriors: The Origins of the New American Right* (2001)

Phillips, Kevin, *The Politics of Rich and Poor: Wealth and the American Electorate in the Reagan Aftermath* (1990)

Schulman, Bruce J., *The Seventies: The Great Shift in American Culture, Society, and Politics* (2001)

Shilts, Randy, *And the Band Played On: Politics, People, and the AIDS Epidemic* (1987)

Stein, Judith, *Running Steel, Running America: Race, Economic Policy, and the Decline of Liberalism* (1998)

Videos

And the Band Played On (140 minutes, HBO Studios, 1993)
Cold War (20 hours, PBS Video, 1998)
The Conservatives (88 minutes, Films for the Humanities and Sciences, 1987)
Eyes on the Prize II (8 hours, PBS Video, 1989)
Ghosts of Attica (90 minutes, First Run/Icarus Films, 2001)
High Crimes and Misdemeanors (90 minutes, PBS Video, 1990)
Jimmy Carter (180 minutes, PBS Video, 2002)
Meltdown at Three Mile Island (60 minutes, PBS Video, 1999)
Nixon's China Game (57 minutes, PBS Home Video, 2000)
Nixon (3 hours, PBS Video, 1998)
One Bright Shining Moment: The Forgotten Summer of George McGovern (125 minutes, First Run/Icarus Films, 2004)
Reagan (270 minutes, PBS Video, 1998)
The Sensational 70s (48 minutes, MPI Home Video, 1993)
The Times of Harvey Milk (88 minutes, Pacific Arts Video, 1986)
Vietnam: A Television History (780 minutes, WGBH, 1987)
Watergate (225 minutes, Discovery Communications, 1994)

Web Resources

Cold War, Cable News Network, Inc.
  http://www.cnn.com/SPECIALS/cold.war/

Documents and Photographs from the Jimmy Carter Library Collections, Jimmy Carter Library and Museum
  http://www.jimmycarterlibrary.org/documents/index.phtml

Documents from the Women's Liberation Movement, Special Collections Library, Duke University
  http://scriptorium.lib.duke.edu/wlm/

Hard Hat Riots: An Online History Project, Karl Miller, Ellen Noonan, and John Spencer
http://chnm.gmu.edu/hardhats/homepage.html

The My Lai Courts-Martial, 1970, Douglas Linder
http://www.law.umkc.edu/faculty/projects/ftrials/mylai/mylai.htm

Online Documents, Photographs, and Exhibits, Gerald R. Ford Library and Museum
http://www.ford.utexas.edu/

Resources, Ronald Reagan Presidential Library
http://www.reagan.utexas.edu/resource.htm

Revisiting Watergate, Washington Post
http://www.washingtonpost.com/wp-srv/national/longterm/watergate/

The Wars for Viet Nam, 1945–1975, Robert K. Brigham, Vassar College
http://vietnam.vassar.edu/

ANSWERS TO OBJECTIVE QUESTIONS

Multiple Choice

1-D, 2-A, 3-B, 4-C, 5-A, 6-C, 7-B, 8-B, 9-C, 10-D, 11-D, 12-B, 13-B, 14-A, 15-D, 16-B, 17-A, 18-A, 19-A, 20-D, 21-A, 22-D, 23-B, 24-C

True or False

1-F, 2-T, 3-F, 4-F, 5-T, 6-T, 7-F, 8-F, 9-F, 10-T, 11-T, 12-F, 13-T, 14-T, 15-T, 16-T, 17-T, 18-T, 19-T, 20-T, 21-T, 22-T, 23-T, 24-F, 25-T, 26-T, 27-F, 28-F, 29-T, 30-F, 31-F, 32-F, 33-T, 34-T

CHAPTER 27

Globalization and Its Discontents, 1989–2000

CHAPTER OBJECTIVES

- What is "globalization"? How were its effects experienced, perceived, and debated by Americans during the Nineties?
- How did the end of the Cold War affect the position of the United States in global affairs?
- What were the causes and significance of the Gulf War of 1991?
- What were the goals and approach of the Clinton administration? What were President Clinton's chief accomplishments and failings?
- What was the Republican "Contract With America," and how fully were its provisions put into effect?
- What were the causes, and the legacy, of the impeachment of President Clinton?
- How did the computer revolution of the 1990s transform America?
- What were the scope and sources of the economic boom of the Nineties?
- What were the main issues and battlelines in the "culture wars" of the Nineties?
- What were the key points at issue in the disputed election of 2000? How was it resolved?

CHAPTER OUTLINE

I. "Globalization" in the late twentieth century
   A. Conceptions of
   B. Emerging controversy over

II. Post–Cold War world
    A. Crisis of communism and end of Cold War
        1. China
            a. Popular democracy movement
            b. Suppression of protest
        2. Eastern Europe
            a. Popular protest
            b. Soviet nonintervention
            c. Collapse of Communist regimes ("Velvet Revolution")
                i. Germany: removal of Berlin Wall; reunification
                ii. Elsewhere
        3. Soviet Union
            a. Economic chaos
            b. National and ethnic tensions
            c. Attempted coup
            d. Dissolution
        4. Implications of Cold War's end
            a. Global prevalence of capitalism, "free market" model
            b. Prospects for spread of democracy
            c. Emergence of United States as uncontested superpower
    B. President George Bush and the New World Order
        1. Uncertain meaning of New World Order
        2. Invasion of Panama
            a. Purposes
            b. Outcome
            c. Controversy over
        3. Gulf War
            a. Background: invasion of Kuwait by Iraqi dictator Saddam Hussein
            b. Buildup to war
                i. Dispatch of U.S. troops to Gulf region
                ii. Debate over prospective war with Iraq
                iii. Forging by Bush of multinational coalition
                iv. Securing of United Nations authorization
            c. The war: Operation Desert Storm
                i. Prompt U.S. victory; ouster of Iraq from Kuwait
                ii. Minimum of American casualties
                iii. High death toll for Iraqis
            d. Aftermath
                i. UN sanctions on Iraq
                ii. Survival of Hussein regime
                iii. Resentment in region over U.S. presence
                iv. Surge in Bush's popularity

       4. Competing post–Cold War doctrines
         a. General Colin Powell's vision
         b. Secretary of Defense Dick Cheney's vision

C. Election of 1992
    1. Growing disenchantment with Bush, Republicans
       a. Economic recession
       b. Remoteness of Bush on domestic issues
       c. Pat Buchanan's "cultural war"
    2. Democratic challenger: Bill Clinton
       a. Popular appeal; empathy for economic anxieties
       b. Blend of liberal and conservative approaches
    3. Independent challenger: H. Ross Perot
    4. Clinton victory

D. Clinton domestic policy, first two years
    1. Departures from Reagan-Bush approach
       a. Cabinet and judicial appointments
       b. Tax policies
       c. Spending plan for infrastructure and job training
    2. Continuities from Reagan-Bush approach
       a. Free trade doctrine
       b. North American Free Trade Agreement
    3. Health care reform initiative
       a. Background
          i. Rising cost of health care
         ii. Growing number of uninsured
        iii. Limited coverage by Health Maintenance Organizations
       b. Clinton plan
          i. Role of Hillary Rodham Clinton
         ii. Provisions
       c. Resistance to plan
          i. Sources
         ii. Themes
       d. Outcome
          i. Defeat of plan
         ii. Subsequent growth in ranks of uninsured

E. Republican sweep of 1994
    1. Background: public disenchantment with Clinton
    2. Republican challenge
       a. Leadership of Newt Gingrich
       b. Proposed "Contract With America"
          i. Shrinking of government
         ii. Reduction in taxes

        iii. Deregulation

        iv. Overhaul of welfare

        v. Elimination of affirmative action

  3. Scope of electoral triumph

  4. Gingrich Republicans in power

    a. Implementation of "Contract With America"

    b. Standoff with Clinton; government shutdown

    c. Recoiling of public from Gingrich, "Contract With America"

F. Clinton's move toward center: "triangulation"

  1. Strategy

    a. Repudiation of "big government"

    b. Co-optation of moderate Republican themes

    c. Rejection of extreme Republican themes

  2. Initiatives

    a. Telecommunications Act

    b. Abolition of federal welfare system

  3. Outcome

    a. Neutralization of Republican challenge

    b. Reelection victory over Bob Dole

    c. Affirmation of mainstream Republican premises

G. Clinton and world affairs

  1. Agenda

    a. Resolve ongoing global conflicts

    b. Restore emphasis on human rights

  2. Mixed record

    a. Fruitful efforts in Northern Ireland, Haiti

    b. Fruitless efforts in Middle East

    c. Lack of effort in China, Rwanda

  3. Balkan crisis

    a. Background

        i. Disintegration of Yugoslavia

        ii. Outbreaks of ethnic conflict, "ethnic cleansing"

    b. U.S./NATO/UN response

        i. Air strikes

        ii. Peacekeeping

        iii. Kosovo war

  4. Role of human rights in global affairs

    a. Growth of

        i. Principle of intervention in internal affairs

        ii. International institutions

        iii. Expanding scope of human rights issues

    b. Uncertainty of

H. Clinton-era boom
   1. Indicators
      a. Low rates of unemployment, inflation
      b. Federal budget: from deficits to surplus
   2. Computer revolution
      a. Key features
         i. Microchip
        ii. Variety of computer products
        iii. Internet
      b. Areas of impact
        i. Private use
        ii. Workplace
        iii. Global reach of American culture
      c. Varied perspectives on Internet
        i. Celebration of democratic promise
        ii. Concern over inequalities of access
I. Undersides of the booming Nineties
   1. Economic difficulties in other lands
      a. Advanced countries
        i. Western Europe
        ii. Japan
        iii. Russia
      b. Third World countries
        i. Trade deficits, foreign debts
        ii. Imposition of stringent spending cuts
   2. Stock market bubble
      a. Frenzied, Twenties-style boom
        i. "Dot.coms"
        ii. Nasdaq
      b. Bust
        i. Timing and scale
        ii. Impact
   3. Corporate greed and fraud ("Enron syndrome")
      a. After the turn of the century, surfacing of
        i. Torrent of revelations
        ii. Scope of misdeeds
        iii. Corporate crime and punishment
      b. Deregulation as contributing factor
   4. Rising inequality
      a. General economic improvement for Americans
      b. Widening gap between richest and poorest Americans
      c. Sources of working-class hardship
        i. Export of manufacturing jobs abroad
        ii. Shift from high-paying to low-paying jobs
      d. Urban and rural dimensions of poverty

       e. The new American suburbs
          i. As self-contained economies
          ii. Increasing heterogeneity of
          iii. Persisting class divisions within

III. Culture Wars
    A. Post–Cold War renewal of ethnic and religious divisions
       1. Around world
       2. In America
    B. New patterns of immigration
       1. Shift in geographic origins
       2. Record numbers
       3. Emergence of new ethnic communities
       4. Diversification of American heartland
       5. Range of occupations, social backgrounds
       6. Predominance of women
    C. New diversity
       1. Latinos
          a. Emergence as largest immigrant group
          b. Variety of national origins
          c. Growing impact on American life
          d. Compression in low-wage sector
       2. Asian-Americans
          a. Growing presence
          b. Variety of national origins
          c. Socioeconomic status
             i. Overall progress
             ii. Polarization between prosperous and poor
       3. Outdatedness of two-race ("black-white") dichotomy
       4. Rise of multiracial culture
       5. Prospect of growing diversity in new century
    D. African-Americans in the 1990s
       1. Progress
          a. Unprecedented strides
             i. Occupational
             ii. Educational
          b. Sources of
             i. Decline in overt discrimination
             ii. Affirmative action
             iii. Economic boom
       2. Growing presence of African immigrants in black America
       3. Problems
          a. Continuing socioeconomic lag
             i. Employment
             ii. Income

           iii. Incidence of poverty
           iv. Quality of schooling
           v. Other measures
     b. Persistence of segregation
           i. Housing
           ii. School
     c. Trend of judicial rulings
           i. On relief from racial discrimination
           ii. On affirmative action
           iii. On school desegregation
     d. Prominence in expanding prison population
           i. Rise of "prison-industrial complex"
           ii. Consequences for black America
     e. Blacks and death penalty
E. Los Angeles uprising
    1. Causes
     a. Rodney King episode
     b. Accumulating grievances of urban minorities
    2. Magnitude
F. Continuing rights revolution
    1. Emerging movement for rights of disabled; Americans With Disabilities Act
    2. Gay movement
     a. Rising focus on Acquired Immunodeficiency Syndrome (AIDS)
     b. Increasing presence in politics
     c. Growing public acceptance
    3. American Indian movement
     a. Growth in Indian population, cultural pride
     b. Pursuit of restitution for past injustices
     c. Quasi-sovereign legal status of some tribes
     d. Prosperous Indian casinos
G. Cultural conservatism
    1. Key grievances
     a. "Identity politics," multiculturalism
     b. Influx of nonwhite immigrants
     c. Decline of "family values"
    2. Key manifestations
     a. Passage of California propositions
           i. Denial of public services to illegal immigrants
           ii. Bars on bilingual education, affirmative action
     b. Denial of food stamps to noncitizens
     c. Publication of nativist works

           d. Creationist campaigns
           e. Assault on National Endowment for the Arts
           f. Defense of Marriage Act
           g. Other crusades
       3. Key voices
           a. Pat Robertson, Christian Coalition
           b. Pat Buchanan
  H. "Family values" in retreat
       1. Decline of "traditional" family
       2. Supreme Court affirmation of abortion rights: *Casey v. Planned Parenthood of Pennsylvania*
       3. Persistence of sexual revolution, feminism
  I. Right-wing extremism
       1. Armed groups: Aryan Nation, Posse Comitatus, others
       2. Racist, anti-Semitic, antigovernment outlook
       3. Oklahoma City bombing
           a. Bloodshed
           b. Conviction, execution of Timothy McVeigh
           c. Impact on national consciousness

IV. Impeachment and election of 2000
  A. Impeachment of Clinton
       1. Background
           a. Republican animosity toward Clinton
           b. Clinton's reckless behavior
       2. Allegations and investigations
           a. Whitewater
           b. Paula Jones
           c. Monica Lewinsky
       3. Kenneth Starr report
       4. House of Representatives impeachment vote
       5. Trial and acquittal in Senate
       6. Public aversion to Starr investigation, impeachment
  B. Election of 2000
       1. Competing tickets
           a. Al Gore and Joseph Lieberman (Democrat)
           b. George W. Bush and Dick Cheney (Republican)
       2. Contested vote
           a. Popular majority for Gore
           b. Florida controversy
              i. Pivotal role in electoral outcome
              ii. Disputed results
              iii. State Supreme Court recount order

    c. U.S. Supreme Court's *Bush v. Gore* ruling
      i. Consequence: Bush victory
      ii. Court's reasoning
  3. Noteworthy aspects
    a. Evenness of partisan division
    b. Lines of partisan division
      i. Geographical
      ii. Urban/rural
      iii. Racial
      iv. Gender
    c. Troubling features
      i. Clash between popular and electoral outcomes
      ii. Failings of voting technology
      iii. Dominant role of big money contributors
      iv. Low turnout
      v. Neglect of major issues

V. Freedom and the new century
  A. Balance sheet of human progress and tragedy in twentieth century
    1. Around world
    2. In America
  B. "Freedom" at close of century
    1. Importance to Americans
    2. Distinctive meanings for Americans
    3. Ambiguous meanings for Americans

CHRONOLOGY

1988   George Bush defeats Michael Dukakis in presidential election

1989   *Brenda Patterson v. McLean Credit Union*
      Pro-democracy demonstrations in China
      Removal of Berlin Wall
      U.S. invasion of Panama

1989–90 Collapse of Communist regimes across eastern Europe

1990   Americans With Disabilities Act
      Reunification of Germany
      Iraq invades Kuwait

1991   Gulf War; ouster of Iraq from Kuwait
      Clarence Thomas/Anita Hill controversy
      Dissolution of Soviet Union

1992	Outbreak of Bosnian war, "ethnic cleansing" Los Angeles uprising *Casey v. Planned Parenthood of Pennsylvania* Bill Clinton defeats Bush in presidential election
1993	Clinton expands Earned Income Tax Credit North American Free Trade Agreement Israeli-Palestinian Oslo agreement
1994	Failure of Clinton health reform proposal Start of Whitewater investigation U.S. troops intervene in Haiti to aid elected government Republicans unveil "Contract With America" Republicans sweep congressional elections California Proposition 187
1995	Oklahoma City bombing Clinton-Republican stand-off; government shutdown
1996	Telecommunications Act Defense of Marriage Act Passage of welfare reform Clinton wins reelection over Bob Dole
1998	Monica Lewinsky scandal
1999	Impeachment and acquittal of Clinton Kosovo war Repeal of Glass-Steagall Act Protests at World Trade Organization meeting in Seattle
2000	End of stock market boom Disputed election contest between Al Gore and George W. Bush *Bush v. Gore*

KEY TERMS

The Gulf War: President Bush's goals in the Persian Gulf War were to defend Saudi Arabia and to liberate Kuwait from Iraqi control. With these goals he was able to build an impressive international coalition. With the rapid collapse of Iraqi resistance, the president had to resist the urge to remove Iraqi leader Saddam Hussein from power, which had not been a coalition goal. Bush and his advisers decided that although Hussein was a threat to the region's peace, they would not liberate Iraq from his rule. To do so might alienate some coalition partners and would entail difficult or even deadly fighting in Baghdad and other major cities. Satisfied with achieving his initial goals, Bush ended the Persian Gulf War with Saddam Hussein still in control of Iraq.

The Perot candidacy: Texas billionaire H. Ross Perot capitalized on dissatisfaction with the Democratic and Republican parties by seizing on an issue that most Americans could understand. Perot argued that the rapidly growing national debt was undermining the nation's economic stability and declared that the politicians of the two major parties had failed to rein in federal spending. Perot's message resonated with voters, earning him 19 percent of the popular vote (although he won no electoral votes). Analysts argued that his third party candidacy had a greater effect on Bush than it did Clinton, as some 70 percent of Perot voters might have voted for the Republican candidate. Perot ran again in 1996 but won only 8.4 percent of the popular vote.

North American Free Trade Agreement: Hoping to create a powerful trading bloc in the Western Hemisphere, Republican and Democratic politicians sought to craft a regional agreement that would eliminate tariffs with the nation's neighbors. Shortly before he left office, President Bush negotiated the North American Free Trade Agreement (NAFTA) with Mexico and Canada. NAFTA would gradually reduce and then eliminate tariffs between the three countries. President Clinton championed the measure and pushed it through Congress despite opposition from his own party and labor unions. The longterm effects of NAFTA remain uncertain, although claims that the agreement would lead to a catastrophic loss of jobs in the United States proved unfounded as unemployment declined in the late 1990s.

welfare reform: Known typically as welfare, the Aid to Families with Dependent Children (AFDC) program had its origins in the Great Depression. Federal aid to low-income families reached 14 million people by 1995, at a cost of $22.6 billion. Critics charged that the program fostered lifelong dependency on federal aid and perpetuated poverty. Despite liberal support for AFDC, President Clinton pledged to "end welfare as we know it." The new program, Temporary Assistance to Needy Families (TANF) provided federal grants to states to administer. TANF placed time limits on participation—most recipients were required to find work within two years and could only receive TANF benefits for a total of five years over the course of a lifetime. The program proved surprisingly effective, especially because the economic boom of the 1990s created millions of new jobs. However, critics noted that despite declining enrollment in TANF, poverty remains a persistent problem in American life.

The Balkan crisis: The totalitarian governments that ruled Eastern Europe after World War II used violence to repress centuries-old ethnic tensions in the region. With the fall of these governments in the late 1980s, resentments and anger quickly resurfaced. Serbian president Slobodan Milosevic dedicated his administration to eliminating Muslims from the region. His program of ethnic cleansing threatened to lead to a wider war in the Balkans, the region where World War I had begun earlier in the century. Uncertain as to how to proceed, President Clinton finally supported NATO air strikes and U.S. participation in a

United Nations peacekeeping force. The fragile peace was disrupted in 1999 when Milosevic ordered ethnic cleansing in a region known as Kosovo. Clinton was again indecisive, fearing that the American public would not tolerate the deaths of American soldiers in Eastern Europe. He ultimately approved aerial bombing campaigns that helped bring about a settlement. The region remained in turmoil, however, reminding Americans of the difficulties of leadership in the post-Cold War world.

Patterson v. McLean Credit Union: Brenda Patterson, an African-American, worked at the McLean Credit Union as a teller. After she was laid off, Patterson filed a lawsuit claiming that she had been denied a promotion and then fired because of her race. Her lawsuit claimed that such actions violated provisions of the Civil Rights Act of 1866. In previous rulings, the court had held that the 1866 law covered private racial discrimination in making contracts. In the Patterson case, the court heard arguments, and then made the unusual and controversial decision to have the attorneys reargue the case. In its ruling the court declared that the Civil Rights Act of 1866 protected Patterson from racial discrimination at the time she negotiated her contract, but did not protect her from such harassment while on the job. Congress responded to the ruling by passing the Civil Rights Act of 1991, which protected employees from racial discrimination while at work.

race and imprisonment: In the years after World War II, incarceration rates in the United States remained relatively constant, averaging about 100 prisoners per 100,000 people. In the early 1970s, as courts handed out increasingly tougher sentences, the rates began to rise, reaching 427 prisoners per 100,000 people. By the year 2000, one out of every four prisoners in the world was in a U.S. prison. African-Americans were especially vulnerable to the rapid rise in prison populations, constituting some 50 percent of U.S. prisoners by the end of the twentieth century, and making up almost 50 percent of the inmates on death row.

Defense of Marriage Act of 1996: The Defense of Marriage Act, which President Clinton signed into law in September 1996, defined marriage as a "union between one man and one woman." While it did not prevent the states from allowing gay marriage, the law prohibited gay spouses from receiving spousal benefits from federal programs. In addition, the act declared that no state would have to recognize the legitimacy of gay marriages performed in another state. The measure easily passed the Congress, with the final Senate vote being 85–14. President Clinton, recognized as an advocate of gay rights, signed the bill into law with some reluctance; however, his 1996 presidential campaign drew attention to his support for the measure with a series of television commercials.

the Clinton impeachment: In sworn testimony, President Clinton testified that he had never engaged in sexual relations with White House intern Monica Lewinsky. When DNA evidence later proved that the president had been intimate with the intern, his statements regarding their relationship opened him to charges of perjury. In addition, special prosecutor Kenneth Starr contended that Clinton had obstructed justice in an effort to conceal his affair, in part by encouraging Lewinsky to lie about their relationship. In December 1998 the House of Representatives impeached the president in votes that split largely on party lines. The Senate, which tried Clinton on two counts, did not provide the 67 votes necessary to remove him from office. Although Clinton prevailed in the crisis, his presidency had been paralyzed and his legacy forever tarnished.

OBJECTIVE QUESTIONS

Multiple Choice

1. A leading slogan of cultural conservatism in the 1990s was
   A. "Safe sex."
   B. "Sixties values."
   C. "Family values."
   D. "It's the economy, stupid."

2. In 2000, the largest employer in America was
   A. General Motors.
   B. Wal-Mart.
   C. Microsoft.
   D. Enron.

3. Which of the following series of events is listed in proper sequence?
   A. Seattle protests at World Trade Organization meeting; reunification of Germany; dissolution of Soviet Union; removal of Berlin Wall
   B. Clinton election victory over Bob Dole; announcement of "Contract With America"; impeachment of Clinton; announcement of Clinton health plan
   C. Clinton electoral victory over George Bush; defeat of Clinton health plan; passage of welfare reform; release of Starr report
   D. Kosovo war; Operation Desert Storm; U.S. invasion of Panama; outbreak of Bosnian war

4. Which of the following was *not* a key trend in world affairs during the 1990s?
   A. the end of the Cold War
   B. an easing of ethnic and religious tensions
   C. a global expansion of the free market model
   D. the advent of international bodies to monitor human rights

5. Which of the following was *not* a policy adopted by the federal government during the Clinton years?
   A. repeal of the federal welfare entitlement
   B. international free trade agreements
   C. federal deficit reduction
   D. universal health care

6. Which of the following was *not* a key element of the Republican "Contract With America"?
   A. sharper restrictions on the sale of handguns
   B. less government regulation
   C. lower taxes
   D. abolition of affirmative action

7. Which of the following was *not* a major demographic trend in 1990s America?
   A. a growth in the number of incarcerated Americans
   B. a growing influx of immigrants from Asia and Latin America
   C. a growing number of Americans designated ineligible to vote
   D. a growing volume of emigration from the United States to Europe

8. Which of the following was *not* a significant aftereffect of the 1990s computer revolution?
   A. a bridging of the gulf between affluent and poor
   B. a broadening of America's cultural influence around the world
   C. a widening of popular input into the public sphere
   D. a marked increase in business efficiency

9. The collapse of communism in the Soviet Union and Eastern Europe occurred during what years?
   A. 1963–1974
   B. 1989–1991
   C. 2000–2002
   D. 2002–2003

10. What occurred in Tiananmen Square in Beijing, China in April 1989?
   A. Tens of thousands of students, joined by workers, teachers, and some government officials, occupied the square and demanded greater democracy in China.
   B. Tens of thousands of students gathered, burning in effigy, "The Goddess of Freedom," to show their contempt for American foreign policy.
   C. An upgraded version of Microsoft Windows was released, causing a flood of consumerism to flood the square, seeking cheap pirated copies.
   D. An appearance by the rock group The Clash led hundreds of young people to flood the square, dancing and singing.

11. During what years did the Berlin Wall, the most prominent symbol of the Cold War, divide East and West Berlin?
    A. 1945–1975
    B. 1961–1989
    C. 1947–2000
    D. 1948–1992

12. In what year did the Soviet Union cease to exist and, in its place, fifteen new independent nations arise?
    A. 1991
    B. 1999
    C. 2000
    D. 1967

13. Who won the Cold War?
    A. China and its allies.
    B. Soviet Union and its allies.
    C. United States and its allies.
    D. No one really won, as each nation took something positive away with them from the experience.

14. Which United States president first spoke of the coming of a "new world order"?
    A. George H. W. Bush
    B. John F. Kennedy
    C. Lyndon Baines Johnson
    D. Jimmy Carter

15. In February 1991, the United States launched Operation Desert Storm as part of the Gulf War, and quickly drove the Iraqi army from what country?
    A. Iran
    B. Israel
    C. Iraq
    D. Kuwait

16. Who was the African-American chairman of the Joint Chiefs of Staff who, in the early 1990s, argued that the United States should not commit its troops abroad without clear objectives and a timetable for withdrawal?
    A. Henry Hugh Shelton
    B. Peter Pace
    C. Colin Powell
    D. John Shalikashvili

17. In the 1992 run for the presidency, Bill Clinton held all of the following views, except which?
    A. He promised to "end welfare as we know it."
    B. He supported abortion rights.
    C. He supported affirmative action for racial minorities.
    D. He pledged to fulfill the unfulfilled promise of Johnson's Great Society.

18. Pat Buchanan delivered a speech at the 1992 Republican national convention that declared cultural war against all the following, except:
    A. gays.
    B. feminists.
    C. supporters of abortion rights.
    D. the Christian Right.

19. What third-party candidate received 19 percent of the popular vote in the 1992 presidential election, the best result for a third-party candidate since Theodore Roosevelt in 1912?
    A. Ralph Nader
    B. Pat Buchanan
    C. Ross Perot
    D. Al Gore

20. In 1994, the Republican Party won control of both houses of Congress for the first time since the 1950s; they proclaimed their triumph the "Freedom Revolution," and Newt Gingrich, a conservative congressman from Georgia, masterminded their platform, called:
    A. "The Moral Majority."
    B. "Contract with America."
    C. "The New Freedom Revolution."
    D. "Morning in America."

21. In line with their 1994 platform, Republicans in the United States House of Representatives moved swiftly to approve deep cuts in all of the following, except:
    A. Medicare.
    B. environmental programs.
    C. the military.
    D. education.

22. The longest uninterrupted period of economic expansion in the nation's history took place during what years?
    A. 1991–2000
    B. 1878–1984
    C. 2001–2008
    D. 1929–1991

23. The Christian Coalition was founded by evangelical minister:
    A. Pat Robertson
    B. Jerry Falwell
    C. Jim Baker
    D. Robert G. Grant

24. The 1990s Christian Coalition became a major force in Republican Party politics and launched crusades against all of the following, except:
    A. secularism in public schools.
    B. abortion.
    C. gay rights.
    D. creationism.

25. By the year 2000, what percentage of all marriages ended in divorce?
    A. 10 percent
    B. 20 percent
    C. 25 percent
    D. 50 percent

26. Which was *not* true of Bill Clinton?
    A. He had smoked marijuana.
    B. He had married a feminist.
    C. He supported gay rights.
    D. He served in Vietnam.

27. Who won the popular vote in the presidential election of 2000?
    A. Al Gore
    B. George W. Bush
    C. Bill Clinton
    D. George H. W. Bush

True or False

1. The protesters assembled at the 1999 meeting of the World Trade Organization in Seattle represented a striking mix of industrial workers and environmentalists.

2. The United Nations endorsed the U.S. invasion of Panama, but denounced Operation Desert Storm.

3. Following the Republican electoral sweep of 1994, President Clinton vowed to defend the heritage of New Deal liberalism.

4. The stock market boom of the late Nineties was fueled in part by high-level corporate fraud.

5. In the 1990s, the vast majority of Latinos in America were poor, and the vast majority of Asian-Americans were affluent.

6. In the 1990s, blacks predominated among the growing ranks of incarcerated Americans.

7. The impeachment of Clinton failed to win the support of most Americans.

8. In the 2000 election, George W. Bush won the popular vote, but lost the electoral vote to Al Gore.

9. The collapse of communism in the Soviet Union opened the world to the spread of market capitalism.

10. During the 1990s presidents George Bush and Bill Clinton both asserted the view that America should embrace the mission of creating a single global free market as a path to greater worldwide freedom.

11. During the 1991 Gulf War, President George H. W. Bush's approval rating reached 89 percent, but the next year, he lost the presidential election.

12. In 1992, unemployment rose as family income stagnated.

13. As president, Bill Clinton opposed his predecessor's passion for free trade, believing instead that regulatory tariffs would ensure higher standards of living for American workers.

14. Had Ross Perot not run as an independent candidate for the presidency in 1992, it is possible that President George H. W. Bush would have won reelection that year.

15. In western Europe and Canada, governments provide universal medical coverage for all citizens, but in the United States there was—in the 1900s and early 2000s—no universal medical coverage.

16. By 2000, 40 million Americans lacked health insurance.

17. In his January 1996 State of the Union address, President Bill Clinton announced that "the era of big government is over," and, in effect, turned his back on the tradition of Democratic Party liberalism and embraced the antigovernment outlook associated with Republicans since the days of Barry Goldwater.

18. In 1996, President Clinton signed a Republican bill into law, abolishing the Aid to Families with Dependent Children (AFDC) program, replacing it with a system of grants of money to states, with strict limits on how long recipients could receive payments.

19. Bill Clinton was the first Democrat to win reelection to the presidency since FDR.

20. In 1994, tribal massacres rocked Rwanda, in central Africa. Over 800,000 people were slaughtered and the United States sent in a massive military force in an effort to staunch the flow of blood.

21. In the early 1990s, in an effort to stop "ethnic cleansing," the United States and its NATO allies, after considerable indecision, launched airstrikes against Bosnian Serb forces.

22. After recovering from the recession of 1990–1991, the United States economy continued to expand for the rest of the decade; the boom became the longest uninterrupted period of economic expansion in American history.

23. The largest one-day drop in stock prices in history occurred on April 14, 2000.

24. Between 2000 and 2002, the price of NASDAQ stocks fell by nearly 80 percent.

25. During the economic upturn of the 1990s, the inequitable distribution of wealth in the United States dropped sharply, as the index of inequality registered a democratic leveling out of American incomes.

26. The Enron Corporation became famous in the 1990s for its leading part in the computer revolution, especially in software.

27. In 2000, more than half of the labor force in the United States worked for less than $14 an hour.

28. During the 1990s, religion in the United States lost much of its appeal, as a secular culture based on consumption and mass entertainment dominated American society.

29. In consequence of the immigration law of 1965, most immigrants arriving in the United States between 1965 and 2000 were from Western Europe.

30. By 2000, more than 10 percent of the American population was foreign-born.

31. By 2000, more than 3 million Muslims resided in the United States.

32. By 2000, poverty rates for Latinos were double the national figure of 11.3 percent.

33. By 2001, more than a third of African-Americans lived in suburbs.

34. In 2000, the number of prisoners in United States prisons reached nearly 2 million, 10 times the number of prisoners in United States prisons in 1970.

35. By the early twenty-first century, more than one in four black men could expect to serve time in prison at some time during their lives.

36. Between 1977 and 1999, the United States executed 598 people.

37. By 2000, more than 400,000 Americans had died of HIV/AIDS.

38. The growth of public tolerance of homosexuality was among the most striking changes in American social attitudes in the last 20 years of the 20th century.

39. In 1994, Californians approved Proposition 187, which denied illegal immigrants and their children access to welfare, education, and health services.

40. By 2000, 23 states had passed laws establishing English as their official language.

41. In 1900, the average annual income of Americans was $3,000 in today's dollars.

42. As late as 1940, a third of American households did not have running water.

43. At the beginning of the twenty-first century, more than 7 million American families lived in gated communities.

44. President Bill Clinton was impeached, but not convicted or removed from office.

ESSAY QUESTIONS

1. Select three significant international episodes between 1989 and 2000, and discuss how they illuminate America's changing place in the post–Cold War world.

2. In 1992, American voters elected Bill Clinton by a substantial margin; two years later, the voters repudiated Clinton, sending Republican majorities to both houses of Congress. How might this reversal in Clinton's political fortune be explained?

3. In 1994, American voters repudiated President Clinton, sending Republican majorities to both houses of Congress. Two years later, the voters reelected Clinton by a substantial margin. How might this revival of Clinton's political fortune be explained?

4. Assess the significance of the impeachment episode of 1998–99. What do the impeachment—and ultimate acquittal—of President Clinton suggest about the political and social attitudes of Americans at the close of the Nineties?

5. "At the outset of the year 2000, the present situation and future prospects of the American people looked bright." In what ways do you agree with this statement? In what ways do you find it unpersuasive? Illustrate your discussion with examples from the text.

6. Assess the significance of the disputed election of 2000. What does the outcome reveal about American politics at the outset of the twenty-first century?

7. Write an essay on the effects of globalization on the world's economy and environment in the 1990s.

8. Compare and contrast two perspectives in the culture wars of the 1990s.

9. Write an essay on immigration and immigrants in the United States in the 1990s.

10. Write an essay on the Clinton administration's efforts on foreign affairs and human rights.

11. Write an essay on the "Freedom Revolution" of the 1990s.

SOURCES FOR FURTHER RESEARCH

Books

GENERAL OVERVIEWS

Chafe, William H., *The Unfinished Journey: America since World War II* (2003)
Hodgson, Godfrey, *More Equal Than Others: America from Nixon to the New Century* (2004)
Johnson, Haynes, *The Best of Times: America in the Clinton Years* (2001)

PARTICULAR ASPECTS

Brands, H. W., *The Strange Death of American Liberalism* (2001)
Cassidy, John, *Dot.con: The Greatest Story Ever Sold* (2002)
Christianson, Scott, *With Liberty for Some: 500 Years of Imprisonment in America* (1998)
Foner, Nancy, *From Ellis Island to JFK: New York's Two Great Waves of Immigration* (2000)
Friedman, Thomas L., *The Lexus and the Olive Tree* (1999)
Gaddis, John L., *The United States and the End of the Cold War* (1992)
Judis, John B., *The Paradox of American Democracy* (2000)

Katz, Michael B., *The Price of Citizenship: Redefining the American Welfare State* (2001)

Levitas, Daniel, *The Terrorist Next Door: The Militia Movement and the Radical Right* (2003)

Ortega, Bob, *In Sam We Trust: The Untold Story of Sam Walton and How Wal-Mart is Devouring America* (1998)

Phillips, Kevin, *Wealth and Democracy* (2002)

Power, Samantha, *A Problem from Hell: America and the Age of Genocide* (2002)

Roberts, Sam, *Who We Are Now: The Changing Face of America in the Twenty-First Century* (2004)

Shipler, David, *A Country of Strangers: Blacks and Whites in America* (1997)

Skocpol, Theda, *Boomerang: Clinton's Health Security Effort and the Turn Against Government in U.S. Politics* (1996)

Smelser, Neil J. and Jeffrey C. Alexander, *Diversity and Its Discontents: Cultural Conflict and Common Ground in Contemporary American Society* (1999)

Stiglitz, Joseph, *Globalization and Its Discontents* (2002)

Wolfe, Alan, *One Nation, After All: What Middle-Class Americans Really Think About* (1998)

Videos

George W. Bush: Election and Inauguration (86 minutes, MPI Home Video, 2001)

Clarence Thomas and Anita Hill (58 minutes, PBS Video, 1992)

The Clinton Years (120 minutes, PBS Video, 2001)

Cold War (20 hours, PBS Video, 1998)

The Gulf War (4 hours, WGBH Frontline: WGBH Educational Foundation, 1996)

L.A. Is Burning: Five Reports from a Divided City (87 minutes, PBS Video, 1993)

The Long Road to War (120 minutes, PBS Video, 2003)

Nerds 2.0.1: A Brief History of the Internet (180 minutes, PBS Home Video and Warner Home Video, 1998)

Rhetorical Highlights from the Impeachment of Bill Clinton (105 minutes, Educational Video Group, 2000)

The Rodney King Incident: Race and Justice in America (56 minutes, Films for the Humanities & Sciences, 1998)

The Seattle Syndrome (24 minutes, Bullfrog Films, 2000)

Yugoslavia: Death of a Nation (300 minutes, Discovery Channel Video, 1998)

The War Room (96 minutes, Vidmark Entertainment, 1994)

Web Resources

George Herbert Walker Bush, The Internet Public Library
http://www.ipl.org/div/potus/ghwbush.html

William Jefferson Clinton, The Internet Public Library
http://www.ipl.org/div/potus/wjclinton.html

Cold War, Cable News Network, Inc.
http://www.cnn.com/SPECIALS/cold.war/

"The Gulf War," Frontline
http://www.pbs.org/wgbh/pages/frontline/gulf/index.html

Impeachment: The Process and History, New York Times
http://www.nytimes.com/learning/general/specials/impeachment/

Investigating the President: The Trial, Cable News Network, Inc.
http://www.cnn.com/ALLPOLITICS/resources/1998/lewinsky/

Los Angeles Police Officers' (Rodney King Beating) Trials, Douglas O. Linder
http://www.law.umkc.edu/faculty/projects/ftrials/lapd/lapd.html

ANSWERS TO OBJECTIVE QUESTIONS

Multiple Choice

1-C, 2-B, 3-C, 4-B, 5-D, 6-A, 7-D, 8-A, 9-B, 10-A, 11-B, 12-A, 13-C, 14-A, 15-D, 16-C, 17-D, 18-D, 19-C, 20-B, 21-C, 22-A, 23-A, 24-D, 25-D, 26-D, 27-A

True or False

1-T, 2-F, 3-F, 4-T, 5-F, 6-T, 7-T, 8-F, 9-T,10-T, 11-T, 12-T, 13-F, 14-T, 15-T, 16-T, 17-T, 18-T, 19-T, 20-F, 21-T, 22-T, 23-T, 24-T, 25-F, 26-F, 27-T, 28-F, 29-F, 30-T, 31-T, 32-T, 33-T, 34-T, 35-T, 36-T, 37-T, 38-T, 39-T, 40-T, 41-T, 42-T, 43-T, 44-T

CHAPTER 28

September 11 and the Next American Century

CHAPTER OBJECTIVES

- What was the impact of the September 11 attacks on the lives and perspectives of Americans?
- What was the domestic agenda of the incoming administration of George W. Bush? How did this agenda evolve in the aftermath of September 11?
- What was the foreign policy agenda of the incoming Bush administration? How did this agenda evolve in the aftermath of September 11?
- How did American foreign relations evolve over the first term and a half of the Bush administration?
- What were the motivations and reasoning behind the Iraq War? How did public debate over the merits of the war evolve over its first three years?
- How did the Bush administration seek to the balance the imperatives of security and liberty in the aftermath of September 11? How did Americans debate this issue?

CHAPTER OUTLINE

I. September 11, 2001
   A. The attacks
      1. Death tolls
      2. Trauma
         a. To New York City
         b. To the country
   B. The perpetrators: Osama bin Laden, Al Qaeda
      1. Bin Laden background
      2. Outlook and agenda
      3. Mode of operation

   C. Terrorism
1. Instances in American past
2. Late-twentieth-century episodes
   a. Hijacking of *Achille Lauro*
   b. Downing of Pan American flight 103
   c. 1993 bombing at World Trade Center
   d. Explosions at U.S. embassies in Kenya and Tanzania
   D. Post–September 11 atmosphere in nation
1. Wave of fear
2. Renewed passion for freedom
3. Fresh attention to old questions
   a. America's global role
   b. Balance between liberty and security
   c. Breadth of American freedom

II. President George W. Bush before September 11
   A. Domestic policy
1. Campaign rhetoric of "compassionate conservatism"
2. Staunch conservative agenda from outset of presidency
   a. Fiscal
     i. Record-size tax cut, geared toward the wealthy
     ii. Revival of "supply-side" theory
   b. Environmental
3. Jim Jeffords defection from Republican party; restoration of Democratic Senate majority
   B. Foreign policy
1. Insistence on American freedom from international treaties, institutions
   a. Pursuit of national missile defense system; withdrawal from Anti-Ballistic Missile treaty
   b. Repudiation of International Criminal Court treaty
   c. Rejection of Kyoto treaty on global warming
     i. Global warming problem
     ii. Growing scientific confirmation of problem
     iii. Contribution of United States to global warming
     iv. Worldwide support for treaty
2. Furious response around world

III. "War on terrorism"
   A. Public mood following September 11
1. Outpouring of patriotism, collective sympathy and resolve
2. Renewal of trust in government
3. Surge in popularity of Bush
   B. Unveiling of Bush Doctrine: September 20 address to Congress
1. Freedom as rallying cry

  2. "War on terrorism"
   a. Vagueness of enemy or scenario for victory
   b. Absence of line between terrorists and governments harboring them
   c. Absence of middle ground
 C. War in Afghanistan
  1. Lead-up: refusal of Taliban government to surrender bin Laden to United States
  2. American airstrikes, Northern Alliance ground combat
  3. Fall of Taliban government
  4. Fragility of new government
  5. Escape of bin Laden and supporters
  6. Characterization by Bush as only start of war on terrorism
  7. Longer-term outcomes
   a. Gradual reemergence of Taliban presence
   b. Ongoing U.S. troop presence
 D. Expansion of U.S. military presence around world
 E. Dramatic departures in American foreign policy
  1. Bush's identification of "axis of evil" (Iraq, Iran, North Korea)
  2. National Security Strategy document
   a. Definition of freedom
   b. Pledge to fight terrorists and tyrants around world
   c. Insistence on global military dominance
   d. Adoption of "preemptive" war doctrine
 F. World reaction: from post–September 11 sympathy to mounting alarm
  1. Breadth of criticism
  2. Themes of criticism
 G. Indicators of American imperial aspirations
  1. Colossal military expenditures
  2. Rehabilitation of "empire" in public discourse
IV. Iraq War
 A. Lead-up to war
  1. Pre-Bush administration
   a. Survival of Saddam Hussein regime following Gulf War of 1991
   b. Ongoing tensions with United Nations and United States in 1990s
  2. Bush administration's push toward war
   a. Pre–September 11
    i. Early advocates of "regime change"
    ii. Military strategizing for ouster of Hussein
    iii. Visions of warm reception from "liberated" Iraqis

      b. Post–September 11
         i. Adoption and announcement of "regime change" policy
        ii. Arguments made in defense of "regime change" policy
       iii. Credulity of American media
       iv. Promotion, then dismissal, of intensified UN inspections for weapons of mass destruction in Iraq
        v. Secretary of State Colin Powell's presentation of "evidence" at UN
       vi. Announcement of intention to go to war, regardless of UN position
  3. Mounting opposition to a "preemptive" war
      a. Sources
         i. Antiwar movements in United States and beyond
        ii. Foreign policy "realists"
       iii. Nations around world
      b. Themes
      c. UN refusal to approve
B. The war
  1. Initial sense of triumph
      a. Rapid fall of Hussein regime
      b. American occupation
      c. Capture of Hussein
      d. Bush: "Mission Accomplished"
  2. Growing signs of crisis
      a. Looting and chaos
      b. Gathering insurgency against occupation
      c. Wave of sectarian violence
      d. Elusiveness of viable government
      e. Emergence of Iraq as haven for terrorists
  3. Longer-term crisis
      a. Descent into civil war
      b. Death tolls
         i. American
        ii. Iraqi
      c. Financial cost to United States
  4. Comparisons with Vietnam
C. Significance of war for American foreign policy
  1. Extraordinary use of unilateral force outside Western Hemisphere
  2. Unprecedented occupation of Middle East nation
D. Reaction to the war
  1. In America
      a. Initial popularity

        b. Growing skepticism

        c. Expanding opposition

    2. Around world

        a. Broad outrage

        b. Straining of UN, Western alliance

V. Constraining liberty in the name of security

  A. At home

    1. Government measures

        a. USA PATRIOT Act

           i. Conferring of vast new powers on law enforcement agencies

           ii. New crime category of "domestic terrorism"

        b. Mass roundups, indefinite detention of Middle Eastern foreigners

        c. Detention of suspected terrorists abroad; Guantanamo

        d. Establishment of Department of Homeland Security

        e. Authorization of secret military tribunals for noncitizens

        f. Authorization of indefinite detention of U.S. citizens deemed "enemy combatants"

        g. Warnings not to criticize administration policies

        h. Rescinding of 1970s-era restraints on police and surveillance activities

    2. Presidential disregard for legal and constitutional constraints

    3. Public reaction

        a. Acceptance of some contraction of liberties

        b. Concern over historical fragility of American rights

           i. Civil liberties

           ii. Equality before the law

  B. Abroad

    1. Bush administration impatience with Geneva Convention, International Convention Against Torture

    2. The torture controversy

        a. Over legitimacy of torture

        b. Over definition of torture

    3. Government measures

        a. Denial to "unlawful combatants" of Geneva protections

        b. Establishment of CIA jails in foreign countries

        c. "Rendition"

    4. Revelations of prisoner abuse in Afghanistan, Abu Ghraib, and Guantanamo

    5. Congressional ban on torture

        a. Enactment of

        b. Bush's grudging acceptance of

VI. Republican gains in 2002 elections

VII. The economy under Bush
- A. Economic trends
  1. Resumption of growth
  2. Continued declines in jobs, wages, benefits
     - a. Magnitude and location of
     - b. Social distribution of
  3. Widening of economic inequality
     - a. Degree
     - b. Causes
  4. Explosion of budget deficits
     - a. Magnitude
       - i. Federal level
       - ii. State level
     - b. Causes
       - i. Faltering economy
       - ii. Increased military spending
       - iii. 2001 tax cuts
     - c. Impact: drastic cuts in social programs
     - d. Bush response
       - i. Support for low interest rates
       - ii. Further tax cuts

VIII. Election of 2004
- A. Candidacy of John Kerry
  1. Expectations for
  2. Limitations of
- B. Reelection campaign of George W. Bush
- C. Bush's narrow victory
- D. Causes and significance of outcome

IX. Bush's second term
- A. Inaugural vow to "end tyranny in the world"
- B. Steady erosion of Bush's standing
  1. Falling support for Iraq war
  2. Republican corruption scandals
     - a. In White House
     - b. In Congress
  3. Failure of Social Security "reform" initiative

X. Hurricane Katrina
- A. Arrival
  1. Destruction of levees
  2. Flooding of New Orleans

      B. Inept response by government
          1. Local level
          2. Federal level
              a. Federal Emergency Management Agency
              b. President Bush
      C. New Orleans disaster
          1. Mass abandonment of blacks, poor
          2. Death toll
          3. Physical damage
          4. Displacement
      D. Public response to disaster
          1. Relief efforts
              a. Private
              b. Other states
          2. Shame over marginalization of blacks, poor
      E. Impact on oil prices

  XI. Immigration debate
      A. Background
          1. Recent swelling of Hispanic immigration
          2. Spread of new immigrants throughout American heartland
          3. Blend of legal and undocumented immigrants
      B. Response to immigration
          1. History of public debate and government policy
          2. 2006 House of Representatives bill to suppress illegal
               immigration
      C. 2006 immigrant rights movement
          1. Mass demonstrations across country
          2. Grievances and demands
          3. Popular reaction
      D. Policy stalemate

  XII. Supreme Court brakes on conservative agenda
      A. Upholding of affirmative action
      B. Overturning of decision making homosexual acts a crime
      C. Reassertion of legal rights for prisoners in American custody
          1. Key cases
              a. *Rasul v. Bush*
              b. *Hamdi v. Rumsfeld*
              c. *Hamdan v. Rumsfeld*
          2. Significance
              a. Rebuff of presidential defiance of legal and constitutional
                  constraints
              b. Reaffirmation of rule of law, separation of powers

XIII. America in the early twenty-first century
    A. Instabilities around the world
    B. Ongoing debate over meanings of American freedom

CHRONOLOGY

1991   Gulf War; ouster of Iraq from Kuwait

1993   Al Qaeda truck bombing of World Trade Center

1998   Al Qaeda bombing of U.S. embassies in Kenya and Tanzania

2000   Election of George W. Bush

2001   Record-sized tax cut
    Bush rejects Kyoto treaty
    Senator Jim Jeffords defects from Republican party
    September 11 attacks
    Bush declares "war on terrorism"
    USA PATRIOT Act
    Bush launches war in Afghanistan; collapse of Taliban regime

2002   Bush identifies "axis of evil"
    Release of National Security Strategy
    Bush announces plan for "regime change" in Iraq
    UN Security Council agrees to renewal of weapons inspections in Iraq
    Establishment of Department of Homeland Security
    Republican gains in congressional elections

2003   Bush launches war on Iraq; collapse of Hussein regime
    Occupation of Iraq by United States and allies
    Capture of Hussein
    Second round of Bush tax cuts
    Supreme Court upholds affirmative action
    Supreme Court overturns criminalization of homosexual acts

2004   Abu Ghraib prisoner abuse scandal
    Rasul v. Bush
    Hamdi v. Rumsfeld
    Reelection of George W. Bush

2005   Congressional ban on use of torture
    Congressional extension of Patriot Act
    Hurricane Katrina

2006   Immigrant rights demonstrations across country
    Hamdan v. Rumsfeld

KEY TERMS

tax cuts: As a conservative Republican, George W. Bush was a champion of tax cuts. He argued that reducing taxes would prevent the federal government from expanding in size and allow Americans to invest and spend their money as they saw fit, thereby promoting economic growth. In June 2001, just months after taking office, he scored a major legislative victory when the Congress approved his tax reduction package. It reduced the tax rates on the highest incomes from 39.6 percent to 33 percent. Moreover, it began the gradual elimination of the estate tax, a form of taxation that applied to only the very wealthiest Americans. As a consequence of these measures, most of the benefits of the tax cut went to the wealthiest Americans. To secure passage of the measure, however, Bush agreed that the estate tax would be fully reinstated in 2010, setting the stage for a major congressional battle over the issue at some time in the future.

Kyoto Protocol: Concern over a possible link between greenhouse gases and a rise in global temperatures prompted a United Nations conference held in Brazil in 1992. This meeting paved the way for a 1997 agreement known as the Kyoto Protocol. Under the terms of the agreement, nations would reduce their greenhouse gas emissions to approximately 5 percent below 1990 levels by 2008–2012. Some developing nations such as China were exempted from its provisions. The United States, which was responsible for one-third of the world's greenhouse gas emissions, signed the measure; however, Congress showed little interest in approving it. In 2001, President Bush rejected American participation, claiming that evidence tying human activity to global warming was incomplete. He declared that abiding by Kyoto would slow economic growth in the United States, costing millions of jobs.

War in Afghanistan: Immediately after the September 11 attacks, the United States began deploying military forces in preparation for an attack on Afghanistan. When the Taliban refused to surrender Al Qaeda leader Osama bin Laden, American and British forces began air strikes against Afghanistan. The United States worked closely with the Northern Alliance, a group of Afghani warlords opposed to Taliban rule. The Northern Alliance fought most of the ground battles until a large contingent of U.S. troops arrived in November. By December the Taliban had fled the country, although fighting continued well into 2002. The victory in Afghanistan, however, was a tenuous one, and military officials feared a resurgent Taliban would launch offensives in 2007.

Lawrence v. Texas: Responding to a call regarding a weapons complaint, Houston police entered the home of John Lawrence, only to find him and another man engaging in sexual activity. The two men were arrested for violating a Texas law prohibiting sexual relations between persons of the same sex. Lawrence claimed that the law violated his Fourteenth Amendment rights, an argument rejected by Texas courts. On appeal, the United States Supreme Court ruled in Lawrence's favor. The opinion noted that Texas had no compelling interest in regulating private consensual relationships between adults, and as such the law violated the Fourteenth Amendment's guarantee of a right to liberty.

signing statements: During his presidency, President Bush made extensive use of the practice of issuing signing statements. Such statements are commentaries on legislation that Congress has passed and the president has signed. They can serve many purposes, including offering instructions on the implementation of the law or presenting the president's interpretation of the meaning of the law's provisions. While several presidents issued such statements, their use was rare until Ronald Reagan took office. George W. Bush regularly issued signing statements, often taking issue with the constitutionality of the laws that he had signed. Between taking office in 2001 and the end of 2004, Bush issued 108 statements, raising a total of 505 constitutional objections. Advocates of signing statements argue they offer the Congress and the public clear indications of the manner in which a law will be implemented. Critics charge that they function as a line-item veto because the president has made clear that he will not enforce some provisions.

Election of 2004: Democrats believed that one asset of presidential nominee John Kerry was his record of service in Vietnam. Although a harsh critic of that war, Kerry was a decorated veteran of that conflict. Much to the Democrats' surprise, their candidate's war record became a matter of controversy that detracted from important campaign issues. A group known as Swift Boat Veterans for Truth alleged that Kerry's wartime exploits were fictions. They claimed that Kerry had received Purple Hearts for self-inflicted wounds. Kerry vigorously defended himself, but polls indicated that Swift Boat television advertisements had the desired effect, raising doubts about Kerry and increasing support for Bush.

racial diversity in education: In June 2003, the United States Supreme Court issued rulings in two cases involving the University of Michigan. The case of *Grutter v. Bollinger* involved a white law school applicant, Barbara Grutter, who claimed that the rejection of her application violated her Fourteenth Amendment rights because applicants of other races received preference. The court declared that the admissions process was constitutional because the institution had a compelling interest to seek diversity in its student body and because the application process took numerous factors beyond race into account. However, in the case of *Gratz v. Bollinger,* the court struck down the university's undergraduate admissions process. University officials awarded each undergraduate applicant points for academic achievement and other factors. Students needed at least 100 points to gain admission. Non-white applicants automatically received 20 points on the basis of race. The court declared that such awarding of points solely on the basis of race was discriminatory and prohibited the practice.

Hurricane Katrina: Public perception of the government's reaction to Hurricane Katrina illustrated the racial divide in the United States. A poll taken in September 2005, just one year after the catastrophe, asked Americans whether race or class played a factor in the delayed government response to the crisis. Sixty percent of white Americans did not think that race was a factor, while 73 percent of African-American respondents believed that race or class played an important role in the slow response.

immigration and globalization: Of the estimated 11 million illegal aliens in the United States in 2005, some 6.3 million, or 57 percent of the total, came from Mexico. Demographers estimated that from 80 to 85 percent of Mexican immigrants arriving in the United States each year were undocumented. The reason why they came was obvious. The median wage of Mexicans working in the United States is $9.00 an hour, while in Mexico it is 21 pesos, or $1.86.

OBJECTIVE QUESTIONS

Multiple Choice

1. A widespread response shown by Americans in the immediate aftermath of September 11 was:
   A. a mix of rage, bewilderment, and anxiety.
   B. a surge of patriotic sentiment and national solidarity.
   C. a new receptiveness to vigorous federal action.
   D. all of the above

2. The three nations alleged by President Bush to constitute an "axis of evil" were:
   A. Libya, Iraq, and Cuba.
   B. Pakistan, Iran, and Indonesia.
   C. Iran, Iraq, and North Korea.
   D. France, Germany, and Russia.

3. Which of the following series of events is listed in proper sequence?
   A. defection of Senator Jeffords from Republican party; September 11 attacks; first Bush tax cut; Bush rejection of Kyoto treaty on global warming
   B. release of Bush administration's National Security Strategy; declaration of war on Iraq; renewal of UN weapons inspections in Iraq; collapse of Taliban government

C. USA PATRIOT Act; September 11 attacks; second round of Bush tax cuts; Republican gains in 2002 congressional elections
D. Al Qaeda bombing of U.S. embassies in Africa; Bush declaration of "war on terrorism"; Bush declaration of war on Afghanistan; Bush's "axis of evil" speech

4. Which of the following was *not* a new theme of American foreign policy announced by the Bush administration after September 11?
   A. Now more than ever, America must honor the constraints of multilateral cooperation and international law.
   B. The United States must enjoy uncontested military supremacy around the world.
   C. The United States is entitled to attack any country which might pose a future threat to its security.
   D. Nations failing to support the United States in its war on terrorism are inherently aligned with the terrorists.

5. Which of the following was *not* a significant point of dispute between supporters and opponents of the American war in Iraq?
   A. whether or not Saddam Hussein had stockpiled weapons of mass destruction
   B. whether or not Saddam Hussein had links with Al Qaeda
   C. whether or not Saddam Hussein was a humane and popular leader
   D. whether or not the United States had the right to invade another country without UN approval

6. Which of the following was *not* a major theme of global alienation over Bush foreign policy?
   A. Bush has flouted world opinion and international law with his invasion of Iraq.
   B. Under Bush the United States has abdicated its responsibility to help the world address the threat of global warming.
   C. When it comes to challenging brutal dictators, Bush is all talk and no action.
   D. Bush's policy of preemptive war has left the world more vulnerable than ever to the terrorist threat.

7. Which of the following was *not* a significant domestic development during the opening decade of the twenty-first century?
   A. a steady rise in the level of federal taxes paid by wealthy Americans
   B. the loss of millions of jobs, especially in the manufacturing sector
   C. a dramatic increase in the powers of government to detain and monitor individuals on American soil
   D. Supreme Court decisions rejecting the president's power to disregard legal rights of prisoners

8. Which of the following was *not* a focus of political debate during the first term of the Bush administration?
   A. the proper balance between traditional American liberties and current security needs
   B. the importance of improving airport security
   C. the appropriate level of federal taxation
   D. the relevance of the United Nations to global conflict resolution

9. In the aftermath of September 11, 2001, a new department in the federal government was created to coordinate efforts to improve security at home, called the:
   A. Department of Strategic Services.
   B. Department of Homeland Security.
   C. Department of Defense.
   D. Department of State.

10. What is the name of the terrorist organization responsible for the attacks of September 11, 2001 that killed 3,000 Americans?
    A. Taliban
    B. Al Qaeda
    C. the Arab Alliance
    D. Salafist Jihadist Unity

11. In his run for the presidency of the United States, George W. Bush referred to himself as a:
    A. "compassionate conservative."
    B. "heir of the Enlightenment."
    C. "New Deal Democrat."
    D. "affirmative action" advocate.

12. In October 2001, the United States launched a war named "Enduring Freedom" against the Taliban in:
    A. Iraq.
    B. Iran.
    C. Pakistan.
    D. Afghanistan.

13. Which was *not* one of the three countries identified by President of the United States George W. Bush as an "axis of evil"?
    A. Iran
    B. Afghanistan
    C. North Korea
    D. Iraq

14. In September 2002, the Bush administration released a document called the National Security Strategy, which announced a new foreign-policy principle called:
    A. "strategery."
    B. "preemptive" war.
    C. the Patriot Act.
    D. the Bush Doctrine.

15. In March 2003, with Great Britain as its sole significant ally, President Bush sent the U.S. military to attack Iraq, calling the war:
    A. "Operation Iraqi Freedom."
    B. "The Iraqi Attack."
    C. "Operation Infinite Justice."
    D. "Operation Enduring Freedom."

16. Iraq possesses:
    A. the world's second-largest reserves of oil.
    B. the world's second-largest wheat, soy, and corn production.
    C. the world's second-largest diamond mine.
    D. the world's only known source of bauxite.

17. What was the 2003 Supreme Court decision declaring unconstitutional a Texas law making homosexual acts a crime?
    A. *Loving v. Virginia*
    B. *Lawrence v. Texas*
    C. *Gideon v. Wainwright*
    D. *Roe v. Wade*

18. The USA Patriot Act conferred all of the following powers on law enforcement agencies except:
    A. the power to wiretap.
    B. the power to obtain personal records from third parties like libraries.
    C. the power to open letters and read e-mail.
    D. the necessity of obtaining a judicial warrant prior to spying on citizens.

19. On September 11, 2001, planes controlled by terrorists crashed into all of the following except:
    A. the Twin Towers in New York.
    B. a wing of the Pentagon.
    C. a field southeast of Pittsburgh, Pennsylvania.
    D. a bridge in Washington, D.C.

20. Who was the leader of Al Qaeda in 2001?
    A. Saddam Hussein
    B. Osama bin Laden
    C. Ayman Al Zawahiri
    D. Khalid Sheikh Mohammed

21. On the morning of September 11, 2001 as the top floors of the Twin Towers of the World Trade Center were engulfed in flames by the terrorist attack, hundreds of New York City firefighters and police:
    A. rushed into the towers in a rescue effort, and lost their lives when the towers collapsed.
    B. directed traffic from the perimeter, but wisely stayed clear of the unstable buildings.
    C. ran into adjoining buildings in an effort to secure them and safeguard their own lives.
    D. initially moved toward the buildings, but under the direction of their superiors abandoned a rescue effort.

22. Which was *not* a terrorist attack on the United States undertaken by Al Qaeda?
    A. a truck bomb that exploded at the World Trade Center in 1993, killing six persons
    B. blasts in 1998 at American embassies in Kenya and Tanzania, which killed more than 200 people
    C. the attacks on the World Trade Center and Pentagon on September 11, 2001 in which 3,000 people lost their lives
    D. the October 1985 killing of an American aboard an Italian cruise ship

23. What country remained, in the early twenty-first century, the richest country in the world in all of human history?
    A. China
    B. Japan
    C. United Kingdom
    D. United States

True or False

1. After the Gulf War of 1991, Osama bin Laden declared war on America.

2. Following September 11, President Bush called on the world community to support and invigorate the International Criminal Court.

3. In the year after September 11, evidence emerged of links between Al Qaeda and the Iraqi government of Saddam Hussein.

4. During the lead-up to the war in Iraq, relations between the United States and France became increasingly strained.

5. Although many nations around the world strongly opposed the prospect of an American invasion of Iraq, most came to acknowledge the wisdom of the war following the fall of Hussein.

6. Following September 11, Attorney General John Ashcroft asserted that critics of the Bush administration were assisting the terrorists.

7. The Republicans achieved significant gains during the congressional elections of 2002.

8. The federal deficit steadily diminished during Bush's first term.

9. Terrorism may be defined as the targeting of civilian populations by violent organizations who hope to spread fear for a political purpose.

10. In 2001, President George W. Bush persuaded Congress to enact the largest tax cut in American history.

11. President George W. Bush strongly supported the Kyoto Protocol of 1997, which sought to combat global warming.

12. President George W. Bush made "freedom" the rallying cry for a nation at war following the attacks of September 11, 2001.

13. In the early twenty-first century the United States far outpaced the rest of the world in every index of power—military, economic, and cultural.

14. In 2003, the United States accounted for just under one-third of global economic output, and more than one-third of global military spending.

15. In November 2001, the Bush administration issued an executive order authorizing the holding of secret military tribunals for non-citizens deemed to have assisted terrorism.

16. In the early twenty-first century, as the American people confronted the threat of terrorism, the need to properly balance freedom and security remained a central issue.

17. In the aftermath of the terrorist attack on September 11, 2001, the country experienced a renewed feeling of common social purpose.

18. In the initial stages of the 2003 Iraq War, fewer than 200 American soldiers died; Iraqi civilian and military casualties were far higher but remained uncounted.

19. The 2003 Iraq War marked a new departure from American foreign policy; previously, the United States had been reluctant to use force outside the Western Hemisphere except as part of an international coalition.

20. By the early twenty-first century, the United States was the world's only superpower.

ESSAY QUESTIONS

1. Identify and discuss three significant ways in which the September 11 attacks transformed life in the United States.

2. Identify three significant shifts in the underlying principles of U.S. foreign policy under President George W. Bush. Assess how these shifts came about and how they affected U.S. foreign relations during the first three years of the Bush administration.

3. Identify and analyze the key arguments raised both for and against President Bush's 2003 invasion of Iraq.

4. Imagine a debate in 2006 between a supporter and a critic of the Bush administration over the following proposition:

   "During his time in office, the policies of George W. Bush greatly enhanced the freedoms and security of America."

   Transcribe this exchange.

5. Write an essay on the tension between freedom and security in the United States in the aftermath of the terrorist attacks of September 11, 2001.

6. Compare and contrast the positions of President Bill Clinton and those of Pat Buchanan with regard to gay rights, abortion, and affirmative action.

7. Write an essay on what civil liberties issues are raised in light of the USA PATRIOT ACT's effort to curtail domestic terrorism.

8. What responsibilities does the United States, as the world's sole superpower, have with regard to extreme poverty in the world?

9. Write an essay describing the United States in international politics in light of the Bush administration's National Security Strategy (2002) and its foreign policy principle of "preemptive" war.

SOURCES FOR FURTHER RESEARCH

Books

Bacevich, Andrew, *American Empire: The Realities and Consequences of U.S. Diplomacy* (2003)

Brinkley, Douglas, *The Great Deluge: Hurricane Katrina, New Orleans, and the Mississippi Gulf Coast* (2006)

Cole, David, *Terrorism and the Constitution* (rev. ed., 2006)

Lakoff, George, *Whose Freedom? The Battle Over America's Most Important Idea* (2006)

Levitas, Mitchell, ed., *A Nation Challenged: A Visual History of 9/11 and Its Aftermath* (2002)

Little, Douglas, *American Orientalism: The United States and the Middle East Since 1945* (2003)

Nye, Joseph S., *The Paradox of American Power* (2002)

Packer, George, *The Assassin's Gate: America in Iraq* (2005)

Suskind, Ron, *The One Percent Doctrine: Deep Inside America's Pursuit of Its Enemies Since 9/11* (2006)

Zakaria, Fareed, *The Future of Freedom: Illiberal Democracy at Home and Abroad* (2003)

Videos

Fahrenheit 9/11 (122 minutes, Miramax Films, 2004)

In Search of Bin Laden (60 minutes, PBS Video, 2001)

The Long Road to War (120 minutes, PBS Video, 2003)

Looking for Answers (60 minutes, PBS Home Video, 2001)

Terrorism Against Americans (50 minutes, CBS News Productions/ History Channel, 1998)

The War Behind Closed Doors (60 minutes, PBS Video, 2003)

When the Levees Broke: A Requiem in Four Acts (256 minutes, 40 Acres & A Mule Filmworks Production and HBO Documentary Films, 2006)

With God on Our Side: George W. Bush and the Rise of the Religious Right in America (100 minutes, First Run/Icarus Films, 2004)

Web Resources

Hurricane Katrina Archive, New OrleansNet LLC
http://www.nola.com/katrina/

Immigrant Rights, Immigrant Solidarity Network
http://www.immigrantsolidarity.org/

The Insurgency: An Investigation into the People Who Are Fighting Against U.S. and Coalition Forces in Iraq, Public Broadcasting System
http://www.pbs.org/wgbh/pages/frontline/insurgency/

Legislation Related to the Attack of September 11, 2001, Library of Congress
http://thomas.loc.gov/home/terrorleg.htm

The National Security Strategy of the United States of America, National
Security Council
   http://www.whitehouse.gov/nsc/nss.html

The September 11 Digital Archive, Center for History and New
Media/American Social History Project
   http://911digitalarchive.org/

ANSWERS TO OBJECTIVE QUESTIONS

Multiple Choice

1-D, 2-C, 3-D, 4-A, 5-C, 6-C, 7-A, 8-B, 9-B, 10-B, 11-A, 12-D, 13-B, 14-B,
15-A, 16-A, 17-B, 18-D, 19-D, 20-B, 21-A, 22-D, 23-D

True or False

1-T, 2-F, 3-F, 4-T, 5-F, 6-T, 7-T, 8-F, 9-T, 10-T, 11-F, 12-T, 13-T, 14-T, 15-T,
16-T, 17-T, 18-T, 19-T, 20-T